THE MEDDLESOME FRIAR AND THE WAYWARD POPE

THE MEDDLESOME FRIAR
AND THE WAYWARD POPE

The Conflict Between Savonarola and Pope Alexander VI

MICHAEL DE LA BÉDOYÈRE

✤

CLUNY
Providence, Rhode Island

CLUNY EDITION, 2024

This Cluny edition is a republication of the 1958 Hanover House edition of *The Meddlesome Friar and the Wayward Pope*.

For more information regarding this title or any other Cluny Media publication, please write to info@clunymedia.com, or to Cluny Media, P.O. Box 1664, Providence, RI 02901

VISIT US ONLINE AT WWW.CLUNYMEDIA.COM

Cluny edition copyright © 2024 Cluny Media LLC

ALL RIGHTS RESERVED

ISBN: 978-1685953430

NIHIL OBSTAT: Joannes M. T. Barton, S.T.D., L.S.S., *censor deputatus*
IMPRIMATUR: E. Morrogh Bernard, *Vicarius Generalis*
WESTMONASTERII, DIE 28 OCTOBRIS, 1957

The Nihil obstat *and* Imprimatur *are a declaration that a book or pamphlet is considered to be free from doctrinal or moral error. It is not implied that those who have granted the* Nihil obstat *and* Imprimatur *agree with the contents, opinions or statements expressed.*

Cover design by Clarke & Clarke
Cover image: Unknown Tuscan Painter,
Portrait of Girolamo Savonarola, oil on canvas, 1591
Courtesy of Google Arts & Culture

CONTENTS

Introduction   i

PROLOGUE: ROME AND FLORENCE

I. *Who Killed the Duke?* (JUNE 1497)   5
II. *Excommunicated* (FEBRUARY 1498)   15

PART ONE: TWO LIVES

I. *Why a Borgia Pope?*   31
II. *Cardinal Rodrigo*   39
III. *Rise of a Prophet*   52
IV. *"We Are Pope"*   69
V. *The Sinner*   77

PART TWO: CLASH AND MARTYRDOM

I. *The New Cyrus*   97
II. *The Prophet Sways the City*   106
III. *An Invader Outwitted*   118
IV. *The Conflict Begins*   125
V. *Moral Reform*   141
VI. *Dilemma of Conscience*   148
VII. *The Last Order*   160
VIII. *The Last Defiance*   169
IX. *A General Council*   179
X. *Ordeal by Fire*   193
XI. *The Last Defence*   198
XII. *Trials*   203
XIII. *Martyrdom*   216

For my youngest son
STEPHEN
who thought Savonarola a most exciting person

✣ Introduction

THESE pages present the story of two men—two men whom fate brought together in mortal conflict. Though they never actually met, the conflict between them united, as well as divided, them. For each represented essential spiritual and moral values of that colourful and formative century of the high Renaissance on the very eve of the great break-up of the Reformation.

Savonarola the Prophet is one of those figures of history who may be said to be too well known by name ever really to be known. What visitor to Florence has failed to walk the few steps into the Piazza della Signoria to gaze upon the plaque set in the ground which marks the spot where, more than four hundred and fifty years ago, the Dominican Friar suffered his martyrdom? Florence, indeed, is forever associated with this revolutionary figure who inspired the popular religious and political reform of the city in a manner comparable, it would seem at first sight, with Calvin's later rule over Geneva or the Jesuit theocracy in South America. Yet few who know his name so well know much more about him than that.

Alexander Borgia the Pope fits into a different compartment of the popular mind. He was *the* bad Pope; but posterity knows much less about him than about his notorious Borgia children: Cesare, the worst of the immoral adventurers of the Renaissance and model of Machiavelli's famous political treatise, "The Prince," and Lucrezia, the female of the treacherous and poisonous species. All three are remembered as archetypes of political villainy and social debauchery. Poor Lucrezia, who in fact was not at all a bad woman!

That the Florentine preacher-prophet, Savonarola, saint and political hero, should have come up against Alexander Borgia, of all Popes, is a curious accident of history which, however, does not seem to have struck the popular imagination. Lives of the Borgias, numerous though they are, make only passing mention of the Friar, while lives of Savonarola (rarer, more serious and much less often read) take Alexander's life and reputation for granted, leaving him in sinister shadows while they sing the praises of their hero.

Thus, not only has an opportunity been missed of contrasting these two extraordinary figures of an extraordinary period of history, both with so much ecclesiastically and religiously in common and so little in the spiritual and moral expression of their lives, but the failure to see them together has resulted in the deforming of each. Was Alexander Borgia as bad as he has been painted? Was Savonarola justified in his holy defiance of the bad Pope, and consequently was he as good as he seems?

The following pages, in trying to give an answer to such questions, will also, I hope, enable the reader to see into the real character of the protagonists of the drama enacted between them. They will show that Savonarola was, without doubt, a man of genius, while Alexander was a man who might have been great. Both, however, were weakened, if not ruined, by the flaws in their characters, the first through a kind of self-intoxication with his mission, always a temptation for the revolutionary, the second through passion and self-indulgence, a temptation common to all men, but, happily, rarely the mark of a Pope. Not surprisingly, the conflict between them brings out one of the great issues of human society: the issue of when obedience is due on the part of the inspired subject or subordinate to the lawful authority of the personally infinitely less worthy superior, whether Pope, ruler or military commander. Put in other terms, when and how far may the good man rebel against that rightful and legal order and authority on which society normally depends?

I think I can say that I have approached the story of these two men and their conflict with a detached and unprejudiced mind; but if there is prejudice, it is in favour of Savonarola, not only because I like rebels against tiresome and unworthy authority, especially when the rebels are clearly so much the better men in the conflict, but also because of a kind of personal association with Savonarola.

All my life I have experienced a kind of Savonarola haunting. It started in infancy and early childhood when my family lived in Florence. I remember being constantly taken to see the spot where Florence hanged one of her greatest heroes, and I still have a picture in my mind of marks there of mourning, placed presumably on the anniversaries of his death. As a schoolboy, I read George Eliot's *Romola*, and the memory of it has always remained more vivid with me than of any other book read at that period of my life. Re-reading it recently, when I was thinking of writing this book, I was delighted to find the story as gripping as ever, even if it now seemed to me that the author had imported a good deal of Victorian moral values into this tale of the men and women of the Renaissance.

When I was first trying to write for publication, the Savonarola haunting started again, and I was lucky enough to have a long article on Savonarola and Alexander VI accepted for publication. It was then that, reading in the Radcliffe Camera in Oxford, I grew almost equally interested in the controversy about the real character of the "bad Pope," and I well remember pouring over the endless pages of Mgr. De Roo's rather naïve attempt entirely to whitewash Alexander.

It was in the course of this reading that I came across the lengthy study of Savonarola by the Jesuit, Fr. Herbert Lucas, published in 1899. This book is one of the most interesting examples of the Jesuit character and of Jesuit scholarship. I can imagine Fr. Lucas emerging, when his other duties allowed, from Farm Street and picking his way on foot among the cabs and horse-buses to the Reading Room of the British Museum. There he would sit for hours, as so many other Jesuits have done, with a pile of books beside him, reading, copying, pondering. The whole business had started when Fr. Lucas received for reviewing a brochure by Dr. Ludwig Pastor on Savonarola. Pastor, the historian of the Popes, had been challenged by a Dr. Luotto about his treatment of Savonarola. Faced by this clash between two scholars, there was nothing for the Jesuit to do but study the whole question for himself. The first result was a series of articles; but when these, in their turn, were challenged, Fr. Lucas wrote his closely-packed and closely-printed book of over four hundred and fifty pages. Such was reviewing in those days.

Whatever the effect of the book at that time, it has now been forgotten. Even English Jesuit friends are surprised to hear that the book was ever written, and one of the foremost Italian Dominican apologists of Savonarola and would-be promoter of his beatification has confessed to never having heard of it.

So far as I can see, over fifty years of further studies on Savonarola have done nothing substantial to break down Fr. Lucas's kindly expressed, but severe, indictment of the great Friar.

Obviously, then, Fr. Lucas's great work is the foundation of this book of mine, so far as the treatment of Savonarola is concerned. Fr. Lucas was much less interested in Alexander and he was content to accept the common estimate of that bad Pope. In a way this strengthened his argument, but in this I have not been able to follow him.

Villari's many times reprinted and translated *Life and Times of Girolamo Savonarola*, with its violent defence of Savonarola and still more violent indictment of Alexander and Rome, seems to have been the model on which most subsequent lives have been written. Even the latest big life, the 1952 *Vita di Girolamo Savonarola* by Roberto Ridolfi, though scholarly and most valuable, follows Villari's lead, interpreting the documents in a sense constantly favourable to Savonarola and hostile to the Pope and his entourage, though in almost every instance Fr. Lucas's interpretation seems to ring far truer.

The Meddlesome Friar and the Wayward Pope

Pastor himself is, naturally, invaluable, especially for his brilliant picture of the Church of those times, on its often forgotten good side, as well as its bad side.

For the text of sermons and writings I have used, wherever possible, Mario Ferrara's two volumes of *Prediche e Scritti*, published in 1952. The 1950 *Alessandro VI e Savonarola*, published by the Accademia D'Oropa, very conveniently prints all the correspondence between Pope and Friar in Italian and provides lengthy explanatory comments in defence of the Friar.

For Alexander and the Borgias, there is, of course, a wealth of literature, good, bad and indifferent, available. Writing this book has afforded me the amusement of reading Baron Corvo's *Chronicles of the House of Borgia*, a highly individualistic and often brilliantly written book, published in 1901, which, despite its violent prejudice (in favour of the full-blooded Borgias as against their mean, little-minded critics, ecclesiastical and political) anticipates some of the later more critical verdicts. But for Alexander and his family I have found Orestes Ferrara's *The Borgia Pope* (1942) the most useful book, although, like Mgr. De Roo, it protests too much in favour of Alexander. Very much can be said against the bad Pope, but a surprising amount can be said on his behalf. Common sense, it seems to me, must be invoked to make him a credible man who, in fact, dealt with Savonarola, at any rate until near the end, with much understanding and even sympathy. Maria Bellonci's recent work on Lucrezia Borgia has many merits and is highly readable, but it swallows too much of the Borgia legend. Marcel Brion in his recent *Le Pape et Le Prince: Les Borgia* argues that Alexander was pretty well as bad as he has been painted, but it is wrong to be shocked by this for he was no worse than others. It does not seem to me that this view is either historically or morally well-founded.

Other books which I have found very useful for the general historical background include Don Sturzo's masterly *Church and State*, *The Decline and Fall of the Medieval Papacy* by the Anglican divine, L. Elliott

Binns, D.D., which is extremely fairly written, and *The Medici* by Ferdinand Schevill.

The fact that this is a biographical study of two people who never actually met and whose direct relationship only covered some three years of their lives has faced me with certain technical difficulties in telling the story. It is a case of two stories and two lives dove-tailing into one story about the clash between the two characters mainly involved. The simplest and most logical way would have been to tell each story separately until the moment when the issue between them was joined. And all this might have been prefaced by a historical introduction. But I rejected this plan because it would in fact have turned the book into a historical study, whereas my purpose was to try to tell the whole story *through* the living personalities of these protagonists and within the values of the times, so far as possible graphically described.

Because of all this it may be useful if I end this introduction with a brief explanation of how in fact the story is told.

In the prologue I set the scene with two contrasting sections, the first in Alexander's Papal Rome and the second in Savonarola's Florence. The dramatic events described in these sections occurred, in fact, only some months before the climax of the whole story, the trial, condemnation and death of Savonarola. More vividly, I think, than any historical description, this prologue will give the reader an idea of the people and the times within which the lives of Alexander and Savonarola were lived.

The story is then divided into two Parts. In the first Part, Chapter One gives as briefly as possible the historical background which made the Borgia Pope possible. Then follow two chapters, the first telling of the life of Alexander until he became Pope and the second of the life of Savonarola until he became a figure of high importance, politically as well as religiously. At this stage when both protagonists are on the threshold of the events which drew them into conflict, Chapter Four gives the necessary explanation of the political events in Italy which came to dominate the conflict itself. The last four chapters of the First

The Meddlesome Friar and the Wayward Pope

Part then draw the protagonists together. In two chapters, I try to give a picture of Alexander as Pope and one of the ruling Princes of Italy, as well as of his family and private life, with reference especially to Cesare and Lucrezia. The last two chapters of this First Part carry Alexander into the political field which brought him up against a Florence passing through the phases of the French War and the political and spiritual revolution inspired by the religious leadership of Savonarola.

Thus by the time the Pope and Prophet come into direct conflict, the reader will, I hope, feel that he has some personal knowledge not only of the two men chiefly involved, but of the background, religious, historical and political, which explains the sequence of events described chronologically in the Second Part of the book.

THE MEDDLESOME FRIAR
AND THE WAYWARD POPE

PROLOGUE
Rome and Florence

I. Who Killed the Duke? (JUNE 1497)

IT was midsummer of the year 1497. After the heavy heat of the Roman day, fleshy, perspiring Pope Alexander VI was doubtless spending the early evening hours in the company of the women he adored—perhaps with his niece, Adriana, who managed his personal affairs, perhaps with the beautiful Giulia herself whom the irreverent Romans did not hesitate to call "the bride of Christ." He may have been missing the company of his own adored daughter, Lucrezia, retired at the moment for political and marital reasons in the seclusion of the Dominican convent of San Sisto, and been obliged to content himself with gazing at Pinturicchio's fresco, in the Sala of the Saints, of the Dispute of Saint Catherine whose features, so tradition tells us, were modelled on Lucrezia.

So much is conjecture. But we know for certain that on the Esquiline, across the Tiber from the Vatican, Madonna Vanozza Catanei, the mother of Alexander's children, Juan, Cesare, Lucrezia and Jofre, was that evening giving a dinner party at her vineyard. It was probably the habit of that tactful and self-effacing woman, who had so long kept the heart of the passionate, pleasure-loving Borgia Pope, to hold such parties. On this occasion, however, she may have been celebrating the high honours lately falling on Juan, Duke of Gandia and Captain-General of the Church, created by his father but a few days earlier Duke of Papal Benevento that his Spanish blood be permanently Italianised. Or possibly the party was being held in honour of his far more capable brother, Cardinal Cesare, due to leave Rome immediately as his father's Legate for the coronation of King Frederick of Naples.

In any case, the supper party consisted of the two bastard brothers, Juan the soldier and Cesare the reluctant churchman, certainly dressed on such an occasion as a gentleman of fashion, of their cousin Cardinal Borgia of Monreale, son of Juana, the Pope's sister, of some other guests together with a mysterious man with a mask, brought by Juan himself.

When the party broke up, Juan and Cardinals Cesare and Monreale rode home to the Vatican. Juan and his masked friend, however, parted from them along the way, presumably to finish off a gay evening by calling on some lady friend. The Rome of those days, despite considerable reforms by the capable Borgia Pope, was an ill-policed city and filled with robbers and ruffians of all kinds, especially at night. It was not healthy to be abroad so late without proper protection. However, Juan and his friend rode off laughing with only a single groom as escort. When they reached the Piazza of the Jews, the groom was instructed to ride back towards Cardinal Sforza's palace near the Vatican and await their return at the Piazza at one o'clock. And that was the last that anyone ever saw of Juan, Duke of Gandia, alive and of his friend. "Where he rode to I have no idea," as John Burchard, Alexander's Master of Ceremonies, to whose diary we owe the detailed account of the evening, simply expressed it.

Next morning the absence of the Duke was noticed by his servants, and the Pontiff was informed. He was not too worried for, as Burchard says, Alexander jumped to the conclusion that his son had spent the night with some girl and preferred to avoid the indiscretion of leaving by day. It may be mentioned in passing that this touch, as with many others one comes across, hardly squares with the general view that the Pope, his family and those around him were without shame. Juan was a dissolute young man and not a churchman, yet Alexander presumed on a discretion more in keeping with later times. But when evening came, the Duke's absence made the Pope "altogether full of sorrow and moved in his whole being." At once he ordered a search and an inquiry into what could have happened.

The Meddlesome Friar and the Wayward Pope

Grim clues to the mystery were soon found. They came across the groom lying badly wounded and unable to give useful information. Juan's mule was also found, and the stirrups showed signs of a struggle. But the truth was discovered when a waterman guarding timber near the Tiber was questioned. He told his story without hesitation or fear. On the night in question he saw two men coming out of a street. They had looked carefully to make sure that the coast was clear. Then two more had followed and had given a signal. A rider on a white horse appeared. On its back was slung a body. Steadied by the men, the horse was led by lantern-light to the edge of the river, turned round and the corpse violently thrown into the Tiber. It fell with a plop. But the dead man's cloak could be seen floating, so the five men threw stones at it to make it sink. When the waterman was asked why he had not reported what he had seen, he shrugged his shoulders and said that he had seen at least a hundred bodies similarly disposed of! No one had bothered him about them. Such was Rome!

There was nothing for it but to drag the river. One manuscript of Burchard's Diary says that three hundred did the dragging; another about three. Wits said that Alexander, simoniacally elected, was at last proving himself a true Fisher of Men. Soon the nets caught the dark, dirty mass from the mud. It was indeed the handsome, successful Gandia with, but a few hours earlier, the whole world at his feet. Now his body, obscenely hacked by dagger thrusts and with a great gash across the throat, was carried back to Castel Sant' Angelo where he was laid out in all his finery. "He seemed to be sleeping, not dead." That night he was buried in Santa Maria del Popolo, and as the flares of the funeral procession passed below him, Alexander was heard to call out into the darkness for his lost and best-loved son.

Who killed the Duke? The plain answer is that no one knows. The masked man suggests the most likely explanation. Juan may well have been lured by him into a trap. Free as were his love affairs and ready as he was at a moment's notice to pick a quarrel through his boorish ways, he could easily have been the victim of some secret enemy.

But the gruesome murder of the Pope's own son, just as his father has settled him in Italy as the lay-arm of the Papacy, was treated as a matter of high political significance. Which of the Pope's many enemies could be behind the deed, everyone asked? A member of the powerful Orsini family, recently deprived of valuable territory for the Duke's benefit? Cardinal Ascanio Sforza, brother of the tyrant of Milan, and always a slippery customer, jealous of the Pope, for the body had been found near his garden? Some creature of the fiery and redoubtable Cardinal della Rovere, Alexander's open enemy in the Roman Curia, whose deepest wish was to see the Borgia Pope deposed by a General Council of the Church and the whole brood exterminated? Giovanni Sforza, Lord of Pesaro, smarting under the humiliation of having his marriage to Lucrezia annulled on grounds of his impotence? The list was endless, but nothing was ever found to connect these great lords, spiritual and temporal, with the crime. Later, it became the fashion to impute the murder—as with many others—to Cardinal Cesare himself, Juan's brother, on the ground that no one stood to benefit more clearly from it.

Cesare, it was said, was deeply jealous of his brother's secular glory as the Pope's Captain-General. He had been fobbed off with the Red Hat, and no head was ever less suited to it. With Juan out of the way, he could become secularised and take his rightful place as the great soldier of the family.

It would be a strange accusation in the case of any family but the Borgias, who have proved to be fair game for any historical calumnies, and it is significant that Cesare's name was not mentioned in this connection until a year after the deed.

The Borgia legend was one that grew with every year that passed, partly out of Italian dislike of the Spanish intruders into the Papacy, partly because Alexander made many enemies and cared not two jots about the accusations made against him; but mainly, one feels, because everyone likes to embroider a likely tale. The start having been given, the world expected that the Borgias should live up to their historical role of being the super-criminals at the very heart of the Catholic Church.

Now if there is one thing certain about Alexander Borgia, it is his utter infatuation for his family; if there is anything undeniable about the Borgias as a whole it is their closeness as a clan. Of Alexander it was said that there had never been *un uomo piu carnale*, which is usually translated as "a more sensual man." But it also means "a man more attached to his own flesh and blood." In fact, Alexander was both. And, oddly enough, the effects of this second, and, most of us would say, more worthy passion proved more evil for the Church than the scandal caused by the first. It is stretching probability a great deal to include among the Borgia vices the pastime of murdering one another.

Cesare may have been jealous of his brother's worldly success, especially as he knew himself to be the better man, but he had no need to kill him. The Gandia titles went to Juan's infant son, not to Cesare. Cesare at the moment was in the highest favour with his father and about to go to Naples as Papal Legate. The existence of his brother would not stand in the way of his secularisation—he was not a priest—should he wish to move from the ecclesiastical sphere to the lay, as indeed he did. The charge can only have been invented by enemies ready to invent anything that could further dehumanise a family whose fundamental failing was that it was all too human.

Whoever the murderer, Pope Alexander was stupefied by the grim tragedy which struck him at his weakest, and not least worthy, point, his adoration of his own children. Burchard graphically described his master's reaction: "When the Pope learnt that his son had been killed and found, like ordure, in the river, his very bowels were moved by his sorrow and the bitterness in his heart. He shut himself up in a room and wept bitterly. Not for many hours would he allow the cardinals and servants to approach him despite their constant pleas and prayers from without. At last he opened the door and let them enter. But from Wednesday evening until Saturday he neither ate nor drank, nor did he sleep until the Sunday."

Even across the centuries one may feel that at this terrible moment for the ebullient and high-spirited Pope, he came nearest in spirit to his enemy, Fra Girolamo Savonarola, the severe, ascetic Prophet of Florence who, overcoming his feelings for an unworthy Pontiff of the Church, remembered the man, and wrote in a letter to him: "Faith, most holy Father, is the one and true source of peace and consolation for the heart of man. Let your Holiness respond to this call and you will see how quickly sadness is turned into joy. All other consolation is trivial and deceitful. Faith alone brings consolation from a far-off country. Let your Holiness then forward the work of faith for which I labour even unto bonds, and do not give ear to the wicked. These things I have written to you under the prompting of charity and in all humility, desiring that your Holiness may find in God that true comfort which does not deceive. May He console you in your distress."

Shaken by the murder of his son, Alexander was for a moment able to rise to the Friar's appeal. The sinner in his grief and punishment raised his hands to touch, however fleetingly, the robe of the saint. Like a flash, the mercy of Christ illuminated a scene that seems so dark to human judgment. For the Spanish Pope, with all his historic faults committed at least without hypocrisy and self-deception, was intensely Catholic. Savonarola's gibe that many priests had ceased to believe in the truth which they were commissioned to teach in no way fitted the Pope himself. Alexander believed, practised his belief and, as Pope, conscientiously and ably defended and promoted it.

The sense of God's wrath, expressed in that deliverance of his son's body, filthy and stinking from the slime of the Tiber, and his faith in God's mercy, as expressed by a saintly friar whom he had, as Pope, grounds for opposing, caused Alexander, with an impetuosity natural to his sanguine character, there and then to reform the Church and himself. His children were to live away from him. Cesare, anyway, was off to

The Meddlesome Friar and the Wayward Pope

Naples. Jofre, the youngest, was sent with his wife to their castle of Squillace. Even his dear Lucrezia, he decided, must prepare to exile herself in Spain, the homeland of the Borgias.

He called a consistory and appointed a Commission of six Cardinals for the thorough reformation of the Church of the Renaissance. To the assembled Cardinals and diplomats he spoke with tears in his eyes. He told them that no worse blow could have befallen him than the death of the Duke of Gandia whom he loved above all others in the world. "We would willingly give seven tiaras to bring him back to life," he said to them. He even had a momentary impulse to abdicate. "God has punished us for some of our sins."

How thorough were the repentant intentions of the Pope who, paradoxically, had always been a reformer at heart, is shown by his own Bull of Reform. The Bull starts right away at the heart of the matter. "We are well aware that morals have notably fallen back. No longer can we tolerate the way in which the former salutary measures instituted by our predecessors to keep sensuality and avarice within bounds have been violated so that we fall headlong into corruption. The nature and appetites of mortal men are indeed prone to evil, holding, as the Apostle says, the spirit as well as the people captive under the law of sin. Even though we were only in a lesser position as cardinal under our predecessors, Pius II, Paul II, Sixtus IV and Innocent VIII, we always wanted to see the present licence of morals restrained by new constitutions. That is why at the beginning of our Pontificate we wished to give this matter priority over all others."

The Pope then explained how the French invasion made the carrying out of these intentions impossible. But now they would start in earnest. Hence the appointment of six of the best and most God-fearing Cardinals to review the enactments of the past and the needs of the present. There followed a list of over one hundred and thirty chapter-heads with which the Reforming Commission was to concern itself. The Pope himself must be the first subject of the reform. His personal way of life, his dress, those permitted to live near him, all these matters were to be attended to. The same for the Cardinals—how they were to be selected in future; their income; their attendants even how much they were to eat at banquets and how they were to be entertained on such occasions. Right through the administration of the Church, the great purge was to make itself felt. The lands of the Church were no longer to be alienated; indulgences were not to be sold; bishops must be resident and must not enjoy the revenues of other dioceses; simony was to be punished by excommunication; the monies of the Church were to be used for pastoral purposes; concubines and illegitimate children of the clergy were to come within the purge; sports and gaming for churchmen were to stop; and musicians, actors and young men were no longer to belong to clerical households.

This is surely one of the oddest of resolutions in the long history of the Church. At best of times the Papal curia works slowly and ponderously. Yet here was the supremely bad Pope, literally within a matter of days, whipping up the whole administration into a minutely detailed frenzy of cleansing the Church which leaps forward over the years to the reforms of the massive, perduring Council of Trent itself.

It is possible to dismiss the whole affair as a comical and rather childish reaction of a worldling Pope who had had a terrible fright. The fact that the grandiose resolutions came to nothing at all may seem to bear out that reading. But at a deeper level one cannot but be struck by the clarity of vision which underlay the corruption of the Church at its worst. The stimulus, however interpreted, was enough from one day to the next to project a paper plan of the Church as it should be. It did not need the Reformers to clear the Church's mind. The mind was never clearer than in the year when Luther was fourteen years old. It was the will of the human element of the Church, suffering from an impoverished theology and philosophy, weakened by the habit of self-indulgence, power and the pride of life through generations—but never blinded—which was lacking. Thus the vices of the churchmen, gross as they were and as they seem to us, belonged to one world and formed one picture. Beside them there remained, untarnished, another world and another picture. That world, that picture, always really mattered far more to them, strange as it may seem, than the evil vanity of their lives. The decline had never led to the last and intrinsically unforgivable of evils: the inability to distinguish clearly between good and evil. It was the worst of Popes who could envisage wholesale and detailed reform from one day to the next.

We need to bear in mind in assessing the true character of Alexander Borgia this extraordinary capacity to see so clearly the right path and to will it with all his heart, however evanescently. We need to remember, too, that the bad Pope and the terrible Friar, whatever the sins of the first and, as we shall see, the extravagances of the second, were speaking the same language, living the same faith and sharing, in however immensely different a measure, the same ideals.

"We fall headlong into corruption; we must begin our reform here —here within our Roman Curia," said Alexander—and meant it in the stress of his grief over the murder of his son in circumstances only too typical of the Holy, the Eternal City, in the last years of the fifteenth century. He meant it, too, throughout his ecclesiastical life as a prince of the Church and a prince of Renaissance Italy, but never got round to it because of his political preoccupations and the hold over him of his passion for his family, for earthly glory, for wealth and beauty, and for the society of fair women.

"You have been to Rome," the doomed Savonarola thundered from his illicit pulpit and as an excommunicate:

> Well then, you must know something of the lives of these priests! They have courtesans, squires, horses, dogs. Their houses are filled with carpets, silks, perfumes, servants. Their pride fills the world. Their avarice matches their pride. All they do, they do for money. Their bells are a tocsin calling to avarice. They preach nothing but food, money, candles....

Why does Rome attack me in this way? Do you imagine it has anything to do with religion? Not a bit of it! They want to change our political ways and impose the tyrant over us again. A fig they care for right living! O, Rome, what do I ask of you? Only a Bull to allow people to live decently. That is all I ask of you. But here, on the contrary, we await a Bull that will trample under our feet all semblance of a decent way of life.

To live decently—Alexander Borgia, in a way, had always wanted that, just as he always wanted to save his accuser, the redoubtable Florentine Dominican friar, from the consequences of his canonical defiance of the authority and the rights of even an unworthy Pope. How terribly he had fallen, despite his efforts, despite his long and by no means wholly bad ecclesiastical career, the grim spectre of the body of his murdered son revealed to him only too plainly.

II. *Excommunicated* (FEBRUARY 1498)

THE scene changes to Florence, eight months later, February 11, 1498: Septuagesima Sunday, when the Church anticipates the coming penitential season of Lent by using mourning vestments as a reminder that the days of easy living are numbered. Two more weeks, then the last fling of Carnival and the forty days of prayer and fasting, ending with Holy Week and then, once more, the triumph and joys of Easter.

Through the shaded narrow streets of a Florence recognizably the same as we know it today, men, women and children were excitedly pushing their way. Many had come from far in the Tuscan countryside, while the houses of the town itself had been rapidly emptying, for the Florentines loved any excitement, religious or political. For generations the great bell of the Palazzo Vecchio had called the citizens to the Parlamento or general assembly of the people, Florence's sovereign popular body instituted as safeguard of Florentine liberties, but used, as is the wont with democracy in the raw then and today, to support the tyranny of the most unscrupulous and determined leader. Those of middle age and more would remember, too, the dreadful day of the Pazzi Conspiracy when their great cathedral or duomo of St. Mary of the Florentine Lily had been desecrated at the moment of the elevation of the Host by the murder of Giuliano de' Medici and the narrow escape of his brother the Magnifico, the great Lorenzo himself. On that day, an Archbishop in his vestments had been swung out from a window of the Palazzo to hang there before the infuriated mob until he was dead.

But those days had passed. Parlamentos were no more. Medicis were no more. Their holy Friar, inspired directly by God Himself, had swept away both tyrants and political trickery, and the city had been converted from the service of despots to that of Christ the King.

But on this Septuagesima Sunday, the hurrying crowd felt as excited as ever they or their fathers had felt in the bad old days. We can see them, the men, arguing together and gesticulating, many doubtless in the sober colours of homespun gowns, enlivened, however, by the Sunday-best of young bloods with those blue or saffron or red cloaks over tunic and part-coloured hose so often seen in the quattrocento pictures; the women, their bleached hair drawn up from the forehead, as was the fashion, in full-skirted, high-waisted gowns and sleeveless overcoat to keep out the bitter wind from the Apennines which caused the self-important children, allies and agents of the Friar, to rub their hands and stamp their feet as they pressed along. Here and there one would see a group of graver and older citizens with long dark cloaks, lined with fur, and black caps with their flaps turned up over their grey hair. They might be bankers or richer merchants of the silk guild with their great warehouses from which the famed Florentine cloth of velvet, brocade, damask, satin, taffeta, gold and silver was sent to every country in Europe and even to the dreaded infidels of advancing Turkey; they might be magistrates of one or other of governmental commissions, of the Council of Ten, overbusy these days with hectic foreign affairs and war, or of the Council of Eight, so recently concerned with the highly controversial trial and execution of the Medicean conspirators whom the Friar had refused to save. They might be members of the exalted Signoria itself, the formal rulers of Florence whose party alignment constantly chopped and changed owing to the custom of two-monthly election.

Standing off the main road here and there, many doubtless on horseback, and closely watching the crowd as it thickened towards the heart of the beautiful city, there would have been bands of swashbucklers, the Compagnacci as they were called, toughs who were the declared enemies of the Friar and his pious "Frateschi" followers—"Masticapaternostri" (Our Father-mumblers), "Collitori" (Twisted-necks), "Piagnoni"

The Meddlesome Friar and the Wayward Pope

(Snivellers) their opponents called them, but "Piagnoni" stuck and they became proud of it. These Compagnacci, friends of the aristocratic and the well-to-do Arrabiati or "Enraged," had shown their quality the year before by covering the Friar's pulpit with ordure. But now they sensed that their hour was coming. They were all the bolder for it, as they measured the feelings of the people moving into the Piazza and passing into the gloom of the great four-arched nave.

They must have been reassured by what they saw and heard. Whereas but a year ago they would have had to admit that the fickle Florentines as a whole were still four-square behind the tremendous personality of their great Dominican leader, today anxiety and division had replaced the former confidence. Hence the new excitement in the air, the shaking of heads, the emphatic gestures, the arguments, as the crowd passed by.

These merchants, craftsmen, peasants of Florence which, under the great Lorenzo, had been the capital of the arts, of culture, of elegance, of dissipation and barely-concealed vice of every description, had received the greatest shock of their lives. From Ferrara a preacher had come into their midst, an impassioned, inelegant preacher, speaking the rough language of the common people. From his lips had poured forth a torrent of Scripture—the ancient prophecies of Jehovah, newly applied, whose stern language had withered the elegances of humanist Tuscan and put the fear of God into the heedless, or at best superstitious, crowds that filled the Florentine churches.

At first, they had tried to laugh at this odd, ugly, God-intoxicated friar who had railed at their vices and the worldliness of the tyranny to which they had submitted. But their mockery had turned into fear and from fear to love as the foreigner had touched them at their weakest spot. Savonarola had spoken, not with a human tongue, but with a divine one.

He was no ordinary man, but the ambassador of God. Again and again, he had proved his credentials, prophesying from his pulpit not merely the woe and destruction common enough among the would-be reformers of Italy, but the detailed time and place of the coming events that would overwhelm the evil city. He had forewarned them of the coming of the new Cyrus with his great army from over the mountains to overrun Italy in the name of God, and the new Cyrus had duly come. Better still, this prophet, who had told them of his frightening visions of the Cross of God's Crising from the heart of the Eternal City of Rome itself and the Cross of God's mercy rising from a new and fair Jerusalem, was so much in God's favour that he could spare a repentant Florence the worst consequences of God's anger.

Such a prophet was not to be disregarded by a people in whom credulity and a formal, automatic religious observance went hand in hand with pride in a new age of culture, beauty and wealth. And even those of them strong-minded enough to doubt the Friar's supernatural claims could not but have been deeply impressed—as we also would have been—by the other side of his personality. His utter sincerity, his zeal for souls, his patent spirituality and love of God and of his people could not be doubted. Not only was he manifestly a saint, but his mind could move with remarkable perceptiveness and indeed much common sense over the range of knowledge and accomplishment in his day: Scripture, theology, philosophy, art, politics—in them all he was at home with intuitions superior to those of the experts. Add to this a winning charm of personality and an oratorical gift beyond compare, and we can begin to understand how the hard-fisted bankers and merchants, the humanists of the first rank and artists who are still household names today, such as Botticelli and Michelangelo, the suspicious lawyers and judges, the soldiers, came as fully under his sway as the common people whose interests he defended and the children of whom he thought so highly. Under his guidance—terrible, frightening and (in our view) mistakenly fraudulent, however subjectively sincere the Friar might be, yet outstandingly enlightened, compassionate and overwhelmingly captivating in manner and personal magic—Florence, if not in a night, at least in a very short space of time, was changed from a city of worldly grace and worldly viciousness into a holy city of prayer, penance and respectable virtue—from a city of political corruption to one of political honesty. Christ reigned at last in Italy.

Flavour to the spiritual reform was given both by the political revolution which went with it unseating the Medici and the aristocracy in favour of the flattered middle and popular classes and by the Friar's burning indictment of the spiritual and moral corruption of the Church. The *Gran Maestri*, clerical and lay, were the constant objects of his attack, and every humbler member of his crowded congregations would tingle with excitement and pleasure as the piercing, popular words poured again and again from the hypnotic black figure standing high by the Crucifix in his cathedral pulpit or in his own church in San Marco. That great hook of a nose, the thrust of the grey under-lip, the high spare cheekbones—these were the gaunt, exaggerated setting for the shining black eyes that seemed to pierce into each man's soul. It was a strange and ugly face, but how capable of expressing the manifold emotions of one who could command with authority, denounce with prophetical intensity, coax with the gentle love of a father, evoke kinship, affection, trust, with a twinkling humour, the ample gesture of embrace, the popular, even the coarse, word.

The words they had so often heard from his torrential lips must have filled the minds of the people hurrying to hear him again on this Septuagesima Sunday.

"O Italy, O Rome, O Florence," he had cried to them, "your villainies, your impieties, your fornications, your usuries, your cruelties are bringing us these tribulations. Priests, hear my words! Priests and prelates of Christ's Church, give up your benefices—you have no right to keep to them. Give up your pomps and shows, your banquets and your dinners. Give up, I tell you, your mistresses and your love-boys. It is time, I tell you, to do penance, else will come the great punishments through which God means to mend His Church. Ungrateful Florence, God has spoken to you. But you refuse to listen. If even the Turks had heard what you have heard, they would have done penance for their sins. So often have I called to you, so often cried to you that there is simply no more that I can say."

But he had said it again and again, sometimes in words that stayed in everyone's memory: "In the early Church it was the chalices that were made of wood and the prelates were men of gold; today it is the prelates who are made of wood, their chalices rich in gold." They had even heard him say, "Give up your ceremonies, lukewarm folk that you are, for you make mere ceremonies the end of your religion"; "The Christian life does not consist in ceremonies, but in the practice of goodness."

They remembered, too, those words of terrible indictment preached only eight months earlier:

> The earth is covered with blood, but the clergy cares not a rap. Its evil example murders the very soul in each man. They are far indeed from God those priests whose worship is to spend the night with harlots, the days gossiping together in choir. The altar itself has been turned into a clerical shop. Priests are even heard to say that God has no care for the world, that everything is chance, that Christ is not truly in the Sacrament.... Come here, you blasphemy of a Church! The Lord gave you beautiful garments; you have turned them into idols. The sacred vessels are turned into the instruments of your vanity. The sacraments are the counters of your simony. Your lust has made of you a brazen-faced whore. Worse than beasts you are, you who have made yourself into an unspeakable monster! Once you were at least ashamed of your sins—no longer so today. Once priests had the grace to call their sons nephews. They no longer bother now. They call them sons—sons pure and simple. Yes, you have made yourself a convenience, a brothel for all... I will stretch forth my hands, says the Lord, I will descend on you in your scurrility and your wickedness. My sword will hang above your sons, upon this

The Meddlesome Friar and the Wayward Pope

brothel which you are, upon your whores and your palaces, and my justice will be made known to all.

This kind of language had not shocked then as it would shock today. Even the children of Florence ranged in tiers around the cathedral were not debarred from listening to the Friar's rough language. Not only were the censures deserved, but speech was much freer. The Friar was in the long tradition of prophets and reformers from Abbot Gioachino de Flora, through St. Bridget of Sweden, St. Catherine of Siena to St. Vincent Ferrer, not to mention dozens of lesser names. Reaction to such outbursts was not what it would be now. To understand this we have to try and blot out of our minds centuries of rationalism and moralisations as applied to individual and social behaviour. Where we live in a flow of expected uniformity in nature and in morals, which causes the deepest scandal when the crust of moral convention breaks down under the passion and greed of national and class aspirations, those fifteenth-century people of Florence still lived in a world broken up by the hazards of living, lusty, instinctive emotions against a background of a vivid picture gallery. Many of these pictures have been preserved for us. Incomparable pictures of heaven on earth in the life of Christ, of Our Lady and the Saints wherein a freshened sense of the reality and vigour of human life enabled the contemporary people in their contemporary dress to be inevitably introduced; startlingly realistic pictures of the Last Judgment in which the damned were so much more excitedly depicted than the saved as though the shortness of even a bad life had for them a haunting allure; pictures with the uprush of paganism and the cult of beauty, of naked—could they ever have thought up our respectable word "nude"?—gods and goddesses and their orgiastic feasts; pictures of gruesome martyrdoms and mock-heroic battles; savage pictures and gentle pictures; pictures superabounding in the luxury of living and pictures of grim asceticism—and all spontaneous expressions of the multiple, unrationalised, unsophisticated feelings of representative craftsmen of genius who, like Fr. Lippo Lippi, could combine the vows of the cloister with the ardours of the lover, and get away with it.

Such people hardly knew the meaning of being scandalised in our sense of accepted patterns of behaviour being defied. There were no accepted patterns, only the unending conflict between good and evil, between life and death against a background of eternal sanctions so vividly felt that even the dread of God's wrath and His eternal punishment seemed to possess a morbid excitement and attraction. That the Florentines had thoroughly relished their Friar's grim prophecies and his denunciations of the Church can hardly be doubted, but they relished it as yet another fresh and thrilling experience. The urbane Pico della Mirandola related how when he heard the Friar a cold shiver ran through all his bones and his hair stood on end. It was all a new picture, a new experience, an end in itself rather than the beginning of rational and moral reflection on the state of religion and the world. It led to raw penance, heartfelt prayer and picturesque reform, not to introspections and moralisations.

The people of Florence, on this Septuagesima morning, were anticipating a fresh thrill salted with fresh dreads. For their prophet had now openly defied, and in the fullest, most blatant manner, the great powers-that-be, the *Gran Maestri* themselves, even the greatest of them all, the Pope of Rome.

Later, we shall follow the story. Let it be enough here to say that Savonarola had at last incurred Excommunication and that Florence itself was threatened with an Interdict. He had long been forbidden by the Pope to preach, but had found excuses for not obeying, and Florence had not been shocked. When the excommunication came, he had long been expecting it, and in the sermon from which we have quoted above, he had warned these people who, on this Sunday, were on their way to the Cathedral:

"They tell you," he had said, "that we shall see many excommunications; but I tell you, and tell you again, that they are seeking something other than mere excommunications. As for myself, I pray to you, O Lord, that it come quick. You ask me if I am afraid? Why should I be, I whom they wish to excommunicate, having done no evil! Let this excommunication be brought—carried aloft on a spearhead! Let the gates be opened to receive it! I have my answer, and if I do not give you the shock of your lives, say what you like about me. I will take the colour out of many a face, far more than you think. I shall speak so loud that the very earth will tremble and rock."

But even when the Excommunication had come and been solemnly proclaimed in the light of torches and to the ringing of bells in the churches of Florence, it was only the enemies of the Friar who took the condemnation as a permission to make trouble and try to bring the city back to its former immoral ways. The bulk of his followers stood firm, while Savonarola himself retired to his solitude in the bare cell of San Marco to write the best of his spiritual treatises.

On this Septuagesima Sunday, however, it was different. Excommunications were fairly frequent in those days and their value had declined. But the Church was the Church, in possession of the keys to Heaven and Hell. Excommunication did not necessarily ostracise, but publicly to defy an Excommunication was another matter, for this was an open challenge to the very authority of the Church, the spiritual order within which the lives of men, good and evil, saints and sinners, were ranged. Interdicts, too, were another matter, for these could still affect the wealth of the rich and the daily living of others in the duty they imposed on all to treat the affected city or nation like a leper colony forbidden association and trade with the healthy outer world.

Everyone in Florence was, therefore, still talking about their Friar's solemn defiance on Christmas Day of the authority of His Holiness the Pope Alexander VI—talking in awed terms, where the more nervous minds were concerned. Had they been deceived? Was their Friar justified? What would happen now that so many supporters, half-hearted at best, were turning against him, now that his enemies, the Arrabiati, were calling for his blood and the graceless Compagnacci threatening to raise the city against him? Many, supporters of the Medici, had never clearly taken sides and had earned in consequence the name of "Bigi," half-black, half-white. Which way was the cat now going to jump for them? Not a few of the ordinary people, with the typical Italian fickleness, were ready to desert if only because the reign of Christ the King, picturesque and not without incidental advantages, was more suitable for women and children than for grown men. Thank God (the blasphemy was instinctive) the gambling, the drinking, the dancing, the women—and not only women, if we are to believe Savonarola himself—might soon be in full flow again. Not a few of the girls, bidden to hide their charms, would be glad enough to make up their faces, wear the alluring fashions and ogle the handsome men. Even the boys, organised by genial Fra Domenico, Savonarola's personal aide, into an unofficial moral police to see that the Friar's rules were not broken, were tiring of the new sport and thinking of the good old days when they roamed the streets making a nuisance of themselves or played the dangerous but traditional and exciting game of stones with its fatal casualties.

On Christmas Day, the excommunicated Friar had publicly celebrated the three solemn Masses of Christmas in the Church of San Marco and given Holy Communion not only to his own Dominican brethren but to a packed congregation of layfolk. To dot the i's and cross the t's, he had emerged from the church and led his community in solemn procession around the piazza of San Marco.

This had been, in a sense, a greater defiance than the one to which the people were hurrying on the present Sunday. The excommunicated had publicly celebrated the Holy Eucharistic Sacrifice, given Holy Communion to himself and to as many as had wished to come. But everyone thought of the Friar as the great preacher. Often feeble and ailing outside the pulpit, Savonarola was another person in it. His elevation above the heads of his congregation was but a feeble measure of the raising and increase of his spirit, the intoxication of his emotions, as he thundered

The Meddlesome Friar and the Wayward Pope

in his grating voice, not only to a vast, but limited, congregation, but to Rome, to Italy, to Europe, to the whole Church. In the word was his power and his genius, and with the word he had defied the world and its *gran maestri*. "I cannot live unless I preach," he had once too candidly confessed. Today, from the pulpit of the great Duomo, in defiance of the Archbishop's Vicar who had fulminated against priests and people who dared to listen to the rebellious Friar, threatening them in their turn with excommunication, Girolamo Savonarola was to preach again—the first time for eight months. He was pitting the force of his personality and words against the whole ecclesiastical power of Rome and the secular principalities and powers which depended on it in Italy and within Florence itself.

Now the expectant, thrilled, saddened, exultant people, for every human emotion must have been felt as all divisions of Florence were represented, were packed around the pulpit within the great, bare nave, most of them huddling together along the benches always placed for Friar's lengthy sermons, but many, no doubt, pressed near the doors and in every corner, and there before them all in the immense hush stood the small black-cloaked Friar, a still relatively young man of forty-six years of age, but worn and wasted with vigil, suffering, work and care; well aware—he had so often said so—that his days were numbered; not yielding, however, in the slightest in his faith in his divinely-appointed destiny—so frail and used a vessel to hold the spiritual force within that could defy Rome and the Head and Hierarchy of the Church.

Savonarola was a preacher of many moods, and he instinctively knew that the great tension of this occasion demanded a controlled introduction suggesting the force that at his will he could release. He began with a prayer and a suggestion of the fated destiny which was his: "O Lord, you have let me ride a sea, and from it I cannot turn back—nor would I even if I could. But I pray to you that no word may pass my lips contrary to the Holy Scriptures and the Church." It was a sufficient introduction on this day. "Now let us come to the excommunication," and we can hear the movement of the great congregation. But Thomas Aquinas, Savonarola's master, not the Friar, seemed to take over as he proceeded with a long scholastic argument. "In every instrument," he told them, "we must distinguish three things, the matter, the form and the moving power." The words *ferro rotto*, "broken tool" hammered at the people's ears. Moved by the wrong hand or for a wrong purpose, an instrument under God's agency becomes a *ferro rotto*. The prince, acting beyond the divine commission, is only a *ferro rotto*. To such a prince no obedience is due. But who is to tell when the tool acts beyond God's commission? "Examine and see whether what he commands is contrary to the principle of all wisdom, God-like living and charity. If what is ordered is contrary to this, you can be certain that a *ferro rotto* is at work and that no obedience is due."

The preacher was now warming to his subject. We can see the quicker movements, the wider gesture as the black cloak opened to reveal the white habit below, the pointed finger, the bending forward of the slight body, the thump on the pulpit, as the voice rose and fell with quick Italian staccato accents: "Just tell me now—what are they seeking, these men who, acting on false information, have obtained this excommunication? They want to destroy the God-like way of living and good government. They want to open wide the doors to every vice. The thing, I tell you, follows logically: no sooner comes the excommunication but the taverns are filled again, the evil pleasures return and every vice prospers. God-like living disappears from the earth." His voice rose, the dark eyes shone, as he hammered the words of indictment. "Nowadays, they only make laws and canons and disputations. The Apostles never needed all those laws. Why? They burnt with love and charity. All theology, all canon and civil law, all the Church's ceremonies have but one end: charity. God made the whole world for charity. Whoever issues any command contrary to charity, which is the fullness of the law, let *him* be anathema! Were an angel, even, were the Virgin Mary and the Saints, to command against charity (which, of course, is impossible) let them be anathema! If there are any laws or canons or a council which say the contrary, let them be anathema. And if any Pope has ever said the contrary to what I am saying, let *him* be excommunicated! I do not say that any Pope has ever done such a thing; but if one should have acted thus, he would not have been an instrument of the Lord. He would have been a *ferro rotto*. Some of you fear that even though this excommunication has no force in heaven, it has force in the Church. But as for me it is enough that I am not excommunicated by Christ. O my Lord, if I should try to obtain absolution from this excommunication, may I be sent down to hell! As to those of you who come to hear me preach and fear to be excommunicated yourselves, I say: Is it a sin to preach? Is it a crime? He who has excommunicated me, if he says so, says it in the face of the Gospel."

Then came a typical Italian touch. The Friar asked the people whether they would like to know who could absolve them from the excommunication. With the impish smile his hearers loved, he drew from his pockets a ring of heavy keys and held them up. Jingling them, he said, "Just do this." The people well understood his meaning and laughed with him. Jingle your money and you will not have far to seek for any absolution you need.

The congregation had probably been expecting a more defiant sermon on this unique occasion. He had been more outspoken in the past. Would he at last name the person who, by his authority though not by his reputation, was the greatest of all his enemies, the Pope himself? Hitherto, his references to Pope Alexander had been indirect and qualified. On the one occasion when he had referred directly to the greatest of the *gran maestri*, it had been in no unkindly spirit for he had quoted the Pope as saying that the good men defended the Friar while the bad ones attacked him.

The sermon was coming to an end, and sensing perhaps the expectation of the people disappointed that their prophet had not given them another and even greater sign from heaven that God was holding him up, Savonarola said: "All has not yet taken place; you have not yet seen everything. But you have seen one thing. You have seen how *someone* in Rome has lost a son."

The allusion could not be missed. It was the Pope of Rome himself, who, eight months earlier, as we have seen, had lost a son, anonymously murdered and ignominiously fished out of the stinking Tiber, while his father had uttered a great cry of despair.

A prophet had arisen in Florence to lay bare before the world the corruption of Alexander, of the Borgias, of the *Gran Maestri* in Church and State and to restore Christ as the King of the world. His prophecies of disaster had long been pouring from his lips. Here was God's punishment falling where the greatest of the *Gran Maestri* would feel it most.

But it was not to work out that way. Papal Rome was still the heart of Christendom, and even an Alexander Borgia had never forgotten, despite his private life and his unseemly family ambitions, his responsibility for the doctrine, right living and peace of the Church throughout Italy and Europe. As for the saintly prophet, Girolamo Savonarola, something in him seemed to be driving him forward to disaster, drunk with his own zeal, reckless of all prudence, disregarding even the elementary rights of authority in hands, however unworthy.

Such were the elements of the tragedy that destroyed the Prophet and his burning vocation and yet, strangely enough, revealed the best in a bad Pope.

What we have described in this Prologue took place in the years 1497 and 1498, near the climax of the story we have to tell in the following pages—the story that began in Rome with the coming of the Borgias from Spain and ended in Florence when the Prophet was forsaken by his own converts and condemned to death by State and by Church.

PART ONE
Two Lives

I. *Why a Borgia Pope?*

BEFORE telling of the rise of the Borgias, it is necessary to say something about the historical conditions which made the career of an Alexander VI possible. Nor will the reader understand that career unless he tries to empty his mind of many of the moral and social values which he has come to take for granted in the Catholic Church of the twentieth century under Pope Pius XII—a Catholic Church now largely divorced from any direct temporal authority and standing in the world as guardian of a theologically precise body of Christian doctrine subserved by an equally rigorously defined moral ideal and teaching within a highly centralised and disciplined organisation.

Twenty centuries have gone to the making of the Catholic Church of today, centuries which have included, after the times of which we write in this book, the Protestant Reformation, the Catholic Counter-Reformation, the Enlightenment, the Romantic Movement, all of which ushered in the great political revolutions of modern times, just as the growth of technical knowledge ushered in the no less important industrial revolutions. This, of course, is not to deny the identity of Catholic faith and moral teaching in the fifteenth and the twentieth centuries, but to insist on the vast differences between the mental and emotional make-up of the men and women who live in our story and the men and women of today, between the *Zeitgeists* of the two periods and between the whole religious, social and political climate then and now.

Looking back from the spiritual ideals of today we may well feel like deploring Christianity's political role in history. Why did it not from the beginning eschew political and temporal responsibilities, concentrating instead on the spiritual "mysteries" of Christian "re-birth" which made possible an inner relationship between the initiated and God, so that through the human story living witnesses would always be found to the real secret of human destiny? The answers to this question are many, but the most fundamental is simply that the Church never had the option of doing so, whether it would have wished to or not.

Alexander VI, as one of the long line of Sovereign Pontiffs, was not only a link in the spiritual chain of Vicars of Christ from St. Peter to Pius XII; he was equally a link in the temporal chain of secular potentates to whose historic role through the centuries we largely owe not only the secure development and culture of the West as we now enjoy it but the protection of the Christian continuity which makes Protestantism, quite as much as Catholicism, possible today.

When the Roman Emperor Constantine, having been converted to Christianity, went East to set up his capital on the Bosphorus, he left Rome, "the capital of the world," in charge of its bishops: the Popes and Vicars of Christ. And when the Western Empire fell, the position, authority and inevitable temporal responsibilities of the Popes gradually increased, even though for many years the influence of Constantinople remained very considerable because of Western anarchy. As the Barbarians streamed into the West, cutting off Rome from much of Europe, they were conquered, not by the sword, but by the Church of the Popes, whose "Romanitas" in the end converted and civilised them. When the time was ripe to crown in Charlemagne a new emperor to be the military arm of the Roman Catholic civilisation in the West, that emperor was the "Holy Roman Emperor" whose relationship to the Church safeguarded the latter's spiritual authority and he became its cultural partner instead of controller as in the Eastern Empire. But the Holy Roman Empire, after Charlemagne, declined and turned out to be too vague and diffuse a political authority to take over temporal responsibilities that fell to the churchmen working on the spot where temporal order had to be maintained. The Papacy, too, rather than the Empire, found

The Meddlesome Friar and the Wayward Pope

itself alone wielding the moral and cultural authority required to save the West as a whole from the ever present threats from the infidel East determined to conquer Europe and destroy Christianity itself.

The Pope's Church, with its civilising spiritual and moral authority, with the necessary help its educated officers (bishops, monks and clergy) gave to the social administration, with its universal law and with its educational and economic enrichment, made possible by its monasteries, created and protected the island of Christendom from which has developed what we now know as Western civilisation.

Today, outside a spiritual authority, directly confined to a section, however numerous, of Christians, the Pope of Rome may look like an honorary moral authority and courtesy Prince whose tiny Vatican State is at best an anachronism, at worst a resented spiritual usurpation. But the actual role of the Papacy in the evolution of the civilisation in which Christians of every kind, indifferent and non-believers, share is measured by the Papal title: "Ruler of the World, Father of Princes and Kings, and Earthly Vicar of Jesus Christ our Saviour," literally acknowledged, if not as a reality at any given moment, at least as embodying the Papacy's historic role. There was no conscious human choice about this, whether on the part of the Popes or of peoples. It inevitably happened. But the price that had to be paid for this half-secularisation of an essentially spiritual commission would necessarily be very heavy. For Popes are human beings and Churchmen are men.

The continuity of these Pope-Kings is a remarkable enough phenomenon when we look back on it as a mere fact of changing history. And the more one knows about the conditions in which this continuity operated, the more extraordinary it seems. For a thousand years, even the method of Papal appointment and election was so uncertain that the Emperor and the local Roman nobles were likely to have as much say in the matter as the bishops and clergy of Rome. In the long struggle between the Popes and the Emperors over the division of authority between them, it was not the Popes who could afford the luxury of grand, romantic conceptions of a renewed Christian world. It was the Emperors with their vague, unsubstantial authority and responsibilities. The Popes were bound by the here and now practical cure of souls and bodies. They had to be realists, keeping together the actual social structure of Europe with hard cash, with the Church's canon law and with an administrative bureaucracy dependent on the far-flung hierarchical ecclesiastical system.

"The shoulders of the Church of Rome are bent under the weight of the common burdens," said Innocent IV. Alas, the need for the money to finance the vast administration was a standing temptation to buy and sell spiritual privileges and powers and by any means available to exact funds in the name of Christ. The accumulation of money, in its turn, was a standing temptation to self-enrichment and ostentatious life on the part of unspiritual Popes and prelates of whom there were bound to be many since the Church offered the best career-making prospects in an otherwise half-literate world.

To make things worse, the short reigns of Popes, usually chosen at an advanced age, involved an inherent instability at the top of the great system, just as the law of clerical celibacy prevented the creation of Papal dynasties and families that could have provided a stability analogous to that of the secular monarchs and princes whose responsibilities were far smaller. Inevitably, the growth of nepotism, the disregard of celibacy, the tricks for maintaining a necessary continuity in a feudal age led to a general relaxing of morals and standards right through the body of the Church. Such evils in a great machine that tended like any other to accumulate the rust and grime of living seemed to be the necessary means of compensating for the inherent weakness of spiritual power when it is charged with vast temporal and semi-temporal responsibilities. How curious, for example, to find Stalin's famous words, "But of how many divisions does the Pope dispose?" anticipated six hundred and fifty years earlier by a French Chancellor opposing the claims of Boniface VIII when he answered the Pope's threat to bring all his forces to bear with the words, "But your forces, my Lord, are verbal; mine are real."

The temporal cares and responsibilities of the Church in the end began to damage its spiritual teaching. The practice of the Faith was no longer sufficiently fed by the Word of God in Scripture and the teaching of the Fathers. Religion thus became a mixture of formal, extrinsic observance and half-superstitious pieties. The great sweeps of spiritual and theological reform died early deaths and at the period of our story the wonder days of the thirteenth century philosophy and theology were being forgotten. Savonarola himself, Friar and follower of St. Thomas Aquinas, was not looking forward to Luther and Calvin, as so many have argued, but back to the greater days of the Church, especially those of Aquinas, when doctrine was at its richest and piety, often, at its deepest.

There is no space here to follow, even in the barest outline, the evolution of the Church and the Papacy, weighed down with these temporal cares that degraded the greatest and highest of earthly missions. It is enough to say that after periods of deep humiliation, such as the exile from Rome to French tutelage at Avignon, with the scandal of the Great Schism following it, and the impotent international efforts to give to General Councils of the Church a priority over the Popes themselves, the growth of nationalism in Europe threw the Popes back on Rome itself and on Italy where the need for the exercise of their authority over the anarchic peninsula forced them to play a more limited, but a more decisive and splendid, role as temporal sovereigns. The Romans themselves, turbulent and revolutionary as they were by nature, had discovered that their great city counted for little in the world when its Pope was absent. It was at this period that we get the succession of the Renaissance Pope-Princes, inheritors of the corrupted legacy yet with the opportunity of displaying a semi-pagan grandeur and power, of whom Alexander Borgia has come down in history as the most notorious.

Yet it would be utterly false to allow the brief picture here given to stand for the Church as a whole. Savonarola was still representative in his day of the best in the Church as was Pope Alexander of the worst.

If the strength of the Papal position allowed the luxury of unworthy Popes, there were also saintly Popes and great Popes, wise Popes and stupid Popes, just as within the Church sanctity, devotion, burning desire for better things are illustrated throughout the centuries in the roll of good prelates, monks, friars, kings, princes, nobles and men and women of humbler quality. Nothing perhaps is more unexpected to our ways of thinking than the international pilgrimage travel, not least to Rome itself for the Papal Jubilees, one of which was celebrated in 1500, two years after our story ends. Christians, then, lived in closed local communities, far more nearly affected than now by the traditions and examples of the local clergy and religious than by the quality of the Church at the top, internationally or nationally. It is consoling therefore to pit against the international laxity that strange internationalism of pilgrimage, which made Christians kin through hardship and penance, with the goal of the tomb of the Apostles, the most sought-after of the many spiritual blessings open to the Christian peoples. And if someone will say that superstition (of which indeed there was plenty) rather than true devotion prompted these distant journeys, the record not only tells of the thousands in every country who sought a better lay life in the Third Orders of St. Francis, St. Dominic and others, but also of the formidably organised and extended active guilds, societies and confraternities whose purpose was to apply the teaching of Christ to the social needs of the day. Every conceivable kind of charity and mutual aid seems to have been covered. The poor, the sick, prisoners, the plague-stricken, girls in difficulties, families facing hard times, the lending of money without usury, the dead, all these were catered for in a honeycomb of practical Christianity.

The fact is that the dramatic contrast between an Alexander VI and a Savonarola was not then, as it seems to us today, a theatrical intrusion, a kind of sport, in the normal pattern of the times; it reflected, doubtless in large and exaggerated terms, the sharply contrasting values, the chequer-pattern of good and evil which then characterised Christianity. For better or for worse—for much better or for much worse—they were times of instinctive, expressionistic, extroverted living in which freedom of choice and individualism were far more real than they have become today under the empire of free institutions. When we realise this we can better understand the upsurge, in Italy especially, of the new forces and new values which governed the period within which Alexander and Savonarola clashed. New ways of thinking, new ideals, new conceptions of human life were making themselves felt. The occasion was doubtless the newly-awakened revival of interest in the classical world of Greece and Rome, through the pouring-in of refugees from the Christian East threatened by the Turks, but these new forces seem also to have been spontaneously generated through a kind of social coming of age.

It was a real Renaissance in the literal meaning of a "new birth" because men felt themselves to be new men—men suddenly conscious of their human powers and thus able to find supreme self-satisfaction in sheer living. To enjoy the adventure of living; to be able to appreciate the arts and the beauty which it was given to these new men to fashion; to savour the present moment and the sensation it could offer, with the spice of the next moment being utterly different; to be able truly to exercise the supremely human act of choice of good or choice of evil; to seek "glory," temporal or spiritual—such were some of the characteristics of these new men who were suddenly becoming vividly *conscious* of the human and personal implications of man, as Christianity had long taught his true nature to be.

Inevitably, this application of the Christian teaching of human responsibility and freedom to a new creative energy, whether carried to achievement by the geniuses of the times or frivolously and barbarously dissipated by the second-raters, went with a fresh bravado about human life and destiny. The élan vital held individual life cheap. To live was more important than to exist for a long time. Men grew treacherous, cruel, callous and ready to kill and be killed. This *bravado*, conscious or unconscious, seems to be one explanation at least of characteristics, deeply puzzling to us, in a man like Alexander. In his life and behaviour we derive no sense of his growing old. Apparently he never measured his grand and very far from blameless life in terms of the shortening years left to him before he must lose all and pay a severe reckoning in the next world as his always vivid faith assured him. How, too, was he able to reconcile his conscience as a priest at the altar, as a Pope called to perform the deepest and grandest ceremonies of the Church, with the gross sins in which he appears to have habitually lived? Yet there is no trace of spiritual and moral anxiety for himself, though there is a strong trace of the better choice he should have made from the start and always wanted to make.

In Savonarola, too, the influence of this *bravado*, this fresh consciousness of the freedom of man, is evident. It is the best explanation of the strange contradictions in his character: his role as a prophet appearing straight from the tremendous days of the Old Testament, his childish naïveté about the inspirations which he believed to have governed his life, his utter spiritual dedication, his terrible and tragic defiance of the whole world of the *Gran Maestri*.

Today, against the background of an expanding universe and within a collective and technocratic society, we lose sight of the individual person whose fate is governed by so many social conventions, externally imposed and willingly accepted. To see the figures of the Renaissance as they were, we need, as it were, a magnifying glass set against them individually, not only because they were larger than life as we know it, but because the springs of their behaviour were so various, so much more deeply rooted in the individual, so much freer—and their vision, after all, was not confined to a scientifically calculable material universe, however infinitely expanded, but it mounted up to, and descended down to, all the mysteries of heaven, of hell and their spiritually and even materially incalculable world between.

II. *Cardinal Rodrigo*

MR. Bernard Berenson has well brought out one aspect of the future Alexander VI in describing him as an "opulent and luxurious half-barbarian." The ancestry of the Borgias (Spanish, *Borja*) is uncertain, but it is likely that, with most of the people of Yativa, near Valencia, whence they came, they were of mixed Spanish and Moorish ancestry. They had been settled in Yativa for about two hundred years and were a noble and important family when Rodrigo (the future Alexander VI) was born in 1432 of a Borgian mother as well as a Borgian father. Oddly enough, the Moorish blood of the future Pope was to give rise to perhaps the wildest of all the accusations against Alexander VI. Savonarola, in the stress of his final desperate quarrel with the Pope went so far as hysterically to accuse him of never having been baptised and therefore of not being a Christian at all, but an atheist. As such, he could never have been validly elected Pope.

In fact, Rodrigo Borgia was born under ecclesiastical patronage and under a lucky star—a star, it seemed, that came from heaven. The big man of the clan at the time was his uncle, Alfonso, recently made Bishop of Valencia, a great and rich See. As a young priest, Don Alfonso had been present on one occasion when the saintly Dominican, Vincent Ferrer, was preaching. After the sermon, the future St. Vincent drew Don Alfonso aside and told him that one day he would be invested with the highest dignity that could fall on a man; and he further prophesied that he, Vincent Ferrer, would after his death be the object of a special honour bestowed by Don Alfonso. Alfonso was indeed to be the first of the two Borgia Popes, and Vincent Ferrer was to be duly canonised by him.

To add to the hovering haloes, Alfonso told the future St. John Capistran of the future St. Vincent Ferrer's prophecies.

It is certainly odd to come across the pious stories that customarily adorn the biographies of saints related about the infamous Borgias, but this one has passed through the sieve of the historians who have sought to eliminate the mass of Borgia legends, and one must suppose there is something in it. If so, it would seem that inspiration from heaven attended the meteoric career of Alfonso Borgia and thus indirectly helped that of Rodrigo since he could hardly have reached the Papal throne save by the luck of having an uncle as Pope. In any event it is clear that with the Bishop of Valencia as his uncle, Rodrigo had best enter for the Church and that as soon as possible. This meant, according to his most critical biographer, Orestes Ferrara, at the age of six, the minimum age allowed. The future Alexander's choice of vocation must have been minimal.

The plan worked admirably. As his uncle Alfonso, a brilliant Canon lawyer in whose debt were the King of Naples and the Pope of Rome, rose in ecclesiastical dignity, so did his young nephew. Papal Bulls brought Rodrigo ecclesiastical preferments in his teens (Pope Nicholas V finding him to be "of honest life and morals and generally praiseworthy for his probity and virtue"). Not long after uncle Alfonso had been made a Cardinal, Rodrigo, aged seventeen, was made a Canon of Valencia. As such, he could enjoy the revenues of the Canonry without the inconvenience of residing in a city so far from the centre of things. In fact, his Cardinal uncle, while desirous of ensuring for his nephew the promotions and revenues necessary for a high aspiring churchman, was also determined to ground him in the best canonical schooling available. Canon Rodrigo Borgia, therefore, left Spain once and for all (save for his later visit as a Papal Legate) and settled down to his books in the University of Bologna. There he spent seven years.

Spaniards who had long had to fight for their faith against the Moors were then as now very real Catholics and we need have no doubt about the earnestness with which the young Canon entered on his ecclesiastical career. The fact has not prevented the growth of stories to the effect that Rodrigo, while actually studying as any young seminarist might be doing today, was pursuing the career of a wild soldier, already guilty of his first murder in quarrelling with a companion and killing him. Nor is it significant that some later scribbler annotated the certificate of approval of Don Rodrigo's studies at Bologna with the comment, "He died in August 1503, and was buried in hell." The Borgia legend was as effective in claiming knowledge about Pope Alexander's afterlife as in adorning the story of his earthly life. And that legend was born of the great event which took place in 1455 when Rodrigo was completing his studies at Bologna at the age of twenty-two. His uncle Alfonso was then elected Supreme Pontiff, taking the name of Calixtus III. Rodrigo's career was assured.

The choice of a Spaniard as Pope was so remarkable that it makes St. Vincent Ferrer's prophecy a near-miracle. But the reason why Alfonso Borgia was elected could hardly have been less flattering. The Conclave wanted a "caretaker" who would live but a few years. Cardinal Borgia was seventy-seven and entirely respectable, very learned and sufficiently distinguished. The decision was to have consequences far beyond the calculations of the Conclave.

The Spaniards, or Catalans, as the Italians called them, were loathed in Rome as barbarians, the term being construed in an entirely cultural sense, since the Romans immediately displayed their own form of barbarianism in organising a riot in the Eternal City to express their feelings about the new Pontiff. And when the learned Calixtus, heir of centuries of fighting for the Faith against the Moors, tore the gold and silver off finely-bound manuscripts to use as the sinews of war to fight the dreaded Turk who had taken Constantinople and threatened to engulf the West, the reputation of the barbarian Spanish Pope was not worth a penny's purchase in Renaissance Rome. Civilised warfare for the Italians was the internecine fighting which kept Italy in a constant state of anarchy. Exactly five hundred years ago, under Spanish Calixtus, Hungary, with the aid of St. John Capistran, saved the West from the Turks.

Pope Calixtus, it must be admitted, made matters considerably worse for himself in Rome by whistling up from Spain a veritable horde of Borgia kinsmen in whose train, of course, came every Spanish hanger-on who might hope to make his fortune in the ecclesiastical or military field under Borgia patronage. Obtuse and pig-headed, as the aged scholar is so apt to be, Calixtus showed no tact or even sense in indulging the Borgia family failing of mutual support against all comers. To make sure that there was no doubt about his intentions, he made two of his nephews cardinals and a third Captain-General of the Church and Prefect of Rome. A desperate Lear, without a hereditary kingdom, he was bent on the seemingly impossible task of forcing posterity to reckon with the Borgias.

He was proved more right than he can have dreamt. Ten months after the election of his uncle as Pope, Don Rodrigo was made Cardinal-Deacon of San Niccolo in Carcere. He was twenty-four years old. A year later his uncle gave him the all-important post of Vice-Chancellor of the Church. Both were acts of blatant nepotism, yet the old man should not be judged too severely. Whether through luck or insight, he had appointed a Vice-Chancellor who, by sheer merit and efficiency, was to keep the post through the four subsequent pontificates until it ended with his own elevation to the Papacy.

Still fighting resolutely against opposition within the Curia and a hatred outside it which made every Spaniard's life in Rome a poor risk, Calixtus III died of the summer plague and the *folie des grandeurs* in August 1458, three years after his accession. Now it was up to Cardinal Rodrigo.

It is time to take a good look at this young ecclesiastic of twenty-six, Cardinal and Vice-Chancellor of the Holy Roman Church at a date when in Ferrara a dark little boy of six, grandson of Dr. Michele Savonarola, was playing—and probably praying—in the streets.

His teacher, Gaspar of Verona, described him at this age as follows: "He is good looking with a happy and gay appearance, a speaker with well-turned and honeyed phrase, who attracts beautiful women to love him and in an extraordinary way draws them as the magnet draws iron—but it is thought that he leaves them as he found them." The last words, "*quas tamen intactas dimittere sane putatur*" are usually omitted when Gaspar is quoted.

The portraits we still have of him as Pope (in his later years, of course), the best-known of which shows him praying before "Christ Rising from the Tomb", one of the frescoes of the Sala dei Misteri of the Vatican Borgia Apartments, do not suggest good looks so much as abundant health and vitality. Pinturicchio's brush—Alexander's head in the fresco is said by Berenson to be the only part painted by the Master himself—makes us feel that the big fleshy face might at any moment break into an intelligent, knowing smile, capable even in the sixties of enchanting intelligent and mischievous women. Translate that dark, experienced eye, that generously curved nose, that full but still firm, upper and under-lip, those heavy cheeks, to the thinner, smoother and more virilely-fashioned features of a man in the prime of life, and one can begin to see the commanding attraction of a young prince—the ecclesiastical status was socially an accident—strong, swarthy, imperious, yet lustily human, amusing and always ready to make and see a joke. His figure, too, was tall, athletic, yet generously built and reassuring to the feminine eye. All in all, he was a full-blooded, commanding man, with a softness and air of comfort about him that made a man in his position both attractive and dangerous.

The quality of Rodrigo Borgia as statesman, churchman and just a man was fully put to the test when his uncle, the Pope, died.

The death of a Pope in those days left his particular supporters or "creatures" (those he had specially favoured and promoted) suddenly bereft. The Cardinal Chamberlain took everything over until a new Pontiff was elected. Hence the custom that the "creatures" of the doomed Pope should make hay while the sun was setting by acquiring any treasure or land still available.

But on this occasion the far-seeing Cardinal Borgia made no attempt to follow the custom. He knew that the Borgias were too unpopular for the risk to be taken. While Rodrigo stood by his uncle until the end, Pedro Luis Borgia, the Captain-General of the Church, proved himself to be a coward by comparison and fled, together with other Borgias and the hordes of Catalans battening on them, to avoid the revenge of the Romans. Thanks to the Cardinal's spirit, the life of Pedro Luis was saved, though he only survived for a short while. Meanwhile, Rodrigo faced both the mob and his enemies in the College of Cardinals, taking his place in the Conclave as though times were normal.

It had been a ticklish moment, but his judgment had been sound. He was no longer seen as an ill-tolerated foreign intruder, but, as it were, as an ecclesiastically naturalised Italian. From now onwards, his life and his developing character strike us as being Italian rather than Spanish, and a true Italian in spirit he would always claim to be.

In the Conclave, Rodrigo adroitly played his cards so as to ensure the election of a character not altogether dissimilar from his, Enea Silvio de Piccolomini, one of the greatest international scholars and humanists of all times. The new Pope, Pius II, was expected to inaugurate an even more liberal and paganised era in the Vatican. He had led the dissipated life of a gentleman of the day and complained of the difficulty of practising continency, a difficulty he did not surmount. But he had reformed and his reign was noted for his interest in the Crusade and his insistence that the doctrine holding General Councils of the Church to be superior to the Pope was heretical. Both points were in tune with Rodrigo's mind, and Pius II became the friend and protector of the young Cardinal Vice-Chancellor in gratitude for his help at the Conclave. After all, no one could now afford to neglect a Cardinal, however young and uncertain in his morals, who could so smartly turn a highly dangerous moment to his own advantage.

The new Pope, who, in his youth, had savoured so much of the good things of a brilliant, morally lax and half-pagan society, seemed to be determined to warn Cardinal Rodrigo of the danger of following too closely in his footsteps.

On one occasion he wrote him a famous letter in which he said that he had heard that Cardinal Rodrigo "was present from the seventeenth to the twenty-second hour in the gardens of Giovanni de Bichis, where there were several women of Siena, women wholly given up to worldly vanities." Complaining that another cardinal was also present, the Pope went on: "We have heard that the dance was indulged in with much wantonness; none of the allurements of love were lacking, and you conducted yourself in an entirely worldly manner. Shame forbids mention of all that took place, for not only the things themselves but their very names are unworthy of your rank. In order that your lust might be all the more unrestrained, the husbands, fathers, brothers and kinsmen of the young women and girls were not invited to be present. You and a few servants were the leaders and inspirers of this orgy. It is said that nothing is talked of in Siena but your vanity which is the subject of universal ridicule. Certain it is that here at the Baths (Petriolo, where the Pope was staying) where churchmen and laity are very numerous, your name is on everyone's tongue." The Pope went on to explain how such behaviour brought the Church into disrepute. "We leave it to you," he went on, "to decide whether it is becoming to your dignity to court young women and to send those whom you love fruits and wine, and during the whole day to give no thought to anything but sensual pleasures." He ended: "May your good sense place some restraint on these frivolities, and may you never lose sight of your dignity. If you do so, people will not call you a vain and showy young man.... We have always loved you and believed you worthy of our protection as a man of earnest and modest character."

One wonders how far this letter, superficially read and without inquiring into the facts behind it, helped to condition the Borgia legend about the future Alexander's private life.

The words "from the seventeenth to the twenty-second hour" suggests lurid deeds in the falling darkness of a July night. In fact the hours at that time were numbered from half-an-hour after sunset. The time given was between one o'clock and six o'clock in the afternoon—an innocent enough hour. We also know from another contemporary letter that the occasion for the party was a baptism at which Cardinal Borgia was a godfather. After the ceremony the clergy were invited to see the women dancing in the garden. The Cardinal's gallantry may well have been overdone, and the dancing under the eyes of two very broad-minded cardinals may well have been of the sensual type common enough at the time. Not a very edifying spectacle, no doubt, but one, we venture to suggest, that has had its parallels, allowing for the fashions and manners of different periods, often enough since. It is at any rate clear that the story which had come to the ears of the Pope was very much exaggerated, and Cardinal Rodrigo at once wrote to the Pope to explain what had really happened and to ask his forgiveness for any ill-behaviour on his part.

Pius II answered: "Your action, my son, cannot be held to be without blame, though it was evidently less blameworthy than we had been informed. We grant you the pardon you ask for, and but for the love we have for you as a son of predilection, we should not have lovingly reproached you. So long as you do good and live becomingly, you will find in me a father and a protector whose blessing will also fall on those who are dear to you. So long as Pius lives, you will have no reason to regret the loss of your uncle, our predecessor."

The real biographical importance of this correspondence does not lie in the reproof of Cardinal Borgia's behaviour. Whatever he had done—and the Pope insisted that he had anyway gone too far—had been exaggerated in the telling. But the Pope had troubled himself to write in the first instance solely because of his love for Rodrigo and the very high esteem he felt for him. The other Cardinal is apparently dismissed as though nothing better could be expected of him. Not so Rodrigo, a "son of predilection...of earnest and modest character." Clearly, the whole episode indicates that a virtuous Pope, if one also of much worldly wisdom, had first been deeply shocked by the thought that the young and outstanding Rodrigo Borgia, of all people, had got himself involved in a pretty disgraceful affair; then had been reassured; but, knowing Rodrigo's weakness, was very glad indeed to have the chance of teaching him a lesson in good time. At any rate, we may be certain that these letters, used to damn Rodrigo, at this time not yet a priest, from the start, show that the Borgia of the legend, a man capable of the grossest conduct and the most monstrous crimes, has not yet come on the scene.

But now comes a sterner test, especially by the standards of today.

It is usually held that at about this time Cardinal Borgia fathered three children, a son, Pedro Luis, and two daughters, Geronima and Isabella. The question whether the future Alexander VI ever in fact had any children has been raised in recent years by Catholic historians, like Mgr. De Roo and Orestes Ferrara. It would be pretentious on the part of the present writer to presume to decide a question whose study involves the equipment of the historian *de métier* with the opportunity of prolonged research in archives, deciding which documents are genuine and which belong to the vast accumulation of forgeries, even of Papal documents, which were made at the time. But common sense can be helpful where professional historians violently disagree. And common sense suggests that at a time when it was almost normal for clerics to set aside in practice the law of celibacy, the general view, sufficiently often attested at the time and immediately after it, that the future Alexander VI had a number of children, is almost certainly true. He was by no means the only Pope of the period to do so in what was called "the golden age of bastards." Even so late a Pope as Gregory XIII, after the Council of Trent, had fathered a child in his early days. So little reason was there to hide the fact of Alexander's paternity in the flesh that the Ferrarese court-poet, singing the praises of the infant son of Lucrezia Borgia by Alfonso of Este, bade him remember that his grandfather was Pope Alexander VI. One can understand that a commoner might see distinction in having a Pope as a grandfather; but in this case the infant was heir to a reigning ducal house!

Bastardy, even within the highest ranks of the Church, was so little thought of that a son of Innocent VIII, Alexander's predecessor, was considered a suitable match for the daughter of Lorenzo de' Medici, the ruler of Florence, and the wedding was celebrated in the Pope's palace in Rome. And the relentless Savonarola himself, while inveighing at the growing lack of shame which allowed churchmen publicly to acknowledge their offspring as "sons" and no longer use the conventional "nephew," seemed more ready to tolerate this natural failing than many another crime in the clergy of his time. The murder of the Duke of Gandia was a punishment from heaven inflicted on his papal father for his opposition to the Friar rather than for his sin in begetting a son. In the face then of the universally accepted belief at the time that Alexander had children, rather than genuine nephews and nieces, and given both the tolerance of the times and what we know of Rodrigo Borgia's character and vocation, it is surely common sense to accept the tradition. But if common sense forces us to this conclusion, it equally demands that the professionally celibate young Cardinal, whose good reputation we know, should have conducted himself in his private life in a manner consistent with his status. And there is good evidence that this was the case.

As against the usual view that the first three children, Geronima, Isabella and Pedro Luis, were born of a different mother from the last four who are so much better known in history, Juan, Cesare, Lucrezia and Jofre, Orestes Ferrara has brought forward documents attesting to the fact that *all* these children were full brothers and sisters. If so, the mother of them all must have been Vanozza Catanci, since there is no doubt whatever that she was the mother of the last four. Apart from this one fact that she was the mother of these children, very little indeed is known for certain about this woman except that when she died she was given a grand funeral at which Pope Leo X was represented.

What kind of picture does all this make up? It suggests that Rodrigo Borgia was, in principle, at least, faithful through his life to one woman, whose first child by her was born when she was fifteen, the nubile age at that period. Since the first children were born in Spain, it suggests also that he was discreet and dignified enough to send his mistress to Spain for the birth of the earlier children. Above all, it suggests that the mother agreed with the Cardinal about the need for her to live a life of retirement rather than presume on a position which would then have given far less scandal than at any other period of history. This is very far from being a picture of a good priest by any proper standards, but it is also very far from being the picture of a debauched man, capable of any crime. It is in fact a likely picture of an otherwise reputable churchman of eminence and of strong sensual disposition who found in this illicit, but generally tolerated, domesticity the compensation for the inability to marry and live happily ever after as his nature craved. He had never asked to be a churchman.

Though as Vice-Chancellor of the Church under four pontificates, Cardinal Borgia amassed a long list of ecclesiastical titles and the revenues that went with them, rather in the manner of Don Giovanni and his lovers in Leporello's song, he was no miser and he spent freely on the Church—and on himself. He was the *grand seigneur* who loved the life of great affairs of State, the pomp and display of his high station and the gay society he kept, but he was personally abstemious and frugal, so that we have every reason to think that his private life with Vannozza was quite other than we have been led to suppose. As the Church's "maid of all work," for that is what his post meant, he was, according to Guicciardini, prudent, vigilant, maturely reflective, and he displayed unusual powers of persuasion and exceptional skill and capacity for the conduct of difficult affairs. We can obtain, under the official language, some idea of the man from the sermon he preached to the clergy of Valencia, whose bishop he was, when he went to Spain as Papal Legate where he was, naturally enough, a great success:

> God, who reads all hearts [he said] be my witness that I have always used my goodwill for the accomplishment of all these

duties; but unhappily I have always been compelled to be absent from you. I had to obey our Supreme Father. The dignity of cardinal attaches me by the most powerful bond to the Holy See, and once named member of its council, I could not be away save on a special mission. The vast and laborious administration of the Roman Chancellery, instituted for the good of the whole Church and yielding in importance only to the work of the Sovereign Pontiff himself, cannot without grave difficulties be carried on in the absence of the authority which presides over it. Our first duty is to obey him to whom God has given supreme authority and towards whom we are all bound to supreme respect. If then I have been prevented until now from being with you and have had therefore to delegate to another the fulfilment of my duties here, it was not by my own choice, but in obedience to circumstances.... In spite of all this, I exhort you to persevere as you have begun in virtue and religion. This is demanded by your priestly profession and your past labours.... Among other things, I commend to you the observance of fraternal charity. If this unity aids the glory and growth of the Church, its degradation brings detriment and ignominy. And since the freedom of the Church has increased in the people the veneration of the priesthood, I beg of you not only to be of one mind in guarding and defending it as the most precious thing, but also to spare yourselves neither pain nor peril for its preservation.

And turning to the great menace which, through all this period, hung upon the Church and the West, he went on:

The Turk after having subjugated Asia and a great part of Europe has twice already descended on Italy, destroying everything with fire and massacre. He is now on his way, threatening the centre of our religion, towards the sanctuary of the Apostles and Martyrs, the City of Rome. If he were thus able to crush the head, the rest of the Christian body would quickly perish. We are the shepherds of the flock, we are set upon the watchtower, precisely so that we may keep it safe. It is for others a duty to follow our example.

We, enlightened by our hindsight, may wonder at the clarity of the Borgia vision where general principles were concerned and where, as a statesman, Cardinal Borgia saw the real external danger to the Church to lie, and at its blindness to the far deeper spiritual and moral threat to the Church caused by the evils to be denounced by Savonarola, of which Borgia was destined to be in history the classical example. But such a position has many historical parallels, not excepting our own day when the threat of Communism so much more readily enlists the idea of Christian crusades than prompts self-examination into the Christian social conscience to see how far Christians have opened the way towards the Communist assault.

As to what the Popes themselves thought of their permanent Vice-Chancellor, let his immediate predecessor, the dull-witted but conscientious Innocent VIII speak in a Bull addressed to him: "Sometimes we like to speak our mind to you who are distinguished by noble gifts, and full of worth and outstanding by your virtues. So now we recall how, while clad in the splendour of the dignity of cardinal, you have served the Church of Rome under the Pontiffs of happy memory, Calixtus III, Pius II, Paul II and Sixtus IV, our predecessors, as well as ourselves, for almost thirty years. During that time you have helped us bear the charges of the Church, bending your shoulders in constant work with unvarying diligence, assisting the Church with your exceptional prudence, your subtle intellect, your prompt judgment, your fidelity to your word, your long experience, and all other virtues known to be yours. Never have you failed me."

Whatever his other shortcomings, Cardinal Rodrigo Borgia was no bad churchman.

III. *Rise of a Prophet*

FROM the half-suffocating, hieratic opulence of Papal Rome, still despite everything the "capital of the world" and the Holy City, we journey north again, through the Medicean Florence and Bentivoglio's Bologna (where the young Canon Rodrigo Borgia is still at his studies), to the distant fief of the Holy See, the self-governing city of Ferrara, home of the arts and sciences. There in 1452 was born Girolamo Savonarola.

Girolamo was of a family of the people risen to what we should call the middle or professional class. His grandfather, Michele Savonarola, was an upright doctor and scientist of sufficient local repute to be favoured at the brilliant court of the ruling House of Este. There he served the Marquis Niccolo d'Este and his two bastard successors, the Marquis Lionello and the Marquis Borso, the latter raised in rank to a dukedom by the Emperor who could appreciate the growing pomp and grandeur of Ferrara under the d'Estes. The doctor saw in his grandson the signs of aptitude and gravity wanting in his own son, Niccolo (Girolamo's father), who preferred society to learning.

As Girolamo grew up, he found himself much more interested in the philosophical studies which were then the natural avenue to medical training than in the career mapped out for him by his grandfather. And where, in his philosophy reading, the precocious boy found himself comparing Aristotle with Thomas Aquinas he was in no doubt about his choice of master. In a sermon, Savonarola once said: "I myself derived great benefit from him (Aquinas) and held him in reverence. For myself I know nothing—the little I have is due to my fidelity to his teaching. His was truly a deep mind, and when I want to feel myself a little child

The Meddlesome Friar and the Wayward Pope

again, I read him and I know him to be a giant while I am nothing at all." The Aquinas influence (St. Thomas was a saint and the greatest of theologians) would pervade the best in Savonarola's life and work.

Girolamo's mother, though described as "a woman of lofty sentiments and strong character," was no saint if we can judge from a letter to her from her son after he had entered the Dominican Order. But her son's standards were always very high. He had three brothers and two sisters. The family was closely knit and Girolamo was always much attached to it.

It seems clear that the boy was considerably influenced by his grandfather who wrote ascetical tracts and, doubtless, compared the increasing vanities of the court with the serious purpose of men of science like himself. As against this solid background, Girolamo had the bad example of a father who was a disappointment both to his own father and to his wife. The contending family influences represented in miniature the characteristics of the outside world into which the boy would enter: the serious and scholarly side of the Renaissance; the mass of Catholic men and women still good, despite bad conditions; and the cult of distraction, elegance and pleasure for which Ferrara, like Florence, was famous.

Though the future Dominican is said to have paid court to a girl living in the same street as the Savonarolas and been snubbed for his pains, it is easier to believe the story that one single visit to the d'Este Court was enough to ensure that he would never go near it again and never become part of the half-pagan world which flaunted itself not only in the privileged circles of the Court but in the constant festivities which gave delight to the people, making occasional riots and bloodshed a small price to pay for the pace of gay living. Girolamo himself is described as a solitary and melancholy boy, and it did not take him long to make up his mind about where he stood in the eternal conflict between the way of the world and the true way of Christ. That thin, angular, dark face with its burning eyes could never have belonged to the great race of compromisers with the best and the worst. By the age of twenty, the path of his future life was surprisingly well marked. Not only would he seek sanctity, but the passion within him for it must burst sooner or later into ardent expression.

The expression was not delayed. In a poem written at that age, called "The Ruin of the World," the young Savonarola anticipated a good deal of what he had to say during the remainder of his life. His lamentations about the state of the Church, the Popes and Rome anticipated by twenty years his struggle with Alexander. "In the hands of a pirate," he sang in verses echoing in harsh stanzas the poetic language of Petrarch, "the Sceptre has fallen and St. Peter is crushed to the ground. Vice and plunder there abound. So much so that I cannot conceive why Heaven itself is not troubled.... So heavy with vice is the earth that no longer can it rise from its oppression. So low lies Rome, its Head, that its great mission is heard no more.... The days of piety and purity are past. Virtue goes begging, never to walk again. Blind to the meaning of virtue, man perverts wisdom by turning it to usurious gain." And the poet consoles himself with a sentiment that will always go deep with him: "But well I know that when it comes to the next life we shall see whose soul is the fairest, whose wings fly in the better style." And he ends with the future preacher's warning to heed well his words, never to look for help among those robed in purple, to fly castles and palaces and be careful to whom you speak, else you will find yourself the whole world's enemy. Goaded to extremities in the end, the future preacher was to forget the maxims he penned at the age of twenty.

Why some men are born so good while others are born so indifferent to goodness is a puzzle of human destiny. A Rodrigo Borgia was born, it seems, with natural gifts that he could use for spiritual greatness, for evil or for a lifelong and unequal struggle between the two. But Girolamo Savonarola was born with a whole predestined oeuvre ready packed and labelled in his spirit from the start. He was driven by an inner force over whose explosive power he seemed to have little control. His other gifts were there at best to direct it.

For a moment, perhaps, he was frightened by what he felt within him, sensing something of the danger of the dramatic way in which his feelings took expression, for he tells us that he hesitated at first to submit to the discipline of the religious vocation within which alone a man, with a spiritual drive such as his, could find opportunity and effective expression. One external objection was the pain which the choice of the life of religion would give his father and mother. They perhaps discerned the unusual qualities of his intellect and hoped for a career that would throw even his grandfather's into the shade. They may be forgiven for failing to foresee that nothing that could be offered to him in the expanding, rich life of Ferrara could compare with the power and influence of their son as perhaps the most famous preacher of all times.

In the end the young Girolamo, moved by a sermon he heard, took the bull by the horns and ran away—half from himself? half to himself?—as a pilgrim to Bologna where he presented himself as a postulant at the house of San Domenico to join the black and white friars of his beloved Aquinas. Inevitably, his decision found lengthy verbal expression—indeed, at both ends of the journey for he left behind him on a windowsill a tract on the "Contempt of the World" for his parents to study and he wrote a long letter to his father from Bologna.

This letter to his father is worth quoting at some length since it affords us a good deal of insight into a mind already well fixed within the boundaries that would mark the writer's future course.

> My honoured Father. I cannot doubt about how you feel at my going away, especially as I left you secretly. That is why I want you to realise through this letter what is in my mind and purpose. It should comfort you and make you appreciate the fact that I have not behaved like a child as some people believe. But first what I want from you is that you be strong enough and sufficiently able to despise the passing things of the world in order to follow the way of truth rather than of passion as some women do. You must

reasonably judge my decision to fly the world and follow my resolve. *In primis*, the reason why I have decided to enter religion is this: first, the great misery of the world, the iniquities of men, the rapes, the adulteries, the pride, the idolatry, the cruel blasphemies. The world has become such that no one can be found in it to do good.... I cannot bear the great malice of Italy's blinded people, the more so as I see virtue utterly withered away and vices mounting. This causes me the greatest suffering I can experience in this world, and every day I have prayed to the Lord Jesus Christ to raise me from this mire.... Tell me now—is there much merit in a man fleeing from the filth and the evils of a miserable world so as to live like a rational being and not like a beast among swine? ... So, my sweetest Father, you have greater reason to thank the Lord Jesus than to complain. He has given you a son and preserved him well enough with you for twenty-two years. Not only this, He has been good enough to make him into a soldierly knight—do you not feel it to be a great grace to have a son a knight of Jesus Christ? Allow me to explain briefly—do you love me or do you not? I know you will not say that you do not love me. If then you love me, remember that I have two parts, the soul and the body. Which of them do you prefer? You cannot prefer the body because then you would be preferring the vilest part of me. But if you prefer the soul, why do you not prefer to seek the good of the soul? Well then, you should rejoice and celebrate this great triumph. Oh, I know that the flesh must grieve a little; but this grief should be limited by the reason especially where a wise and large-hearted man like yourself is concerned. Do you not see that it is also a great sorrow to me to be parted from you? I do want you to believe me. Never in all my life have I suffered more than in finding myself abandoning my own blood and going amidst strangers to sacrifice my body to Jesus Christ and to sell my will into the hands of those I have never known....

The Meddlesome Friar and the Wayward Pope

Allowing for age, is it unfair to suggest that this was a rather priggish and pretentious letter? From it one might derive the impression that no one had ever before left his family to become a monk or priest. Nor does his logic allow anywhere a shading of his adolescent condemnation of the world, bad as it might be, neither in the sense that there might be other good people in it or that the bad might be judged as persons, often weak and ill brought up, rather than as out and out criminals. The lecturing tone, too, to a father and a family he loved and from whom he hated to part seems a little distasteful.

However, he was more true to himself in the Tract on the "Contempt of the World" for in it he did contrast the great people of the world with the "simple people, the unlettered folk, the uneducated women who put to shame the false wisdom of the world," and this love of the simple and unlettered he always retained.

Some years later, Savonarola, a friar nine years in religion, wrote a letter to his mother, condoling with her on the death of her brother. His tone is unchanged, or rather it has grown more relentless and more severe. His uncle's death forms part of the many sufferings inflicted by God on his family and prayed for by himself to make sure that they understand that "human hopes are blind and false." "Open your eyes and be not ungrateful. Ask yourself whether from the beginning of the world until the end any servant of God has been without temptation, persecution and tribulation. God flays his children lest they derive hope from earthly things.... These deaths of ours teach us not to accumulate wealth, not to live in fine style, not to dress grandly; they teach us the real worth of honours, glory and present delights, seeing that we have them for so short a while." And he tells the story of the sudden recent death of a "young, fresh and healthy young man" and of a young singing-girl, the most popular in the town, who was painfully struck down in childbirth "carrying the punishment of her sins." He adds: "If perhaps she had followed the way of life which I once explained to you she might not have come to such a pass." The moral is clear: "I pray therefore that you and my sisters, Beatrice and Clare, should give yourselves over entirely to prayer, leaving aside all vanities, not only in the deed, but even in the desire for them. Give yourselves over to solitude, spiritual reading and prayer. Do not worry about society, whether you see people or they see you...and you, my Mother, I pray that you will forget this world.... I do not say all this to you in order to avoid comforting you, for that would be against charity. I say it only to weaken your love so that, were I to die, your sorrow would be lessened."

In fact, his mother, who evidently adored him and always deeply missed him, was spared the tragedy of his end, but after her death the Friar was so absorbed by his sermons, prophecies and reforms that he could only say (in a sermon): "My mother shed tears for many years. I let her do so. It is enough that she now must know that she was wrong to do this."

There is something terrifying in all this application of a clear logical mind to feelings so gloomy and judgments instinctively so severe. Even though there was such manifest abuse of the talents and powers which God gave to man—and Savonarola had certainly had plenty of opportunity of observing that abuse in the Ferrara of his day—this instinct of Savonarola in the degree in which he indulged it was destructive, and not constructive, and calculated to shape a world intolerable to man as he has been created. Was it the world which Christ saw around Him? One may be pardoned when emerging from the shadows of this side of the Friar's character for being unable to suppress a certain relief at the humanity of the Borgias, even though one does not wish to condone the astonishing excesses of that humanity, more especially in the Chair of Peter. Moreover, all this was only one side of Savonarola's personality, a kind of logically fanatical watertight compartment in his mind which, however, unfortunately prevented him from fusing with his dark severity the great powers of love, sympathy and inspiration which he possessed and from using his excellently critical and Thomistically-trained mind to examine with any detachment the true quality of the abnormal

The Meddlesome Friar and the Wayward Pope

illuminative or visionary powers on which his work so much depended.

Savonarola's career in religion progressed quickly—too quickly perhaps, suggests the judicious Fr. Herbert Lucas, S.J. It may have been a case of uncritical and unwise superiors, enchanted to find a saint in their midst, failing to remember that even sanctity needs to be wisely guided and directed by men who understand the pitfalls of the human mind and make-up. Within seven years, he was promoted to the highly responsible job of novice-master at Bologna.

Emerging ardent, but still raw, from the sheltered and artificial life of the cloister, he was surprised and disappointed to find himself, after all, a flop as a preacher. When he was a preaching failure in his native Ferrara, he could excuse himself on the ground that a prophet is without honour in his own country, but when with more experience he found his first congregations in Florence itself dwindling to a handful, he became deeply depressed. "I cannot live unless I preach." He *had* to succeed—or else give up altogether which he was tempted to do. The decision, of course, was not his, but that of his superiors, and he carried on.

One reason for his failure was obvious. The fashionable preachers of the time in cities like Florence and Ferrara were the masters of elegant language, of balanced periods, of flowing and harmonious discourse, after the classical patterns, whose sermons were a joy and a flattery to the cultivated congregations who listened to them. Savonarola, to his immense credit, was never tempted to succeed through a pulpit expression of this debased type. From the beginning to the end he was always to preach in a rough, popular, direct and colloquial way. If he hypnotised his congregations, it was not by the traditional oratorical arts, but rather in the manner of the political and street-corner speaker of genius through galvanising them into attention and interest and skilfully playing on their reactions. Personality, not words, evidently held them, for most of his sermons make rather dull reading, except the happy phrase, the powerful invective and the coaxing mingling of affection and prayer with which he could win their hearts. Fire, homely wit, moving love, it was through these that the force of his conviction could win through. But with a direct method of this kind, time, practice and familiarity with the audience are needed. One does not succeed at the first attempt. It seems that he needed a new ingredient to launch himself once and for all with the critical, but still superstitious, people of his day. That ingredient was, first, the hint at and then the full flow of his claim to a special divine inspiration and the gift of prophecy. When this came, his power over the people became absolute. No wonder his rival in Florence, the Augustinian, Fra Mariano da Gennazzano, the Bossuet of his day, was disgusted to find the tables turned on him. Whereas once Savonarola could attract but twenty-five people while Fra Mariano was filling a neighbouring church, the time soon came when the latter's polished moderation of language and thought was shown up by Savonarola to be the empty thing it really was. But Savonarola's was a dangerous victory, for Fra Mariano, powerfully placed in Rome, became his relentless enemy.

At first, Savonarola was used by his superiors to give missions in various towns of Northern Italy, and we get a glimpse of his life before his real work in Florence began from a letter he wrote to his mother who was complaining of his continued absence from Ferrara: "I know you are wondering," the Friar wrote, "why I have not written to you for so many days. This is not due to my having forgotten you, but because there have been no messengers. It is true that one of our friars was on his way to Ferrara after Christmas, but I was so busy during the feast that I quite forgot to write. I am very sorry about it. Since then Fra Giacomo of Pavia, who used to be our Prior in Ferrara, has come here and told me how much pain I gave you by not writing. I told him there had been no messengers and that the road from Brescia to Ferrara is impracticable and no reliable messengers available. Afterwards, when going to Genoa I thought that once I had got to Pavia there would be daily messengers and I could write. But now that I have been ordered to preach this Lent at Zenova I have managed to get to Pavia. So I can now write as I have meant to, and can tell you that I am well, content in mind and sound in body, though tired with the journey and with a long way still to go before reaching Zenova."

The critical sermon of his life, after his first failures, was, it seems, preached in 1484, while on this missionary work. It was at San Gimignano, near Siena, then a commune and town of some importance and retaining to this day the marks of its former independence and beauty. Here he made the great declaration that governed the whole of his preaching and his work of reform. He prophesied that (1) the Church should be scourged; (2) that it should afterwards be renewed; and (3) that this should happen soon. In Brescia, a few months later, he gained the full oratorical confidence which was to capture Florence.

Savonarola himself expressly denied that this threefold prophecy constituted in any way a special revelation from God. It was from his studies of the Old Testament and deep familiarity with the history of sinful Jews, ever threatened and ever protected by Jehovah, that he came to draw the analogy between the prophecies of old and the need for similar prophecies to stir his own people and rouse them to a sense of their destiny and the needful reform if they were not to be punished by God.

We can see how the combination of his deep feelings, even as a child, about the state of the Church and the vices of the world with the inexorable scholastic logic drawing conclusions from general moral premises, illustrated by the Scriptures, led to his own inner certainties. Even so, there was a jump to explain, for the preacher, then expressly disclaiming any supernatural prophetical gift, did in fact categorically prophesy. He may at first have meant it as no more than a rhetorical trick, but can we escape the conclusion that a subconscious inner will was driving him on to claim powers beyond the normal human range? Indeed, Savonarola passed insensibly from this first type of rhetorical prophecy into the habit of making prophecies which he himself believed to possess a supernatural origin, and from these to the widest claims of being with God and guided by God in all his work. In the end, he did not recoil from expressing his absolute certainty of God's special support for him in his actions in the form of imprecations that God should destroy him there and then if what he said were not true. This conviction that he was endowed with special supernatural powers was in the end to lead to his destruction at the unwilling hands of Alexander VI.

But we have his own testimony to the inner process by which he came to make his claims, as given in his *Compendium Revelationum*:

> God, then [Savonarola explained], having among others made choice of me, His unworthy and unprofitable servant, caused me to come to Florence by order of my superiors in the year 1489. In this year, on August 1, I began publicly to expound the Apocalypse in the church of San Marco. And in the course of my preaching throughout the year I repeatedly insisted on three points (the threefold prophecy of San Gimignano repeated often enough in his travels). These three conclusions I endeavoured to prove by means of probable arguments from Sacred Scripture, and in particular by means of comparisons which I drew between what is there read and what is actually happening. But at that time I refrained from saying anything which could imply that I had received any special revelation on the subject, because I saw that my hearers were not rightly disposed for the reception of this secret. [In other words, he had by then already felt conscious of really having prophetical powers.] But in the years which followed, seeing that men's minds were gradually becoming more ready to believe, I occasionally introduced some prophetic vision which, however, I set forth in the form of a parable. But when I saw how much opposition and ridicule arose on all sides, I began to grow afraid and firmly resolved to preach on other matters. *But I was unable to carry out my resolve.* For whatever else I read and thought about only moved me to disgust, and as often as I tried to preach on some other subject, I could never satisfy myself.

Clearly, he was always experiencing this kind of inner compulsion, his whole emotional make-up driving him against his more superficial prudence to speak—and without doubt to see—his true message in terms of a vividness and a conviction which he believed to be, in his own words "a certain supernatural light by means of which the prophet perceives (a) that the things which are revealed to him are true and that (b) they derive from God."

This description is extremely interesting in its complete honesty. Savonarola was not a trained scholastic philosopher for nothing. He approached his own sense of being specially "illumined" with an admirable logical detachment very much in contrast with other "illuminists" who tend to adopt a "take it or leave it" attitude, since the sense of inner certainty seems so infinitely stronger than any argument of reason or common sense. But the price Savonarola paid for his frankness was to describe an experience, which he thought to be supernatural, in terms consistent with a deep-rooted impulse derived from his will to succeed in his mission at all costs.

The whole position is further argued in a dialogue between himself and the "Tempter." The "Tempter," though normally living "in solitude" is described as also having had "a special revelation"—a special revelation about "the good results of your preaching" (that is, of Savonarola's). But he has also learned that the Friar is "misguided by a certain simplicity." Savonarola answers him: "To say that by means of a lie I have wrought good results is to say what is contradictory. The results themselves show that I have not lied." This was not a very good answer since accidentally good can come out of evil and Savonarola's "certain simplicity" would not be the same as consciously lying.

The "Tempter" then reports people as saying that Savonarola is "moved by a certain spirit of melancholy...the visions are only dreams or the effects of a lively imagination." No, the Friar retorts to this very honest suggestion: "So far from being melancholy, I am filled with a spirit of great joy, and I experience an illumination and behold visions which are beyond nature, for I have studied philosophy and I know how far the light of reason can go.... Moreover, I cannot but see the entire conformity between the present state of affairs and these expositions of Holy Scripture which, without straining the text, I have publicly given. Such things, even a fool must realise, do not come from a melancholy disposition, dreams or a strong imagination." The answer is once again inadequate for there is no reason to suppose that some kind of mental or emotional derangement could alone account for the Friar's convictions. Because his inner urges could not be fitted into his rational philosophy, he assumed that they were inspired. He was certainly completely sane yet possibly deluded, apparently by the narrow and arbitrary limits he imposed on the forces that can affect a person's conscious reasoning powers. The mere feeling of joy can be as deceptive as that of sorrow, and no doubt he felt both.

At this point, the "Tempter," rather oddly, makes the tentative suggestion that perhaps it is all due to his own diabolical powers. Savonarola, accurately, points out that he knows better; he knows how to distinguish the "Tempter's" work from God's. Experience proves a divine origin in this case because "(1) the things I have foretold are much more certain for me than the first principles of philosophy (they would be), and because (2) I see that what I have foretold is exactly coming to pass, and I have never been deceived even in the smallest detail." This last was surely an extreme claim even for him to make. When the "Tempter" suggests that it is all due to the Friar's cunning, the latter answers: "They said that I was a simpleton, but now that events have shown me to be right, they turn round and ascribe it all to my astuteness." Later, the "Tempter" challenges him about the accuracy of his prophecies. "Whatever I have predicted," Savonarola asserts categorically, "has either already happened or will most certainly happen, nor will a single jot of it be unfulfilled." Tired out, the "Tempter" gives in. "I see that you have an answer to every objection," he generously admits.

In this Dialogue, Savonarola only really put up one serious test of his claim to a special inspiration or revelation from God, namely the judgment by the fruits. Were his prophecies fulfilled in a manner wholly beyond any natural degree of human foresight, however shrewd? And was the reforming work he did, depending on the revelations and prophecies, so fruitful to others and spiritually strengthening to himself as to warrant the judgment that it was all specially inspired by God, as he constantly claimed?

Of the Friar's subjective honesty and of the outstandingly holy motivations of his whole life and work we have no doubt whatever. That his work was therefore as a whole blessed, more particularly as a highly dramatic protest and warning about the corruption of so many of the teachers and pastors of the Church and its consequences, may well be believed. But the sequel, we think, will show that there are no grounds whatever for believing that Savonarola's prophecies and revelations are to be attributed to any special divine inspiration.

It was while Lorenzo de' Medici, the most powerful, clever and popular of that upstart dynasty, was still alive that Savonarola came to settle finally in Florence. Ironically, it was Lorenzo himself who wrote to the General of the Dominicans to ask that the famous Friar be sent to San Marco in Florence. He did this, it seems, at the request of Pico della Mirandola who was troubled in conscience and wished to have the Friar to advise and guide him. As for Savonarola himself, he appeared to be reluctant to face what was to prove the crucial mission of his life and he needed divine illumination to strengthen him on his way across the Apennines. In Florence he had failed and his fashionable rival, Fra Mariano, was still there.

At the start, therefore, Savonarola was content to work very much behind the scenes, lecturing under a damask rose-tree in the garden of San Marco, as peaceful and lovely a spot as could be found in all Italy. There with his brethren he would walk under Michelozzi's graceful cloister—the cloister repeated in Fra Angelico's famous Annunciation and facing the community as they walked up the convent stairs to enter the cells and community rooms lighted by the pictorial windows on the heavenly mysteries which Angelico and others had painted, not for the immortality they have earned, but for the spiritual enrichment of their companions. How strange that this perfect expression in stone of the beauty, simplicity and peace of the Christian ideal of life should have been created in the century of the upsurge of cruelty, of self-indulgence, of a defiant humanism, of superstition and of saintly striving—the century of the Pazzi Conspiracy,[1] of the Borgias, of Machiavelli and of Savonarola himself!

Little by little the Friar's audience grew until he found it necessary to move to the church of San Marco on August 1, 1489. There it was a new Savonarola preaching, a Friar trained in the hard mission school of Northern Italian towns and—more to the point—enormously strengthened by his ever-growing consciousness by direct inspiration from on high.

His famous threefold prophecy and his new manner at once made a deep impression, but it was a two-way impression.

Many began to see in him the heaven-sent prophet; others, especially those—the Ottimati, the Miceans, the powerful generally—whose wealth and status depended on the maintenance of accepted values and the secularist ideals of Lorenzo, were furious and not a little

---

1. The Pazzi Conspiracy took place in 1478 when Rodrigo Borgia was forty-six and Savonarola twenty-six. The banking Pazzi family was backed against the Medicis by Sixtus IV who appointed an anti-Medicean Archbishop of Pisa. At the solemn moment of Mass in the cathedral of Florence, when all the congregation was bowing before the elevated Host, Francesco Pazzi and a friend stole into the church to murder Lorenzo and his brother Giuliano. Giuliano was killed, but Lorenzo escaped unhurt. The archbishop of Pisa and his supporters tried to raise the city against the Mediceans but failed. From the windows of the Palazzo, some of the captured plotters were thrown out for the maddened mob to slay, while the Archbishop himself in his vestments and Francesco Pazzi were hung out of windows on a rope until they died. The failure of the Pazzi Conspiracy strengthened in the end the position of Lorenzo and Florence as against the Papal States and Naples. The way was thus made easier for the invasion of Italy by the King of France, Charles VIII, under the pretext of a crusade against the Turks, but in fact to claim the Kingdom of Naples on the basis of ancient dynastic claims, since the French royal house had once ruled Naples.

afraid. But from San Marco he moved to the cathedral itself in the Lent of 1491. "Reflect carefully, those of you who are rich, for your punishment will come. Not Florence shall be the name of this city: it will be called but a den of thieves, of vice, of blood."

This kind of language was not calculated to endear him to the leading men. As he wrote to Fra Domenico, he expected to share the fate of Bernardino of Feltre who was exiled for his plain preaching under Lorenzo's father. When leading citizens asked him to give up his novel ideas and way of preaching, he answered that his kind of preaching would triumph in the end, while the old kind (referring to Mariano) would fade away. When told that Lorenzo himself was behind the feeling against him, and wanted to banish him, he prophesied that it would not be he, Savonarola, who would have to go, but Lorenzo. Making his point more precise on this occasion, he said that not only Lorenzo, but the Pope and the King of Naples were soon to go.

It is far from certain that Lorenzo, who was a tolerant man and one who enjoyed novelties, really objected to Florence's famous new preacher. In fact, he asked him to preach in the Palazzo before the august Signoria itself. He accepted, and we can imagine the disarming smile as Savonarola explained to his congregation that he could not be quite himself in the palace, but must bear himself more conventionally than usual—as Our Lord doubtless had to do in the house of the Pharisee! Lorenzo would have enjoyed that little touch.

But Savonarola was in no play-acting mood with Lorenzo whom he held responsible for the pagan and vicious state of Florence. When in 1491, the Friar was elected Prior of San Marco, which owed so much to the generosity of the Medicis, he refused to pay the customary visit to the Magnifico, and likewise refused to ask to see him when he visited the convent.

But by this time Lorenzo was breaking up, though only a year or two over forty. When dying, he asked that Savonarola should visit him.

In San Marco, it was believed that the Friar refused Lorenzo absolution because he would not promise to restore Florence to its former liberties. This story, apparently then thought edifying, of a priest demanding a political test of a dying man, is narrated by early Dominican biographers. But the only eye-witness to what happened is content to say that Savonarola made the usual exhortations to the dying man who accepted them with Christian resignation, joining in the prayers for the dying. One prefers to believe this more edifying version.

Lorenzo's death fulfilled the Friar's prophecy; he had long been sick. Ferrante of Naples also soon died, *sine luce, sine cruce, sine Deo*, in Burchard's words, but he was an old man.

More immediately important for our story was the third of the prophesied deaths: the death of the Pope, Innocent VIII, successor to Sixtus IV. Best known to posterity because of Pollajuolo's monumental tomb, transferred from the old St. Peter's to the new one, Innocent died some three months after Lorenzo. His rather unfortunate reputation for a Pope is that of a "family man" with no less than sixteen children. He was not much of a Pope, but the truth behind the legend of the sixteen children is simply that as a young man, before taking Orders, he illegitimately fathered two children.

Lorenzo, the greatest of the Medici, left Florence in the hands of a graceless son, Piero, and, no less to the point, in the hands of Girolamo Savonarola, the prophet who had already amply demonstrated what he thought of the famous Medici and the elegant tyranny they had imposed on the once free people of Florence.

Innocent's death left the Holy See vacant for the fifth time since Cardinal Rodrigo Borgia, now sixty years of age, had been made Vice-Chancellor of the Church. It was high time for him to get himself chosen Vicar of Christ if he was ever to reach to the summit of his ambitions.

IV. *"We Are Pope"*

AFTER the death of Innocent VIII, Cardinal Rodrigo Borgia was, without question, pre-eminently *papabile*. Even earlier, after the death of Sixtus, Innocent's predecessor, Borgia, though only fifty-two, had accurately applied to him the tag "he who enters the conclave a Pope, leaves it a Cardinal." This fact is bound to be surprising to those who think of Rodrigo Borgia through the distorting mists of the Borgia legend. But here is the witness of his contemporary, Sigismondo de Conti. "He never missed a single consistory. Throughout the reigns of Pius II, Paul II, Sixtus IV and Innocent VIII, he was always an important personage. Few people understood etiquette as well as he did. He knew how to make the most of himself, and took pains to shine in conversation and to be dignified in his manners. In the latter point his majestic stature gave him an advantage. Also he was just the age, about sixty, at which, according to Aristotle, men are wisest: robust in body and vigorous in mind, he was admirably equipped for his new position."

But perhaps the best testimony to his merits during his thirty-four years as a cardinal and Vice-Chancellor is to be sought in the simple fact that we know relatively little about him during all those years. Failures and scandals would have been greedily recounted, but we have to make do with the famous letters of Pius II about the garden-party in Siena, account of which has already been given. As a permanent official, his years of steady and often boring paperwork behind the scenes receives its obvious encomium in being unsung. It is, in fact, safe to say, that apart from the facts that he lived an unmarried "married" life with the discreet Vanozza Catanei and had a number of children, two of which have become famous or rather notorious in history, that he certainly too much loved good society, especially feminine, and that he was, and supremely loved being, a great and wealthy temporal prince, Rodrigo Borgia might have been *papabile* in any age. It cannot be too much emphasised that Borgia, like the other pre-Reformation popes during this period of degraded Renaissance morals, was religiously completely orthodox and normally devout. The truth is that in that age the weaknesses of a Cardinal Borgia were not considered impediments to the highest ecclesiastical promotions, even to the Papacy itself. This deplorable fact must, in its turn, to some extent excuse the readiness of churchmen to indulge in them.

The Borgia legend, which only really got into its full stride with the change from Rodrigo Borgia to Alexander VI, brings its first great charge to bear on Alexander's election itself. Burchard, through his endless pages of pedantic description of Papal ceremonial and the doings of ecclesiastical high society, had a way of turning a good phrase, and everyone has quoted his opening words on Alexander's pontificate, "*Anno Domini* MCCCCLXXXXII, *augusti mensis die* 11, *videlicet die sabbati, summo mane, Rodericus Borgia, nepos Calixti tertii, vicecancellarius, creatus est papa, vocatusque Alexander sextus. Et incontinenti, assumpto papatu, dispersit et dedit pauperibus bona sua.*" ("In the year of the Lord 1492, on the eleventh day of August which was a Saturday in the early morning, Rodrigo Borgia, nephew of Calixtus III, Vice-Chancellor, was created Pope and named Alexander VI. Immediately, after assuming the Papacy, he distributed his goods and gave them to the poor.") What the sarcastic old chronicler meant, of course, was that the new Pope paid the debts he had incurred to the cardinals of the conclave through buying their votes. In fact, Cardinal Borgia followed the custom of his immediate predecessor. As a newly-elected pope he gave to his friends and supporters the goods, palaces and benefices which he had held but which, as Pope, he could no longer hold. The fact that he had managed during his long years at the Vatican to accumulate a long list of possessions meant that he had a good deal to give "to the poor." Inevitably, the conclave

The Meddlesome Friar and the Wayward Pope

cardinals, knowing this custom, measured their chances of being enriched by the different cardinals who had good chances of being elected. What precise goings-on of this kind took place at any election was anyone's guess, and the chroniclers were not slow to make accusations of all kinds, according to the parties and influences they favoured or attacked. Charges of simony were freely made in the case of the elections of Sixtus IV and Innocent VIII as well as this case of Alexander VI. Unedifying as such customs were, the charge of technical simony—trying to buy and sell the Papacy—must depend upon an exact knowledge of what went on within the conclave. Was any particular transaction a definite bargain to buy a vote or was it a general promise, according to an undoubted, but customary, abuse, near to simony, that So-and-so would not be forgotten in the general distribution if one turned out to be elected?

In point of fact, the general circumstances of this election made successful simony by Rodrigo Borgia rather less likely than usual. All but one of the twenty-three cardinals who took part were Italians, while the absentees were Spaniards and Frenchmen who might be more inclined to favour a foreign pope. Most of the cardinals were already rich and powerful—some richer than Borgia. The wealth needed to buy the votes of so many rich and supposedly hostile men to tempt them to elect a Spanish Pope against their inclinations would have been far beyond even Rodrigo's means, or indeed of the fortune of any single cardinal. But perhaps the strongest argument against the almost universal charge of blatant simony was that it was not necessary. Rodrigo, Vice-Chancellor, expert in ecclesiastical affairs and with an excellent reputation for firmness in maintaining the rights of the Church and Rome, was a likely choice in any event. If he did not win, it would be because of powerful foreign interests on behalf of other possible candidates. The chief of these was represented by Cardinal Giuliano della Rovere, as political-minded and fiery as his uncle Sixtus IV and jealous of Borgia. He was strongly supported by French and Neapolitan interests. Another was Cardinal Ascanio Sforza, brother of Ludovico, called "Il Moro," tyrant of Milan.

Borgia bided his time, realising the likely deadlock between these two. So it turned out, Ascanio himself being won over not by money but by the expectation of becoming Vice-Chancellor and the new Pope's right-hand man. The hope of the Roman people was that Borgia should be elected. The conclave expected that he would best defend Papal interests. And so, in the end, he was—and unanimously, according to his own testimony, though some hold that he was elected by the single casting vote of the aged Patriarch of Venice (bribed, naturally). Infessura, the source of so many libels against the Borgias, said that the angry Venetians punished their Patriarch on his return home. Unfortunately for the credit of Infessura as an accurate chronicler, the Patriarch died before he got back to Venice.

The story of the simoniacal election grew with the telling, and it was to prove a key point in Savonarola's attack against Alexander. Obviously, the prevailing loose customs at Papal elections furnished a sufficient canonical basis on which to make a case when Alexander's firm stand in the interests of Rome and Italy against the French made him many enemies. Savonarola doubtless came firmly to believe that the election had been simoniacal, and he would have believed the same about Sixtus and Innocent. It was Cardinal della Rovere, robbed of the Tiara and, like Savonarola (though for much less worthy reasons), in league with the French, who was determined to ruin Alexander's reputation for all time. When he became Pope Julius II, he had his revenge over the dead by decreeing in the Bull *Cum Tam Divino* that simony invalidated any Papal election. He was comforted, no doubt, to think that his old enemy had never really been Pope at all. In fact, of course, this Bull could not have any retrospective force, and, despite Savonarola's firm belief that Alexander's election was invalid, this would not legally have been so, even had the election been technically and truly simoniacal.

The result found Rodrigo Borgia in buoyant mood. "We are Pope and Vicar of Christ," he is said to have exclaimed triumphantly and to have chosen the name Alexander in memory of Alexander the Great and

The Meddlesome Friar and the Wayward Pope

the Invincible. One suspects that, despite his drawing-room manners, Rodrigo Borgia's taste was not always of the best. Certainly, the obtaining of the great prize did not improve his character, for even if we allow for all the legends, we still have to reckon with the difference between the excellence of the reputation of Cardinal Rodrigo Borgia and the rather more doubtful one of Pope Alexander VI.

For the moment, however, it was all roses. The people of Rome, who knew him best, acclaimed Borgia's election. With bonfires, torchlight processions, flowers and triumphal arches they greeted their new Pope. At his Coronation he received an ovation from the people which was said to be without precedent. With the common people, at any rate, he had outlived the prejudices against Spaniards which his uncle, Calixtus, had had to endure, though the time was coming when his firm policy and determination to secure the temporal authority in Italy of the Holy See would revive the "Catalan" prejudice. The election was welcomed in the Italian States and celebrated with unusual festivities. The Ambassadors, sent to Rome, went beyond the usual formal and decorous eulogy of their trade. The Sienese ambassador said: "On account of the Godlike virtues and gifts with which they saw him endowed and adorned, he seemed to have been chosen and preordained by Divine Providence as Pastor of the Flock and Vicar in the lordship of the Most Holy Roman Church." Another said: "You have nothing to learn from others during your Pontificate. Against you alone no accusation of ignorance can be made. You know the needs of the Holy See and religion; you know what a Roman Pontiff must do; what is permitted to him; what is useful. In your great wisdom you have no need of any man's counsel. Consult yourself alone, obey yourself, follow your inclinations, take yourself for a model, you will never fall into error if you rely upon your own judgment." Flattery was the business of such spokesmen on such an occasion, but if there had not been considerable hopes from a Pontiff with an exceptional ecclesiastical record, such fine words might well have had a sarcastic sound. But a good deal more realistic and far-seeing was the exclamation of Lorenzo de' Medici's nephew recently made a cardinal to seal the understanding between Innocent VIII and Florence: "Now we are in the jaws of a ravening wolf, and if we do not flee he will devour us." But even this view was unintentionally complimentary as coming from a representative of one of the leading Italian States about a Pope whose aim it would be to save Italy in defiance of the prejudices and jealousies of its petty rulers. From England the Bishop of Durham came in due course in the name of Henry VII and Burchard tells us that he made a speech "well and elegantly composed but little pleasing, to those who heard him, because of his bad accent."

The hopes thus rested in the new Pope were not deceived. As a trained canon lawyer, he was soon hard at work reforming the judicial system in Rome and he set Tuesdays apart for personally hearing cases. Lawless Rome, more under the thumb of the lawless patrician families, such as the Orsini and Colonna than under the Pope, was to be divided into new districts, each with its own magistrate. The punishment of criminals without fear or favour was to be enforced by hanging and the destruction of the criminal's dwelling. Prisons were to be better managed. He planned a more popular constitution which would give the Romans some degree of self-government as a curb against aristocratic banditry. We know from the waterman who saw the Duke of Gandia being murdered that these changes still left much to be desired. But a new Rome is not built in a day.

In fact, Alexander (as, in some ways, Savonarola) had a very liberal mind for his time. This liberalism went with his personally easy-going and tolerant disposition, except when he was thwarted in affairs that happened to matter deeply to him—it showed itself in his cavalier attitude to ceremonial rules that so much shocked Burchard. It goes far to account for the growth of the Borgia legend. When reports were brought to him of the scurrilous things written and said about him, he just laughed at the tales. And now, after his accession, he showed his breadth of outlook by his determination to protect the hated Jews of

Rome. This protection was the more remarkable in that his own Spanish countrymen were engaged in "purifying" Spanish blood by persecuting the Marranos, or converted Jews, and driving them out of the country, conveniently pocketing their cash. To the Jews, Alexander said, answering their expressions of homage: "Hebrews, we admire and respect your Holy Law since it was given your ancestors by the most High God through the hands of Moses. But we are opposed to the false observance and interpretation you have of it, because the Apostolic Faith teaches that the Redeemer whom you await in vain has already come, and that he is Our Lord Jesus Christ who with the Father and the Holy Spirit is the Everlasting God." Which of all the Popes could have put the Christian position more fairly?

There is no need to continue the record of Alexander's pontificate, since these pages do not claim to be a life of Rodrigo Borgia but only to present a sufficient sketch of his life and character to make us see and understand the man in conflict with the redoubtable Friar of Florence. But two more points may usefully be noted. It is an irony of history that the Catholic Church in large measure owes to the Borgia popes one of its most popular and widely observed devotions: the daily threefold recitation of the "Angelus" to the ringing of the bells of churches and religious houses, as visitors to Catholic towns in Europe are sometimes made well aware of in the early hours of the morning. The exact origins of this gradually developing devotion are not wholly clear, but Calixtus III, in commemoration of the great Christian victory in Hungary over the Turks ordered the ringing of the bells at midday and Alexander VI revived this custom and made it obligatory for all times. This Borgia piety, it appears, is what fixed forever this popular devotion within the Church.

A second much better known historic action must also be noted, namely Alexander's famous division between Spain and Portugal of the territories discovered and to be discovered beyond the seas. This is often seen as the last great international political ruling of the Papacy, and in a sense it was. But the Pope was not in fact assuming the role of a world arbiter, but simply using his normal spiritual authority to ensure and organise the conversion of the heathen in the new world by allotting the responsibility for this work to the Powers which had made the overseas discoveries. Nor was it, as has been maintained, a pro-Spanish decision by a Spanish Pope. Previous Popes had allotted to Portugal the lands which the Portuguese had discovered. Alexander simply did the same for Spain at a moment when no one dreamt of the vastness of the dominions thus indirectly confirmed to Spain and he maintained the decisions of his predecessors in regard to Portugal. Hence Alexander's drawing of the line from north to south a hundred leagues from Cape Verde.

But if we may overlook the ecclesiastical aspects of Alexander's pontificate (allowing for an occasional fondness for pleading illness to avoid ceremonies), which were normal and traditional in an active pope of long experience, diligence and, as we have seen, of would-be thoroughgoing reform, we obviously cannot, in this context, overlook that personal life of his of which so much that is lurid and scandalous has been written.

V. *The Sinner*

How far Rodrigo Borgia degenerated in a moral sense after becoming Pope is by no means easy to establish. One might have expected that a responsible, experienced and observant churchman (despite his family) would have turned over a new leaf on assuming the august dignity and responsibility of Supreme Pontiff and Vicar of Christ. In doing so, he would have been imitating his patron, Enea de Piccolomini (Pius II). But there is certainly no evidence of his having done so. It seems, on the contrary, that his head was turned by power and that the general papal passion, more marked in the Borgias than in others, for promoting the interests of his children and relations overcame him.

This was—at any rate to the degree in which he indulged it—a curious vice for so discerning a mind, since in the nature of things a Pope cannot hope to add any temporal succession to the posthumous spiritual or ecclesiastical fame that falls easily to him. Perhaps the success of his uncle in breaking the normal rules led him to think that they could be broken again, and this explains why he was so reluctant to secularise his son, Cardinal Cesare. There can be no doubt that he strove at all costs to establish his children in positions from which they could not be dislodged. More natural, one thinks, was his inability to change and reform his personal mode of life. He had always been a self-indulgent man, and at the age of sixty something like a miracle has to occur to curb weaknesses and passions that have bitten deep into the character and so often increase their hold on a person as they transfer them from a less vigorous body to a more subtle and experienced mind. Just as Alexander was totally incapable of the resistance and perseverance necessary to carry through the thoroughgoing reform of the Church which in a moment of spiritual anguish he could set in motion, so he was unable to change from a luxury and worldliness of living to the asceticism and simplicity that suited his spiritual office. The devil that lay within the Church and within him could only be exorcised by prayer and fasting—Savonarola had the truth of the matter there—and by struggles and conflicts within a world in ferment and within his own spirit, struggles wholly alien to the times and to himself.

Nevertheless, there must have been obvious limits to the dual-nature of the life of the Borgia Pope, or, to put it otherwise, to the elasticity of his conscience. The Alexander of legend is not easily fitted into the Cardinal Borgia we know. Was the Vice-Chancellor, acclaimed *papabile*, faithful in his way to Vanozza, going, as Pope, to add to his burning ambition for the greatness of his children, a debauched old man's licentious life? The charge has often been made.

The lady supposedly involved in Alexander's riper *amours* was the young beauty of Rome, Giulia Farnese, known to history as Giulia Bella, Giulia the Beautiful. Without any solid evidence Giulia is said to have been the model for Pinturicchio's *Virgin and Child*, surrounded by angels in the Borgia Apartments of the Vatican. Not at all a pleasant idea if she were the Pope's mistress; but not something to be shocked about, given the customs of the days, if she were no more than a close friend of the Pope and his entourage. After all, the Farneses were a rich and noble family of Rome with estates on Lake Bolsena, and Giulia's brother, Alessandro, had been picked out as a boy (as Alexander himself had been) for high ecclesiastical promotion by Innocent VIII. Like Alexander, too, he was destined to be Pope (Paul III).

The key to Rodrigo Borgia's relations, as cardinal and pope, with this beauty of Rome and the Papal Court is undoubtedly to be found in Alexander's cousin, Adriana de Mila. Adriana was the granddaughter of a sister of Calixtus III, and therefore a first cousin once-removed of the Pope. Alexander, who always liked to have plenty of women around him, treated Adriana as a kind of superior housekeeper and confidante. This lady, on whom no suspicion of evil living has ever fallen, married Ludovico, of the great Orsini family, and it was her son who married Giulia Farnese. Another highly important member of this female company was Lucrezia herself, a beauty in her own right, fair and rather childlike, and paling beside Giulia. She married, in a ceremony of the utmost splendour, Giovanni Sforza, kinsman of the tyrant of Milan, and Lord of Pesaro in his own right. To these, the dusky, exciting loveliness of Sancha of Aragon, wife of Alexander's youngest son, Jofre, came to be added. It is of some importance to see these women, together with their attendants, as a happy and frivolous group of close friends in whom Alexander delighted, rather than to think of Giulia as a solitary star. The story is always told of how on one Whitsunday these young women, led by Sancha, caused disedification in St. Peter's. The Spanish preacher's sermon was in Burchard's words *prolixum nimis et tediosum* ("too long and too boring"). The Pope was annoyed, but his women, once Mass was over, thought up the lark of all getting up out of their seats and climbing up on the platform where the canons normally sang the epistle and gospel to the "scandal of the congregation." This, no doubt, cheered Alexander, too, for though he loved all ceremonies, he shared Savonarola's dislike of bad sermons, excessive ritual, and could not find it in his heart to scold the women who expressed their feelings like naughty schoolgirls.

Gregorovius quotes a contemporary letter which probably better serves to describe the living Giulia Farnese than to further the calumnies against her. "Madonna Giulia," her brother-in-law, Lorenzo Pucci, wrote just before Christmas 1493, "has grown somewhat stouter and is a most beautiful creature. She let down her hair before me and had it dressed; it reached down to her feet; never have I seen anything like it; she has the most lovely hair. She wore a headdress of fine linen, and over it a sort of net, light as air, with gold threads interwoven in it. In truth it shone like the sun. I would have given a great deal if you could have been present to have informed yourself concerning that which you wanted to know. She wore a linen robe in the Neapolitan fashion, as also did Madonna Lucrezia who, after a little while, went out to remove it. She returned shortly in a gown almost entirely of violet velvet. When Vespers were over and the Cardinals were leaving, I left them." Another contemporary wrote of Giulia's "dark colouring, black eyes, round face and particular ardour."

It would be idle to pretend that Alexander, who could never keep his eyes off beautiful women, was not bewitched by this ravishing creature among the gay feminine company he liked to keep, the Giulia Bella whom the irreverent Romans were wont to call "the bride of Christ." But what we have to decide is whether the Pope's relations with this woman were, technically at least, innocent or whether he made her his mistress? Was the ageing Alexander, in fact, the father of Giulia's infant daughter, Laura?

If we assume the worst, what would the set-up have been? It would mean that Adriana was all the time condoning her own daughter-in-law's *affaire* with the Pope, and this with the connivance of his own daughter, Lucrezia. It would mean that Alexander's passion and shamelessness were such as to be indifferent to the feelings of a relation like Adriana confronted with her own daughter-in-law's curious sin, and indifferent, too, to what his daughter might feel about such a relationship between her father, the Pope, and her friend. Even the future Paul III, a good Pope, must have been privy to the sordid entanglement.

There is a limit to everything, and Alexander would indeed have had to be the vicious reprobate of the legend, difficult to relate with the *papabile* Cardinal Borgia, to have forced Adriana and Lucrezia, for both of whom his affections are sufficiently attested, to play their unsavoury parts. Only the clearest proof of his debauching Giulia (sister of a cardinal) can, in our view, make good the accusation. Such clear evidence has not been found.

The open Giulia accusation was not contemporary, and it is absurd to make anything of Roman gibe that Giulia was "the bride of Christ." It was typical Roman scandalmongering. The main evidence rests on two

The Meddlesome Friar and the Wayward Pope

or three letters which indicate Alexander's annoyance at being separated from Giulia, even though the separation was due to her being with her husband. At the time, the military situation, with the French king invading Italy, was sufficiently anxious to give the Pope some excuse for wanting to have his women near him. Moreover, it was known that the King was being pressed by Cardinal della Rovere to get the Pope deposed by a General Council, so it was hardly the time he would choose to provide further moral hostages to his enemies, as any proved liaison with Giulia would have done.

In one letter he wrote: "We would wish that you should see as clearly as we do ourselves the necessity of your being totally attached to the person who loves you most in the world. When you have fully realised this, if you have not done so until now, we shall know that you are as wise as you are beautiful." This sort of pompous flirtation, with a grain of irony in it, was typical of Alexander. It proves his bad taste, not his guilt.

It is true that he could show a strong annoyance with Giulia's husband, Orsino Orsini. The latter was in the Pope's military service, but, like all Orsinis, he was more interested in himself than in anyone to whom he owed fealty. Giulia's fidelity to him was keeping not only her, but Adriana and Lucrezia, many miles from their proper place, as the Pope saw things, namely in their real home, the palace of Santa Maria in Portico, hard by the Vatican itself. Giulia was in fact torn between the unedifying insistence of the Pope that she should always be in Rome with him and her husband's insistence that her place was with him in the wars. "Thankless and treacherous Giulia," wrote Alexander in some anger. "Navarrico has brought us a letter from you in which you signify and declare your intention of not coming here without Orsino's consent. Though we judged the evil of your soul and of the man who guides you, we would not have believed that you could behave with such perfidy and ingratitude in view of your repeated assurances and oaths that you would be faithful to our command and not go near Orsino. But now you are doing just the opposite by going to Basanello for the purpose, no doubt, of surrendering yourself to that stallion once more. We hope that you and the ungrateful Adriana will recognise your mistake and make suitable penance. Finally we herewith ordain, *sub poena excommunicationis latae sententiae et maledictionis aeternae*, that you shall not leave Capodimonte or Marta or still less go to Basanello—this for reasons affecting our State."

So far as we know, everyone has taken this extraordinary letter seriously, including the solemn and extended form of excommunication. Surely it is clear that the letter is entirely in the tradition of ecclesiastical jokes which Alexander loved, jokes that often tend to combine a certain coarseness with the heavy Latin formulae of Church protocol. Alexander would hardly have made such a reference to the husband if he himself were in fact behaving in a similar fashion and it is utterly inconceivable that a Pope who at any rate knew so well his ecclesiastical business would indulge in anything but a mock excommunication as an excellent joke. The whole tone of the letter indicates a political preoccupation rather than an amatory one.

Evidently more deeply felt were the sentiments in another letter of the Pope's, this time to Lucrezia. "Madonna Adriana and Giulia," he wrote, "have arrived at Capodimonte where they found her [Giulia's] brother dead. This death has caused as deep grief to Cardinal Farnese as to Giulia and both were so cast down that they caught the fever. Let us pray God and the glorious Madonna that they may quickly recover. Messire Joanni and you have not truly shown great respect and consideration for us in the matter of this journey of Madonna Adriana and Giulia in that you let them go without our permission. You should have remembered that such a journey, undertaken so suddenly and without our consent, must have given us extreme pain. You will say that they decided on it because Cardinal Farnese had wished it and arranged it; but you should have asked yourselves whether it was to the Pope's liking. The thing is done, but another time we shall look to it better and shall consider in which hands we shall place our affairs."

The Meddlesome Friar and the Wayward Pope

The earlier letters give an impression of an ageing man's attempts to keep up with the younger and gayer generation on whose vitality he was seeking, rather pathetically, to feed his own. The later one catches him in the reaction of a depressed and sententious mood. Human nature does not alter for popes, though popes are happily usually chosen from men with a very much better control over human nature. Clearly, the whole position was open to the gravest misunderstanding—not that the Romans, alas, would have been so much scandalised as thoroughly amused. So it is not surprising to find contemporary letter-writers taking for granted the worst interpretation and pretending to notice a resemblance between the man of sixty-two and Giulia's infant daughter, Laura. It is interesting to see how the latest biographer of Lucrezia Borgia, Maria Bellonci, accepts without question Alexander's guilt, yet is forced in the end so far to admit the doubt as to whether Laura was the Pope's child that she makes the following extraordinary suggestion: "Giulia must have passed Laura off as a daughter of the Pope—as that tradition is so strong—in the hope of providing a better marriage for her." Considering that Laura's mother was of noble Roman blood and the sister of a young Cardinal with the whole future to hope for, it would have been odd for Giulia Farnese to think in terms of a dead Pope's bastard daughter being better fitted for the marriage market than the legitimately born niece of a likely future Pope.

Burchard's Diary once refers to Giulia as the Pope's concubine, but the expert on the ceremonies and pageant of the Papal Court was not privileged to spy on the intimacies of the Pope's life. He depended like others on gossip. Moreover only a few pages of the original diary are available today. The texts which historians have had to use are copies or copies of copies to which additions and interpolations have undoubtedly been made. Copyists at that time did not hesitate to "improve" a text by dropping in descriptive phrases and anecdotes which would make the reading more exciting or which enabled them to serve a grudge or a prejudice. Burchard must indeed have been a peeping Tom if two famous stories in the Diary are really his—or if he did not invent them out of spite. The first describes a supper party to which a large number of prostitutes were invited. The Pope himself, Cesare and Lucrezia are said to have been present and to have witnessed scenes of open debauchery related in crude detail by the Papal Master of Ceremonies. The other incident refers to the amusement caused to the Pope and his daughter by the sight of four stallions released in the courtyard of the Apostolic Palace where two mares, belonging to a passing woodcutter, had been enclosed. One of the oddities about these two stories is that they stand almost alone of their kind in an immensely long document devoted to what obviously interested the writer, namely his business of reporting the kind of Papal activities now read in the official columns of the *Osservatore Romano* and criticising Alexander and others for not observing exact rubrics. Why just these two, if such was the Borgia papacy's way of life? And how did Burchard come to be able to relate as a personal eye-witness the first of the stories? Did he really look through the key-hole—the picture of him doing so is more amusing than what he saw. But the strongest argument against the veracity of both these anecdotes which have done so much to damn the Borgia reputation is the suggestion of Lucrezia's presence at both and especially the first. Whatever may be said about the other children, Lucrezia was a good woman with a strongly developed religious side to her character.

Her father adored her. Is it conceivable that he would have gone out of his way to corrupt her in such a fashion? Nothing about him makes sense if this is to be believed.

Four years after Alexander's death a Chronicle of the Lives of the Pontiffs and Roman Emperors was published in Venice. In it there is the following character-sketch of Alexander VI which, allowing for the general moral reprobation of the Borgias, fostered by their enemies, rings true enough: "He was a great Pontiff whose splendid qualities were matched by equally great vices. There was nothing small about him. He was intelligent, eloquent, tactful in adapting himself to the character of

The Meddlesome Friar and the Wayward Pope

everyone he met, most energetic in matters of business and, even though he had never given much time to literary pursuits, it was clear that he set no small store on learning. He was always so punctual in paying his soldiers that whatever happened he was able to count on a willing and most loyal army. All these virtues, nevertheless, were neutralised by vices which need not be mentioned here, and by his overmastering desire to secure a great position for his bastard children."

This, as we have suggested, was Borgia's least forgiveable sin—and the most foolish. It is hard for a posterity, which, without ever greatly changing in regard to what is called the weakness of the flesh, has nevertheless equated "not being found out" with respectability, not to feel shocked by the brazenness of a Pope, of all people, who accepted the conventions of a highly sensual age in a country which to this day has different values in the matter from the Anglo-Saxon people; but the pride, ambition and greed of Alexander Borgia for his illicit brood was surely a much deeper sign of corruption at the heart of the Church. Because of this, he and his family were perhaps not over-punished by a posterity which has come to accept the Pope himself, Cesare and Lucrezia as the very type of cold-blooded monsters to whom no crime was foreign. Yet most of the legend is completely untrue.

We have already recounted the lurid and yet pathetic end of the young Duke of Gandia, the chief pride of Alexander, the father. No more could be said of him at least after the tragedy. He lives, indeed, as the grandfather of St. Francis Borgia, the third General of the Society of Jesus, the religious order which did so much to cleanse the Church from the evils of which his great-grandfather, Alexander VI, has come to be accepted as the symbol.

Cesare—on whom Machiavelli in his famous treatise on political realism modelled the "Prince"—was brought up in Spain and educated for the Church in much the same way as Alexander had been educated by his uncle Calixtus III. But in this case it was a hopeless shot in the dark. Cesare was a very different man from his truly ecclesiastical father.

At the age of about sixteen, his father made him a Cardinal-Deacon in the famous Consistory of September 1493, when Alessandro Farnese (the "Petticoat Cardinal," so-called because he was Giulia Farnese's brother) and Ippolito d'Este (son of the ruler of Savonarola's Ferrara) were also made Cardinal-Deacons in their teens. One of the nominees in the same Consistory was Cardinal Morton, Henry VII's Chancellor and Archbishop of Canterbury.

On the young Cesare, destined in his eyes to become the third Borgia Pope, his father showered the benefices that were necessary if he were to have the wealth and status of a great Renaissance ecclesiastical prince. But the blood of Rodrigo and Vanozza did not make churchmen, even by the broad standards of those days. Cesare, incredibly handsome, clever, spoilt and a born soldier, could only kick his heels restlessly as a Cardinal.

From the start he was a complete misfit, though he served his father loyally in the various commissions, mainly of a temporal order, entrusted to him. In the end, it became necessary to face a problem unusual in those days—and in any other days, for that matter—namely, the secularising of a Prince of the Church who, happily in this case, was never a priest. The Pope intensely disliked the idea, and he must have had wit enough to realise that the prospects of future Borgia greatness would be poor indeed without any ecclesiastical posterity. However, in the end he allowed the usual ecclesiastical procedures to be set in action, and when the Cardinals finally left the decision to him, he consented. Cardinal Cesare was duly laicised. Hitherto known as the Cardinal of Valencia, because of the chief benefice given to him, he was first made count and then duke of Valence by the King of France, thereby coming to be known as the Valentinois—a name that, quite accidentally, seemed to cover both phases of his career. He married in the end Princess Charlotte d'Albret, sister of the King of Navarre and cousin of the King of France. He played an important diplomatic and military role in securing an understanding in the end between the Pope and the French king and

The Meddlesome Friar and the Wayward Pope

in bringing something like order and unity, especially in the Papal States, according to his father's plans. Cesare was a ruthless prince and soldier and a good model for Machiavelli, but as the times went a good deal more enlightened and, when possible, humane than the type of half-barbarous petty lord or chieftain whom it was his job to destroy in the interests of order and social peace. Notorious murders were imputed to him, apart from the charge of assassinating his brother, Gandia, but with no better reason, and a little lower down we shall describe the death of the Duke of Bisceglie, Lucrezia's second husband, of which he has been accused, while briefly reviewing the life of Lucrezia herself, Alexander's adored daughter.

On the ground, no doubt, that she was the female of the species, Lucrezia's legendary reputation among the orgies, poisonings and treacheries of the Borgias is even worse than Cesare's. The truth, however, is that Cesare was typical of the intelligent, but amoral, *condottiere* of anarchic Renaissance Italy, whereas Lucrezia was, all in all, a good woman. True, she was an attractive and rather weak-minded creature who accepted the standards of the social behaviour of her times and her class. Nor did she object to playing the role demanded of her by her father and her family—she was too much of Borgia not to have enjoyed it. But she was also a woman with clear moral and spiritual standards of her own, and these came to have ever greater influence on her life and character.

Lucrezia was probably brought up in a Dominican convent in Rome, and she certainly showed throughout her life the effects of this early training in her strong feeling for the peace and security of the cloister—not that cloisters in those days always resembled those of today. The prying eye of Burchard swept the Roman scene meticulously enough to enable him to say that practically every convent in Rome was a brothel, though his additional remark *nemine contradicente* suggests that it was discovering what it wanted to discover. There is nothing to suggest that Lucrezia's convents were reduced to this baseness. Beautiful and fair, Lucrezia seems to have found in the company of Adriana,

Giulia and Sancha a gay and irresponsible happiness that paralleled in the great world something of the refuge to her spirit that religious retreat afforded. Certainly, the Borgia atmosphere of legend is quite foreign to all we know about her, though we must presume that she naïvely accepted, not without enjoyment in the more sensual side of her nature, the odd way in which her father behaved and the necessities of State which dictated conduct so different from her own considered tastes.

Betrothed as a small child by her father before he became Pope to relatively humble suitors, Lucrezia had a much more important marriage arranged for her once her father became Pope. Her husband was to be Giovanni Sforza, Lord of Pesaro, a small Papal fief. At the time, the alliance between the Papacy and the Milanese Sforzas, backed of course by Cardinal Ascanio Sforza, suited both parties. But Lucrezia was still only thirteen, and for some months, the marriage, celebrated with a prodigal splendour, most disedifying to Burchard who dwells on intimate details, was not consummated. Whether it ever was is at least doubtful. This was the period of the great French threat to Italy, and Lucrezia's husband, bound by his family ties to Milan, France's ally, and by marriage to the Papacy, started playing a double-game, ostensibly siding with his father-in-law and informing Milan of the Papal military movements. Thus the Lord of Pesaro was proving an unsatisfactory husband, personally and politically, and the alliance seemed in every way a failure. Lucrezia retired temporarily to her Dominican convent and signed a statement that she had been transferred to Sforza's family for over three years "without sexual relationship, nuptial commingling or carnal knowledge, a fact to which she was prepared to swear and to be submitted to obstetrical examination."

Sforza struggled hard in defence of his virility, but was forced in the end to admit his impotence. The case went through the normal ecclesiastical channels, the lawyers applying to the situation the decree of Gregory IX that a marriage which remains unconsummated for three years or more may be annulled. The Lord of Pesaro did not hesitate to hint that the true reason for the annulment was that the Pope himself was his rival for Lucrezia's favours. This monstrous suggestion is in keeping with the tale that Lucrezia, while in her convent retirement, gave birth to a child whose father might have been the Pope, though the more usual accusation is that the father was a Spaniard, Pedro Caldes, called Perotto, who was subsequently murdered and found dead in the Tiber, like the Duke of Gandia. Of course, he too had to be killed by Cesare. There is no evidence for this slander, though there is a mystery about a Borgia child referred to as the Infans Romanus. His parentage, both on the father's side and the mother's, is unknown. To add to the enigma, contradictory Bulls about him suggest that *both* the Pope and Cesare were the father! It is sheer guess-work to suggest that he was the child whose existence confirms the story of Lucrezia and Perotto and it is pure calumny to invent an incestual relation between the Pope and Lucrezia to account for him. The most likely father was Cesare by "a certain Roman woman"; but we simply do not know.

The annulment of the marriage between Lucrezia and Sforza is widely believed to have been a put-up job, but the unsatisfactory nature of the Lord of Pesaro's character and of the marriage itself, not to mention Sforza's wild accusation about Alexander's relations with his own daughter, find a natural enough explanation in the husband's humiliating consciousness of his own physical defectiveness. It is true that his first wife had died in childbirth, but in those circles the paternity of the husband could hardly be assumed.

Lucrezia, it must be remembered, was still only eighteen years of age when this first marriage was annulled. She remained very much of a prize in the marriage market. The Pope, as usual, kept everyone guessing and at last settled on the handsome and intelligent Alfonso of Aragon, an illegitimate son of Alfonso II of Naples and brother of Sancha, the wife of the Pope's youngest son, Jofre. The bastardy on both sides was not considered a slur, and the Prince who was made Duke of Bisceglie seemed an ideal partner, personally as well as politically, for a bride a year older than himself. But Lucrezia seemed fated to disaster. Just two years after the marriage, Alfonso, one evening, was leaving the Vatican to walk the short way to Santa Maria in Portico. It was in Jubilee Year, and Rome was crowded with pilgrims and beggars sleeping out. One wonders what the devout pilgrims made of the Papal Court and habits, though we do know what effect it all was to have in a few short years on pilgrim Martin Luther. Suddenly, some of the figures lying there on the ground sprang up, surrounded the Duke and attacked him and his companions. A running fight took place in which the Duke gave a good account of himself. But his aggressors were too many, and by the time he had found refuge within the Vatican, it seemed as though he could not live. What happened to him subsequently is not clear. One version is that he died of his wounds—the most natural explanation. Another is that he was strangled in his bed. A third that he was murdered by an agent of Cesare who was also accused of leading the band of ruffians who had ambushed and attacked the Duke. Once again we do not know. Many automatically pointed to Cesare, but as in the case of Gandia no one has suggested a plausible motive. Yet, as in the case of the earlier murder, a strong motive would have been needed to make Cesare the murderer of a husband dear to his own sister.

Even for those days, the tragedy was a terrible ordeal for the twenty-year-old Lucrezia who had found happiness in Alfonso. Not long before in the same Jubilee year, old Alexander himself had undergone a most alarming and rather ludicrous experience. A violent summer thunderstorm had blown up and lightning had struck the Vatican. Part of the palace collapsed, and a mass of rubble fell into the hall of the Popes where Alexander was seated on his throne under the canopy, awaiting his children. The Pontiff found himself buried under the debris and everyone thought him dead. Men worked frantically to rescue him, and he was finally discovered still sitting on his throne, dazed but with only superficial cuts. Within a week he had recovered. And he had had a stroke only a few days earlier! For a man of sixty-eight this was not doing badly.

But for the less resilient Lucrezia, at the age of twenty, such omens, followed by the violent death of the husband she loved, were enough to make her seek in life a fate rather less colourful, spiritually and temporally, than the one which the Borgia kaleidoscope had so far bestowed upon her.

Third time Lucrezia was lucky. Political and dynastic reasons suggested an alliance between the Papacy and Savonarola's fatherland—though this, of course, took place some three years after the Friar's death. Politically, it would further strengthen Alexander's life-long aim to bring unity and order into the estates of the Papacy. Dynastically, it would be a brilliant marriage for the Borgias whose future—and consequently the future of Cesare and Lucrezia—must be highly uncertain after the Pope's death which at that time would hardly be long delayed. The d'Estes of Ferrara were not worried by bastardy, but they were a great Italian House with a strong Catholic tradition. It is inconceivable that they could have accepted as a future Duchess the Lucrezia of the Borgia legend: poisoner, incestuous, adulteress. The Lucrezia, betrothed to Alfonso d'Este, son and heir to Duke Ercole, was described by the Ferrarese Ambassadors in these terms: "The more we examine her and the more closely we study her way of life, the higher is our opinion of her goodness, her honour and her wisdom. We have likewise noted that she is not only pious but devout." And so the notorious daughter of the Borgia Pope quietly left the chequered Roman scene to become, in due course, Duchess of Ferrara, the highest secular rank and title achieved by the ambitious Borgias, and lived in happiness, piety and dignity until her early death in childbirth at the age of forty-two. In her, too, the Borgias experienced a little at least of the family ambitions of Alexander, since Lucrezia's descendants ruled in Ferrara at the period of its highest cultural fame until at the end of the sixteenth century when Ferrara reverted to the Papal States.

Cesare was less lucky. Talented, but with little natural judgment and spoilt by the splendour of his state as the Pope's son, he could not flourish once the mighty support was taken from under him. In the end he was imprisoned by the King of Spain, escaped and soon after died fighting, at the age of thirty-two.

The only really great heritage Alexander was to have was the one he least expected: the ascetic and spiritual fame of his great-grandson, Francis, fourth Duke of Gandia—St. Francis Borgia, General of the Jesuits. But by then the Counter-Reformation had reversed the ecclesiastical values into which Rodrigo Borgia had been born and had lived, and the means by which this was achieved were hardly those which moved Girolamo Savonarola as he meditated on the *gran maestri* of the Church, above all on the greatest of them, the Pope Alexander Borgia of his day.

The sketch we have sought to give of Alexander and his family should at least suggest the limits within which the Borgia Pope's great weaknesses expressed themselves. He was not, we believe, a monster nor a man of unbridled licentiousness. Nor were the lives of his children and his entourage criminal and shameless. The Pope, though increasingly interested, through the conditions of his pontificate, in temporal affairs, remained faithful to his ecclesiastical duties as the endless pages of Burchard make clear. True, Burchard did not omit to note occasions when the Pope was absent, "he pretended to be ill, so that he should not have to say Mass the next day," but such noted exceptions only suggest a normal regularity. Lucrezia, as we have seen, had been brought up with Christian principles sufficiently strong to counterbalance the heavy temptations of her birth. And one may also usefully dwell on the fact that Giulia's brother, the Petticoat Cardinal, lived to be the ascetic, reforming Paul III who approved the foundation of the Society of Jesus by Inigo Loyola.

The picture is not wholly dark, for good and bad were strangely mingled in those times when the veils of respectability were not considered important, as they remain strangely mixed today under the veils which we are accustomed to draw over them.

Alexander, at least, was no hypocrite. Nor, for that matter, was

The Meddlesome Friar and the Wayward Pope 93

Savonarola who, being what he was, could not but have seen in the life of Rodrigo Borgia, as Pope and Vicar of Christ, an object of horror. Right as the holy Friar was, we shall see in the story of the clash between them that Savonarola nevertheless took a one-sided view, with tragic consequences to his reputation and to himself. He was the heir to the best tradition of religious piety in the Middle Ages and the unconscious forerunner of the one-sided reforms which a more introspective and individualist age demanded of the human conscience. But Alexander, as with the other Popes of his times, was at least faithful to the essence of his commission, namely to maintain the continuity of the successors of St. Peter with all that that meant not only for the preservation of the Christian revelation, its unity and its defence of the moral and human foundation of Christendom, but also for the safeguarding of the place of the sinner, of the *homme moyen sensuel*, within the fold of Christ, that he might still hope rather than despair.

Savonarola was to have every possible justification for denouncing the evils of the time, so conspicuously typified by the colourful Alexander Borgia and to strive to feed anew the life of the Church by recalling, through the Old and the New Testaments, the living personal relationship between the Christian and the loving, yet judging, God. But in responding to his vocation he was tempted to overlook the mercy and understanding of Christ, thus himself falling to a harshness and intolerance which was also the weakness of his own reforming strength.

In the quarrel between the two figures, which we are now in a better position to understand, we can sense that the conflict between the sinner and the saint may result in lessening the sanctity of the one and illuminating the privilege of the other to remain, so long as life lasts, among those whom Christ came to save, while He yet condemned their sins, with an infinitely deeper knowledge of them than a Savonarola could have.

PART TWO

Clash and Martyrdom

I. The New Cyrus

SAVONAROLA does not seem to have been stirred in any special way by the election of Rodrigo Borgia to the Papacy in 1492. Whether he then knew about his private life we cannot tell. He must have been aware, however, of the general pleasure at the election of an experienced churchman of whom much could be hoped. But he was not likely to have much faith in any of the worldly cardinals of the time. From his early years he had bitterly condemned the ways of the contemporary Papacy and rule of the Church, but while he was meticulous about details where Florence was concerned, he appears to have regarded Rome as generally symbolic of the evil state of the *gran maestri* of the Church rather than to have dwelt upon particular scandals, as we should now be inclined to do.

If any effect on him was made by the election, it may perhaps be deduced from the fact that the election separated two of his most famous visions. The first was the vision of the two crosses: The cross of God's Wrath rising from the heart of Rome into a sky of dreadful storm whose lightning, hail, fire and thunderbolts left but a few men alive; the second the cross of God's Mercy, rising from Jerusalem lighting up a whole world and causing fresh flowers on all sides to bloom with the people of the world gathering together to kiss the cross. In his vision during the Advent of 1492, after Borgia had become Pope, the Friar saw a hand in the heavens holding a sword on which were inscribed the words: "The judgments of the Lord are true and just." Voices from the Trinity cried: "The wickedness of my sanctuary raises its voice to me from the earth. Therefore will I visit their iniquities with a rod, and their sins with stripes. My mercy I will not remove from him, nor by my truth will I hurt him, and I will have mercy on the poor and the needy." Clearly, he was not optimistic.

But though, as we shall see later, the first relationship between Savonarola and Alexander concerned a purely ecclesiastical affair, it was political circumstances which initiated the real trouble between the saint and the sinner. Italy, it must be understood, was now under threat of a major invasion by Charles VIII of France, ostensibly leading a crusade against the Turks but actually seeking to make good his claim to the Kingdom of Naples.

Baron Corvo (Frederick Rolfe) proves himself a good hater in his lively *Chronicles of the House of Borgia*, so we need not take too seriously his descriptions of the men he hated—he was on the side of the Borgias. But the following account he gives of the French King tallies with all the records: "He was a self-conceited little abortion, this Christian king, of the loosest morals, even for a king, of gross Semitic type, with a fiery birth-flare round his left eye, and twelve toes on his feet hidden in splayed shoes, which set the fashion in foot-gear for the end of the fifteenth century in Italy; and, like all vain little men, he was anxious to cut a romantic and considerable figure." The name, "the French Disease," by the way, was due to the consequences to himself of the monarch's private habits. But neither the character nor the appearance of the "Little King," as the Italians, not so tall themselves, called him, prevented high Italian ecclesiastical personages from championing him against the Pope.

First of them was Cardinal della Rovere (the future Julius II, we recall again) who did not scruple to revenge himself for Borgia's success in the Conclave by doing all he could to encourage Charles to defy Alexander. Charles had sent envoys to Rome to make sure that the Pope would bless his invasion and support his claim to Naples of which the Holy See was then the suzerain. Alexander neatly avoided giving a straight answer. Charles's claim, he explained, would have to be submitted to a juridical

The Meddlesome Friar and the Wayward Pope   99

tribunal and, meanwhile, the Sovereign of the Eldest Daughter of the Church would be better employed furthering the crusade against the infidel. Had it not been for della Rovere's interference, the Pope's delaying tactics might have put off the superstitious Charles altogether. But the jealous Cardinal had a much better card to play, even if he pulled it out from under his ample scarlet sleeve. Was Alexander a true pope at all, he suggested to the King? Could he not be canonically proved to have been simoniacally and consequently invalidly elected? It would be well for the Eldest Daughter of the Church to call for a General Council of the Church to deal with the situation.

Such a proposal was not then as far-fetched as it would be today. The growth of learning, the splitting-up of Europe into nations, the Babylonian Captivity in Avignon, the Great Schism, all these had created a situation in which much support was to be found within the Church for setting up of General Councils of the Church whose authority, it was claimed, could override that of the Pope. These Councils were not called to define doctrine, but to settle disputes and propose reforms at a time when the position of the Papacy had been much weakened and the authority of the other mixed ecclesiastical-secular bodies, not least the Universities, had been rapidly growing. Such Councils (Pisa, Constance, Basle), strongly political in their flavour, had in fact exercised considerable authority since the Great Schism had made it necessary to depose and validate rival Popes; but the Councils failed in the end to reform the Church or to establish the view that the Council was above the Pope. Pius II had already felt the power of the Papacy to be sufficiently strongly re-established to warrant a clear ruling on this matter. In fact, by the middle of the fifteenth century the position of the Papacy stood once more where it stands today.

Such considerations did not worry della Rovere, nor did he hesitate to set in motion a policy which, had it proved successful, would certainly have initiated a fresh Great Schism between the supporters of Alexander and his own. As a cardinal, della Rovere had at least as much right as anyone to make this proposal. Charles VIII may have been a mean little man compared with the great and ambitious Cardinal, but he, a reigning Prince with a right in those days to take such initiative, had the sense to realise that he would be raising a storm, not least in his own country, if he acted on this advice, a storm which he would never be able to control in his own interests. But Cardinal della Rovere at least succeeded, one way and another, in confirming Charles's resolve to invade Italy in earnest in quest of the Neapolitan throne.

The part played in the invasion by the second churchman, to support the French king, Cardinal Ascanio Sforza, Vice-Chancellor of the Church and up till now the close friend of the Pope, was more understandable. He stuck to his Milanese relations, though not in the most gallant manner. The way of the invading French army lay through Milan, where power was disputed between Ascanio's brother, the Regent Ludovico Moro and Ascanio's nephew, the Duke Gian Galeazzo, or rather his wife, Isabel of Aragon, daughter of Alfonso of Naples. Her cause was naturally championed by her father. The wicked uncle was refusing to hand over his powers as Regent to the sickly young Gian Galeazzo, now that his minority was ended, despite the protests of the courageous Isabel, his wife. Ludovico looked to the French (who had a secondary dynastic claim to Milan) for support against the legitimate ruler. But Isabel pathetically appealed to the French King when he reached Milan and he was sufficiently moved to visit her ill-treated husband. It was the perfect fairy-tale story, but it had the wrong ending. The bullied young Duke died suddenly, and no one knows whether the wicked uncle had him poisoned. Anyway, the villain won through, with Cardinal Ascanio in his train, and the Sforzas played their highly valuable part in speeding the invading French army into a defenceless Italy, save for the frantic efforts of the Spanish Pope and the Spanish Neapolitan dynasty to preserve the independence and unity of Italy and all that it stood for in the interests of the Church and of civilisation.

The Meddlesome Friar and the Wayward Pope

The third churchman of influence who opposed the Pope's policy of resisting the French pretensions and siding with the little French King and his unprecedentedly large army was Savonarola himself.

With the reforming, prophetical Friar we are, of course, in a very different spiritual and moral world from that of Alexander on the one side and that of the two leading Cardinals who favoured Charles VIII on the other. Savonarola had no direct interest in international and political affairs at all and certainly nothing to gain from them for himself. For him, the French King and his army were simply God's handy instruments for the chastisement of his own Florentine people and of the rest of Italy if his own call to prayer, penance and reform went unheeded. Yet, even in this, Savonarola's naïve faith ran parallel with the guile of della Rovere, for it was the latter, it seems, who suggested to the French King the value of inscribing on the standards of the French army legends such as *"Voluntas Dei"* (God's Will) and *"Missus a Deo"* (Sent by God), expressions which echoed the terms of the Friar's own pious beliefs.

Savonarola expressed himself as certain in his own mind that he welcomed the French invasion *because* God Himself had told him that Charles was the divinely-selected instrument for the chastisement of Italy and the destruction of the *gran maestri* in Papal Rome. Again and again he had told the people of Florence that another Cyrus would cross the Alps, led by the Lord as the Lord's chosen scourge. It would be useless for the Italians, he had insisted, to trust to their weapons since the royal invader would conquer without difficulty. He even foresaw that Florence itself would bungle its attempt to meet the threatening danger. All that year (1494) he was preaching on Noah's Ark, and on Easter Sunday he implored his people to enter into the safety of the Ark. "But a time will come when the Ark will be closed, and many will then be uselessly sorry at not having entered into it." Beyond doubt, the preacher made an extraordinary and indeed revolutionary impression on Florence in that decisive year. Skilfully prolonging his analogy with the Ark in his sermons, he was able to make the formidable text, *Ecce ego adducam aquas super terram* ("Behold I will bring a flood of waters over the earth"), to coincide with the news that Charles VIII, leading an army greater and infinitely better equipped than anything the amateur fighters of restless Italy had conceived, was approaching. The effect was tremendous and Savonarola could do what he wished with the city of his adoption.

Obviously, the question is whether Savonarola was deluding himself in his surely sincere belief that he had talked with God, prophesying the future with divine help, deluding himself, therefore, in his conviction that Charles was the God-sent scourge appointed from on high to punish the wicked Italian people. Prophetical claims are common enough in the annals of the saints, yet only in the case of St. Joan of Arc do we find political prophecies that strike one as politically similar to Savonarola's. And even in this case the Church's test of the prophecies are in natural and historical evidence, not supernatural illumination. Illuminations, revelations, prophecies (outside Scripture) are accepted by the Church, however, provisionally and not finally and therefore not as part of the essential Catholic faith. They usually directly concern spiritual matters. Moreover, the soundest mystical tradition tends to frown on such "illuminations," judging them to be a sign of the mystic's human weakness rather than of his or her closeness to God. In other words, every possible objection has to be overcome before the Church feels it to be safe to propose to the faithful the acceptance of such claims as a help in their own Christian life. Savonarola's temporal and secular prophecies have little chance of passing through the close mesh of the Church's sorting of the genuine from the spurious. In principle, they belong rather to the type common enough in the Middle Ages when preachers and holy men and women readily expressed their convictions and exhortations in terms of coming chastisements ordained by an angry God.

Yet in Savonarola's case there are two difficulties. In the first place, his was a superior mind, well trained in philosophy and theology, as he often pointed out. In the second place, the accuracy and precision of these early prophecies are remarkable.

The Meddlesome Friar and the Wayward Pope

However superior and well trained an intellect may be, it will not necessarily be able to control stronger emotions and urges coming from deep down within a personality. From his earliest days Savonarola's moral feelings about the world were so exceptionally strong that we are entitled to believe that his make-up was unusual from the start. Moreover, as we have seen, he worked up to his prophetical claims from what had been the rhetorical devices of an acutely penetrating mind. Nor could he fail as a preacher to see the good that could be done by this powerful and, after all, traditional, kind of preaching. Where and how the line came to be drawn between his vivid sense that his remarkable powers were indeed inspired and his earlier acknowledgment that they were not no one can tell. But we cannot but believe that if he could deceive the people of his times, he certainly first deceived himself. There could have been nothing in him consciously fraudulent.

More impressive to us nowadays was the early accuracy of his apparent foreknowledge, though it must be said that as he went on his prophecies grew wilder and wilder. Yet even the earlier ones are seen to be far less impressive on close examination. Charles VIII's plans of invasion were under discussion between France and the Northern Italian principalities by 1493, and Fr. Herbert Lucas, S.J., concludes, after a close investigation, that he did not mention the new "Cyrus" at least until that date. Nor did it take any very great percipience to feel certain that if Charles's plans were put into operation, he could meet with no effective resistance from the politically divided and militarily ill-equipped peninsula. His greatest oratorical *coup* when he pronounced the words of Genesis about the flood involved no foreknowledge, for the news of Charles's approach was widespread as, too, was the general sense of imminent catastrophe. As to Florence bungling matters under Charles's threats, in this case Savonarola at least knew what he was talking about, for in the Florentine state of politics at the time no other possibility was feasible. One must therefore conclude that the Friar's prophecies did not really involve otherwise inexplicable foreknowledge, but they certainly do suggest that he had an extremely shrewd political mind, capable enough—and lucky enough—to foresee with extreme accuracy what was to happen.

The most difficult aspect of Savonarola's prophecies, from a modern point of view, is undoubtedly the curious outlook which, if we may say so without irreverence, they impute to the Almighty. It is true that the Jehovah of the Old Testament did things that seem very strange to us, but under the Old Covenant, God was seen through the eyes of a primitive pastoral tribe and the lessons which God had to teach a stubborn people were accommodated to their needs and understanding. Under the new Covenant, God was revealed in the person of Christ. Since then the role of prophecy itself has changed and weakened. Can we believe that God, as revealed in Christ, would choose—as distinguished from merely allowing—Charles VIII and the army of France to chastise Italy, scourge His Church and then renovate it? If the vicious little King had been fully conscious of and seriously intent on a great crusade against the infidel and if he had it in his mind to single out an evil Pope for warning, the notion might have had some plausibility. But it is far more plausible to suppose that it was Savonarola himself, steeped in the world of the prophets of the Old Testament, who transferred the old order, with himself as the new prophet, from the days of preparation to those of fulfilment, yet did this with a full sincerity and conviction. Nor did the ultimate utter failure of the whole French project, quite apart from the fact that it effected nothing very alarming in the way of a divine chastisement to the people of Florence and Italy, cause Savonarola to change his mind. For him the fulfilment of the prophecy of punishment and subsequent renovation was merely postponed.

More practical were the lessons which Alexander learnt from the way in which Charles marched unopposed from the north to the south of Italy. It was a warning of how easy a prey Italy could be to any intelligent and determined Power with a real leader. Alexander saw that under his temporal responsibilities it was necessary to unite the Italian States and to keep such secular duties distinct from his spiritual office. Savonarola, on the contrary, insisted on hopelessly confusing the two, believing in a spiritual renovation of the country as the means of political success and in political success as the proof of the validity of his vast spiritual claims. Thus, Florence, the "holy city," remained, so long as Savonarola's reform flourished, opposed to the efforts made by the Pope to ally the different parts of the country in a so-called "Holy League."

In most of the Friar's prophecies there was an easy let-out. If a sinister prophecy was not fulfilled, the fact could be accounted for either by the spiritual improvement of the people, while the failure of the people to pray and reform themselves explained the non-fulfilment of a hopeful prophecy.

II. *The Prophet Sways the City*

IN Florence during those heavy autumn days of 1494 trepidation and excitement were felt among the people. It was not only due to Savonarola, for the contemporary, Jacopo Nardi, described how "everywhere and especially in the court of Rome there came to be great worry and perturbation as though God had chosen this prince (Charles) as His special instrument to cause some raising of standards in His Church." The God-sent Cyrus, everyone whispered to his neighbour, was something beyond the natural order of events as the easy-going, if quarrelsome Italians, had known them. He was coming, they had heard, with thirty thousand men. Two thousand were knights of noble blood. Most were the hard-bitten, experienced fighting Swiss salted by many fierce, excitable Gascons. They were marching down with unheard-of guns that could shoot iron balls at so terrific a speed that you had no time to repair the damage done by the first shot before the second hurled you into eternity. Such numbers alone seemed like an avalanche, for how could they move down the narrow streets of the towns and be quartered in the scattered dwellings of the countryside?

The great Lorenzo de' Medici has been succeeded by his worthless son, Piero. That is why the Friar had had little difficulty in foreseeing that Florence was bound to make a fool of itself in the face of the invaders. After a braggart show of wanting to resist the enemy, Piero began to realise what he was up against and abjectly changed his tune, begging for a safe-conduct and mercy from the little monarch whose bite turned out to be so much more dangerous than his high-pitched bark. Piero was ready to pay any price for his safety. So the French really began to believe

The Meddlesome Friar and the Wayward Pope

that God was on their side and they cashed in heavily on their new-found faith. Tuscany and Florence were the gates to Rome and Naples. These must therefore sacrifice their proudest possessions and their time-honoured defences. The frontier fortresses of Sarzana and Sarzanello, Pietrasanta, Livorno and proud Pisa itself were to be handed over to Charles as pledges of good faith. Piero yielded all, together with much of the money which the banker-minded Florentines prized so highly.

This chopping and changing graphically fulfilled the Friar's prophecy that the rulers of Florence would behave "like drunken men." It also proved the Friar's long-awaited opportunity. Piero had done what he had to do in a graceless fashion, but it is hard to see what alternative he had. As Landucci, a contemporary chronicler put it, "Piero was held somewhat blameworthy. He acted like a youngster, perhaps rightly, since he remained the King's friend." Unconsciously, too, he played directly into the hands of Savonarola and the rapidly increasing number of Florentines who could see no hope in anyone but their supernatural prophet. Prone to superstition and belief in a half-magical world, despite their culture and often scepticism, they could not resist signs like these. The Friar, not the disgraced Medici, must be their real leader. The people flocked to hear him as he insistently called for the real remedy: penance and yet more penance.

"Listen to me," he cried. "Or rather listen to the words that come from God. I cannot say other than 'Do Penance!' Come, sinners, come, for God is calling you.... O Florence (like Babylon) you are sitting by the rivers of your sins. Make a river of your tears that you may purify yourselves in it.... In such a spirit, consider the tribulations that are in preparation for you—seek for their cause, and you will confess that it is God who sends them. He leads these armies and He is their general. Realise this and you will do penance, showing yourselves wise in the expectation of God's help in these troubles.... If you can pick out the cause, then look for the medicine. Give up the sin which is the cause of this evil and you will be cured.... You are deceiving yourselves, Florence and Italy, if you refuse to believe me. Nothing now can help you but penance. You will see it for yourselves—do what you will, what you do will prove useless if you do not do this."

And the Friar listed, catalogued and underlined all their sins and every type of sinner, not least the priests and the monks. He wore himself out, as he confessed, preaching repentance. His attitude, however spiritually right, ensured Florence's graceful yielding to the invader and her readiness to take his advice in all things now that the Medici had failed the people. But Savonarola's policy was, in effect, exactly the same as Piero's who by now had taken refuge with the French.

Under Savonarola's guidance, the Florentine Signoria, while providing against any breach of faith on the part of the French, came calmly to accept the terms made by Piero. It approved the view "that nothing should be wanting as to decency in its relations with that most Christian Prince, nor should it be remiss in satisfying with cash the avaricious nature of the French." And the treaty finally confirmed that "the city of the Pisans [Pisa had since revolted from Florence on its own account], together with Livorno, should remain in the hands of the King's Majesty, so that he could hold them during his enterprise against the Neapolitan Kingdom...and that the city of Sarzana and its fortresses, of Sarzanello, and of Pietrasanta should remain in the said hands of the King's Majesty during the said enterprise."

Savonarola himself was sent as an ambassador to Charles to make sure that the monarch would treat the Florentines properly. It was a chance for a sermon, not to be missed by the prophet. "Whereas," he told the twelve-toed Royal Majesty, "the immense goodness of God has now, for so many years, patiently borne with the sins of Italy, and has so long awaited her repentance, and whereas she has turned a deaf ear to the admonition of her pastor and has daily multiplied her crimes, putting on the brazen face of a harlot; therefore the Supreme and Omnipotent God has determined to proceed by way of justice and to execute judgment on her. But because God is wont to temper justice with mercy, it has pleased Him to reveal to one unprofitable servant the sacrament of His purpose to reform the Church by a grievous scourge." The Friar then told the King that he had been predicting for three years what was to happen. "God who cannot deceive has brought everything to pass down to the last detail—details as small as a man's nail." The rest must undoubtedly follow. "At last you have come," Savonarola continued, "come as God's minister, the minister of His justice. With joyful heart and cheerful countenance, we welcome you. Your arrival has filled with joy every servant of God...."

So far, so good. But the Friar who could thus confidently juggle with the will of heaven had his feet more firmly on the ground when it came to discussing the fate of Florence and the likely behaviour of the God-sent forces. Pointing out to Charles that the divine Mission imposed special obligations on him, he emphasised most of all "his city of Florence, which, though it labours under the burden of many sins, yet counts among its people many servants of God of both sexes, lay and religious. For their sake, you ought to preserve the city to the end that with a more tranquil mind they may intercede with God for the good success of your expedition." Having begged the King to make sure that the soldiery did not become "the occasion of fresh sins" and especially could be trusted to "defend the honour of those spouses of Christ who dwell in convents," he warned him: "If wickedness should by your means be increased, know that the power given to you from on high will be shattered."

Charles was hardly capable of understanding such language, and even if he had wanted to could not have prevented the greedy lords and the rough soldiers of the day from looting and misbehaving wherever they went, but there is universal agreement that the Friar's personal influence at this grave moment of internal political uncertainty and the expectation of possible disaster when the mighty foreign army reached Florence saved the city from the worst horrors of anarchy. Even when the injudicious Piero, before the French came, made a bid for the restoration of the Medici power, the city remained under control. Returning to Florence, Piero tried to enter the Palazzo, as the Vesper bells rang, but was refused admittance. The people heard the great bell of the Palazzo summoning them to a *parlamento*. The cries of the republicans, "*Popolo e Libertà*," mingled with the Medicean rallying cry, "*Palle! Palle!*" The general attitude of the people left no doubt as to what the city felt. Piero fled the city, together with his brothers, the Cardinals Giovanni (Leo X) and his cousin, Giuliano (Clement VII). It was the temporary end of the Medici rule.

At length, in the afternoon of November 17, 1494, Charles VIII of France, accompanied by Cardinal della Rovere, entered Florence at the head of his army. The Florentines had been ready to greet him and had made all suitable preparations for a deliverer rather than a conqueror. But the King tactlessly rode his charger with his lance levelled, the symbol of conquest. Still, the arranged festivities were carried out, and apart from the incident when some Florentines released prisoners-of-war, held by the French (a central episode in George Eliot's *Romola*), the worry was not so much about welcoming Charles as getting rid of him. The longer he stayed, the worse his men behaved. It was left to the Friar to persuade him that he was wasting time that should properly have been spent on his divine mission, and in the end he went, the Florentines by now heartily sick of him and his army.

The whole affair had not been a very auspicious beginning to God's mission for the spiritual renovation of Italy, as Savonarola saw it. With the fall of the Medici, Florence was left to govern itself with its time-honoured institutions, popular in their essence and intention, but for long abused by powerful families like the Medicis and their privileged friends. The habit and experience of popular government had been lost, and Savonarola found that many looked to him for guidance.

Though no one could accuse him of seeking direct political leadership—indeed he had carefully refrained from a practical task which was alien from his vocation—circumstances once again favoured his spiritual and moral purposes. The Medici, for him, represented the pagan culture, however elegant, of the times. They were the enemies of the peoples of God. They belonged to the tribe of *gran maestri*, of "the governments displeasing to God." Their Catholic traditions were no defence, nor their patronage of the Church. The Medici stood in the way of the Friar's great vision of a holy city of Florence, a city of a reformed God-fearing people, a city in which the mighty were put down from their seats and the humble exalted, the hungry filled with good things and the rich sent away empty-handed.

Here was his political opportunity, waiting for him ready-made. His followers, the *Frateschi* or *Piagnoni*, were now in the ascendant and they looked to him for practical guidance. In this matter, Savonarola stood on firm ground. The visionary Friar, capable of such extravagances in preparing the way for the city of God, was realistic enough when it came to teaching his Catholic people the main principles of sound popular government. Savonarola, when not carried away by his voices, was a shrewd and exceptionally intelligent person, with a deep love of the poor and humble. The disciple of St. Thomas, the Friar had found in his teaching the necessary moral principles which were applicable to the true government of men.

Rather than attempt in these pages to follow the intricacies of Florentine politics and the Friar's part in them, it will be sufficient to follow one of the many sermons in which, from the cathedral pulpit, he advised the citizens and the magistrates on their responsibility for peace and liberty.

Rule by a single person, he told them on December 14, 1494, is best when that person is a good man, "but when the ruler is evil, there can be no worse kind of rule." In warm climates, he explained, where people have little blood, and in cold ones, where they have plenty of it, but, alas, little intelligence, men are apt to submit to a single ruler. But in countries neither too warm nor too cold, like Italy, where plenty of blood and intelligence are to be found, "men are not ready to submit to a single ruler: each person would like to rule others, each one being in command and not under command." This was the cause of all Italy's troubles. Hence wise teachers had recommended the rule of more than one. "This is especially true of Florence where men are usually full of blood and intelligence." The duty of the people (now that he had proved his prophecies) was to reform their morals and attend to the city's common good. Let them do this and "Florence would grow richer and more powerful than any State, her empire spreading into many places."

The Friar's universal principles always had a surprisingly narrow application to his adopted home-town. However, he again insisted that the Church would be reformed, and that soon, and he even hazarded the prophecy that the Turks and the pagans would shortly be baptised. "Rid yourselves of the old ways, O Florence, and renew yourselves in all things in God's way."

He went on to explain at length how wrong Cosimo de' Medici had been in his *mot* that States are not ruled by prayers and *paternosters*. They are far better ruled on spiritual than on natural grounds. He was, of course, condemning the almost entirely amoral political philosophy of the Renaissance. "Where there is no charity, there is no love between the citizens. Where there is no obedience, citizens are divided—good counsel cannot exist amidst disunion. Such government grows feeble and weak. Voluptuousness, moreover, causes men to become effeminate, weakening them still more. Thus it is that wealth is spent through vice with the result that the city loses its reputation whatever it tries to do. Good men flee from such a city, for they see the evil towards which it is heading, while murderers and bad men rush to belong to it." Four hundred years of further political experience have not disproved Savonarola's thesis.

Coming to practical measures, the Friar demanded that the Signoria banish all men who oppose divine worship. It must insist that the priests in the city be good priests, for the clergy should be a mirror in which everyone can learn the right way to live. Let bad priests and religious be excluded. However, he added, more cautiously, that this was not really the business of the people, but of the Supreme Pontiff—still, subject to that spiritual authority, they must strive as a temporal authority to ensure that their clergy be good. Nor should citizens take so much account of self-enrichment, but, for the love of God, give the surplus of their wealth to the poor.

Let the Signoria make laws against that cursed vice, sodomy, which has given Florence such a bad name in all Italy. Though perhaps much of this is only talk, laws must be passed to see that sodomites are mercilessly stoned and burnt. The Friar also condemned verses, jokes, inns and the evil way in which many women dressed.

Having thus rid themselves of evil moral ways, let them all attend to the common good. "Citizens, if you only work together conscientiously to look after the common good, each one of you will fare better, spiritually and temporally, than if each looks to himself only. Look, I tell you, to the common good of the city, and if anyone shows pretensions to raise his head higher than the others, let him be deprived of all his possessions." No one must seek office, but wait for it to be offered him. Keep these rules, and God will bless the city with wealth—wealth in which all the citizens will share if they carry out their duties, and if any grow rich, well, they will have the chance of helping the poor.

As the long sermon, so curiously compounded of moral exhortation and political planning, in answer to the prevalent pagan callousness and selfishness, drew near its close, Savonarola came closer to his real purpose which strikes us even now as excellent and far-sighted. He wanted arbitrary charges on the citizens given up in favour of taxes and duties assessed in terms of the means of each citizen and the common need. "Let such charges on a man's property be reasonable so that the charge may not be heavier than the incoming wealth. Similarly with duties, let them be reasonably calculated in the light of what is owed both to the State and to the individual." Similar advice was given about the size of marriage dowries which should be proportioned to a man's status, those for the artisans and craftsmen not exceeding thirty ducats.

Most important in the Friar's mind were the measures he thought necessary to ensure that "no one should make himself ruler or dictator of others in the city." Those who manage to attain such power are "men without God's grace and outside God's providence; they are usually the worst types of men without intelligence or faith.... They are never really the friends of anyone, nor do they trust anyone.... Very often they dare not trust themselves, nor their wives sometimes, nor even their own children.... Their rule cannot really endure for long, since the whole country, though it may not dare show it, hates their tyranny."

But how to prevent the rise of such tyrants? With the fall of the Medici, a committee of twenty men, called *Accopiatori*, had been chosen as a ruling committee for the appointment of the Government or *Signoria* and the *Dieci di Guerra e Pace* (Foreign Affairs Board) and the *Otto di Balia* (Justice). But the Accopiatori were without effective authority, and Savonarola was not satisfied. "The Constitution which you have established cannot endure unless you improve it," he now warned them. "I believe that the best Constitution is that of the Venetians. You should copy it, but leaving out the features that are unsuited and unnatural to us, such as the office of the Doge."

He was referring to the Venetian Great Council, an aristocratic body intended to limit the powers of the Doge and prevent mob rule. Florence, a city with a turbulent political record, admired the constitutional stability of the rich, mercantile Venetians, as Continental democracies today admire the British Constitution. The idea of imitating Venice at this critical moment of transition had been widely canvassed, but the difficulty was that Venice was an aristocratic oligarchy, whereas Florence wanted a popular government, yet safe against the anarchy experienced in the past. The Friar's moral authority and political sense greatly helped at this point to ensure that the Florentine Great Council should meet the appeal for popular government yet be moderately and fairly constituted from the politically experienced citizens or their descendants with a more popularly-flavoured minority from the lower classes and youth. Similarly Savonarola called for a lessening of the role that selection by lot rather than election played in Florence.

"Courage now, we are making a start," the Preacher cried. "Today, the principle of the good life begins! But first you must make up your minds to a complete amnesty throughout the people. Let everything of the past be forgiven and cancelled out: so I tell you and so I command you in the name of God."

As the months passed, the Friar continued to give his political advice, mingled of course with moral exhortation and subject always to the principle that no political system can work unless it is founded on spiritual principles, and his guidance was accepted. He inveighed against the old-established Parlamento, which may fairly be called the prototype of much modern democracy, for in making the final political appeal to the assembled people, it inevitably played into the hands of whomsoever could bribe, cajole and control the people. It was, he said, the same as depriving the people of their power. Another important and widely debated measure was the complement to the Friar's demand for a general amnesty, namely the establishment of a legal form of appeal against the sentences of the judiciary or Otto di Balia. This committee, by six votes, could condemn without appeal—and since the votes were given by means of beans (*fave*) the law was called the law of the six beans (*sei fave*). Savonarola demanded that this law be given "a small stick to rest on in the form of a Council of Appeal." And so it was done.

No wonder that to this day Savonarola, despite his mistakes and extravagances, has remained a hero to the Florentines, for though the political lead he gave in those times may seem to us in part archaic and in part mere common sense, we have to remember how much of a pioneer he was in Renaissance Italy. His principles, though firmly based on spiritual and moral principles (and surely rightly so), possess the balance between authoritarianism and exaggerated democracy which to this day States find it so difficult to achieve.

Alexander, too, was a reformer at heart, as we have seen, though in an ecclesiastical and authoritarian tradition, and, once again, we are faced by the paradox of these two so morally diverse personalities, the one a sinner the other a saint, rising above the level of the times.

Unfortunately the Friar's wisdom and deepest Christian instincts were easily betrayed by the intoxication which seemed to overpower him in the excitement of the politico-spiritual battle and the outpouring of words which were always his strongest and most persistent weapon, as they were also his most persistent temptation, just as the Pope was defeated by his "carnal" tastes.

Despite Savonarola's wise insistence on a general amnesty and a court of appeal against demagogic sentences, he could cry, in the heat of conflict and crisis, from the pulpit, "Let him lose his head"—of any member of the Signoria who should in future dare to call a Parlamento and he declared of such that "anyone cutting them to pieces shall not be guilty of sin." Tyrannicide was even more openly advocated by the Friar in the case of the Medici, should any of them dare to return to Florence and attempt to seize power again. "Off with his head—be he the chief of any family whatever. Off with his head!" he said when the danger of a Medici restoration seemed possible. "Place your trust nowhere but in the Great Council which is the work of God and not of man; and may he who would change it or put rule in the hands of the few be eternally cursed by God." Any idea of reforming the barbaric criminal code was beyond him, and when he himself came to suffer under it he did not complain.

And he was as good as his word when it came later to the sentence of death pronounced on five leading statesmen for alleged conspiring to bring Piero de' Medici back (George Eliot in *Romola* included Romola's scholar-father among the doomed on this occasion). Savonarola who had had earlier a not very edifying preaching duel with the Franciscan,

The Meddlesome Friar and the Wayward Pope

Domenico da Ponzo, on this very subject of the necessity for appeal from the decisions of the *Sei Fave*, refused to intervene when his followers pressed for the carrying out of the death sentence without any appeal being allowed.

The Borgias, doubtless including Alexander, were not the kind of people who in the fifteenth century would recoil from political assassination if this were the only means of gaining important ends, but at least they did not try to make the Almighty their accomplice. In the Friar, however, were mingled a rare wisdom and breadth, when it was a case of applying philosophy to complex human problems, with an Old Testament theocratic fury when the divine purposes which he sought to further were frustrated by his opponents. Emotionally he belonged to the past, even if he could draw from the wisdom of the past principles even in temporal matters. These principles the Renaissance in its exultation over its discovery of a new man had utterly forgotten.

The anti-Medicean conspirators, including the venerable Bernardo del Nero, whose culpability was at worst technical, were executed, without favour of appeal, only a few months before it was Savonarola's own turn to face human judgment and justice, erring as it was, and one cannot but feel that even his tragic end had its place in the complex pattern of his character compounded of sanctity, insight, love for his fellowmen and yet an uncontrolled emotional extravagance and eccentricity incompatible with balanced and fully saintly Christianity.

III. An Invader Outwitted

SAVONAROLA'S greatest claim to fame may well in the end lie in the political work he accomplished in Florence in the winter of 1494–1495. It is difficult to believe that but for his sense and his overmastering moral authority, the turbulent, inexperienced and argumentative Florentines could have accomplished this peaceful transition from the Medici dictatorship, with all the picturesque glamour attached to it, to a moderate popular government. And the Friar's guidance—he never in fact directly participated in political debate and he possessed no political authority—extended not only to the big issues which we have mentioned, but to such socially beneficial measures as putting a stop to "the gnawing worm of usury", as exacted by the Jews, through the proper establishment of the co-operative lending society, the *Monte di Pietà*. He himself, like Alexander, was not anti-Semite in an age of antisemitism, but on the contrary saved the Jews from persecution by making their hated usurious rates impracticable.

The whole Savonarola reform must be accounted a unique example of a spiritually-motived political revolution. The more strange, therefore, does it seem that the mind which could accomplish this should have been so blind to the wider interests of Italy as a whole in the face of an occurring foreign invasion and of the growing threat of the new nations against the anarchic peninsula. Florence, his mission field by divine appointment, seemed to be the whole world to him. He was even capable of persuading himself that it was part of the divine scheme of things that Pisa should ever remain subject to Florence. For when that city, held by the French King, decided to imitate Florence's rejection of her own

The Meddlesome Friar and the Wayward Pope

Medici tyrants by rejecting in its turn the overlordship of Florence itself, Savonarola included the restoration of Pisa to Florence among his prophetic certainties of the future. As Fr. Lucas comments: "That Pisa should be again brought into subjection to Florence was part of the scheme of Providence as conceived by him. According to his prophetic gospel, God was deeply concerned about the liberties of Florence. The liberties of Pisa were, it would seem, a matter of quite secondary importance."

Alexander, thanks to Savonarola's welcome to the French King in the name of God, found himself more realistically engaged. Already the perfidious Ludovico Sforza who had smoothed the passage of Charles VIII had begun to realise his mistake and was trying—too late—to encourage the Genoese and the Venetians to do something about Italy's danger. But once the French army, which was vulnerable in that it could have been persistently harassed by the Italians on whom it lived, had passed through Florence, the Papal States lay wide open to it. And if the tougher Northerners were open to bribes, pecuniary or spiritual, still less patriotic integrity was to be expected both of the perpetually warring semi-independent lords who owed allegiance to the Papacy in its nominal domains and of the grandees, ecclesiastical or lay, in Papal Rome itself.

By the time Charles was approaching the Eternal City with his thirty thousand men and rolling cannon, Alexander VI found himself completely isolated. Everyone who had had the chance to do so had gone over to the invincible invader, including Verginio Orsini, the captain of the Pope's military forces, with all his family who had received the King in their chief castle and had handed it over as French military headquarters. There was panic at the Vatican where valuables were hastily packed in readiness for the Pope's flight.

But the Pope did not fly, despite the advice of many around him. There is much to be said for him at this critical moment. There he was, a Pope always surrounded by enemies eager to humiliate the Borgias; a Pope, the validity of whose election had been openly called in question by powerful cardinals and whose royal enemy had been urged to have him judged by a General Council; a Pope whose private life was the subject of unsavoury rumours strong enough to afford any mischief-maker a handle for undermining his pontifical status and dignity. Yet at this hour he invoked his moral authority as Pope of Rome against a whole world and prepared himself to stand firm against the all-powerful King of France and his grand army. He even managed to do this, while his mind was half the time concerned, not about himself, but about the safety of his womenfolk, his mistress of former days, Vanozza, his beloved Giulia and his niece Adriana. And in the end his courage and judgment succeeded in completely turning the tables against the King and his thirty thousand men.

First about his women. Giulia and Adriana, on their way to Rome, had been captured by a company of French soldiers who were of course completely defeated in their turn by the ravishing beauty of the Italian ladies. Such beauty was not however sufficient to prevent their captors from demanding a large ransom. It was done with all despatch, and soon His Holiness, expressing his delight by wearing a kind of military fancy-dress, went out to meet the women from whose vitality he drew so much of his own moral courage. He was equally concerned about Vanozza, it appears, though it is guess-work that she shared his own refuge behind the thick, but ill-made, walls of Castel Sant'Angelo. Giulia was more discreetly given refuge elsewhere, probably with the help of her brother, Cardinal Farnese, who wrote that it would be unfitting for her to remain in Rome lest "things occur that would bring small honour to all." Maria Bellonci pounces on this letter, which she discovered, to suggest that the "small honour" referred to her supposed liaison with the Pope. Considering that any beautiful—or indeed any ugly—woman in Rome was liable at any moment to fall into the hands of the French soldiers with no Savonarola to admonish them, it is curious to find this interpretation, especially as one might have expected a person as lascivious as Alexander Borgia has been made out to be to kill two birds with one stone by having Giulia safe and close to him in the safety of his fortress.

The Meddlesome Friar and the Wayward Pope

Relieved of these worries, so important to him, Alexander was able to negotiate with the French who, as he had rightly anticipated, saw in him, not a defenceless ageing man of none too good a character, but the spiritual lord of the world who symbolised a spiritual and moral force far too great to be equated with the present weakness and uncertain reputation of the human figure before them.

In the circumstances the Pope was naturally unable to do more than use for all it was worth the Papal sovereignty and the pomp of Papal ceremonial to authorise the King and his army to pass through the Eternal City and the Papal territories, limiting however their passage to the bank of the Tiber opposite to the Vatican. He also, doubtless most unwillingly, forgave the Cardinals who had taken the French side. At length, on the last day of the year 1494, the great army entered to the acclamations of the fickle Romans, while Alexander, never at a loss for the right gesture, remained watchful at home, quietly chanting papal Vespers *more consueto*.

Monarch and Pope at first treated with one another through ambassadors with cool politeness, while the French soldiers "in their customary fashion, forced their way into houses, drove out the owners with their horses and everything else, ate, drank and set fire to anything that would keep them warm," thus causing the people greatly to regret the welcome they had given to the picturesque cavalcade a few days earlier.

Rather than submit to Charles's increasingly exacting terms, which included his investiture with the Kingdom of Naples, Alexander retired with his personal troops to Castel Sant'Angelo and declared that he would defend it. If attacked, he himself would emerge and stand on the walls in full pontificals and carrying the Blessed Sacrament. All this could be no more than a fine gesture, even if he did walk along the terraces in the face of the French cannons, but the effect was spoilt by the collapse of part of the outer wall of the fortress with the loss of three lives. It had become a stalemate, and in view of the increasing anger of the Romans at the way their goods were being stolen and their women ravished by the French, it was time for both sides to abate their claims and make the best they could of the situation.

When Charles, on January 16, 1495, at last came to the Vatican to meet Alexander, the Pope was discovered, so it is said, on his knees in prayer, thus greatly edifying his exalted visitors. That he fell to his knees in prayer would not be difficult to believe for Alexander had an excellent sense of the theatrical; that the French were edified by this, rather more difficult. Unfortunately, Burchard says nothing about it and only gives lengthy accounts of the complex ceremonial during which he, as with any master of ceremonies today, bullied everyone, Pope and King included, to do the right thing. Twice the Pope did his little bit of acting. First when he pretended not to see the King make his first two genuflections so that he could condescendingly prevent him from having to make his third; and second, when he pretended to be taken ill, presumably to add the appeal of weakness to that of strength. However all this be, Alexander accepted Charles's terms where they mattered little, but stood firm on the vital point that he could not invest the French King with the sovereignty of Naples. In the traditional pontifical way he insisted and continued to insist that Charles's claim must be the subject of prolonged legal investigation. Despite this firmness and the sore temptation on the part of the French to be done with it all and challenge the Pope's right to be Pope, as the rebel Cardinals wanted, Charles VIII recognised him as the true Vicar of Christ and the successor of St. Peter. And at the solemn Pontifical Mass next morning in Saint Peter's, the son of St. Louis poured water on the Pope's hands and handed him the towel.

The good Friar had purchased the King of France's favours with the city of his adoption; the bad Pope had brought him to his knees by claiming nothing but the undefended authority of the supreme office he so sinfully held. It was Alexander's finest moment and one of the more striking in the long history of the Papacy.

One of the conditions to which the Pope had to agree was the handing over of hostages, including his son, Cardinal Cesare, officially

The Meddlesome Friar and the Wayward Pope

pronounced Papal Legate, but actually bound for four months by the terms of his appointment. Whether through the luck which always seemed to attend this bad Pope or through a prearranged piece of sharp practice the chance of which no Borgia could resist, even this demand of the King of France proved to have a symbolic effect on the fortunes of both Charles and Alexander.

The Pope who had always understood the vital Italian need for military and political unity if the country was ever to stand up against the rising great Powers and play its part in resisting the Turk—his crusading interest was derived from his uncle Calixtus—was now learning the hard way what the Italian anarchy, on a large or smaller scale, really meant. Not only had a little bounder, like Charles of France, marched through Italy just because he possessed a modern army, but he himself, the Pope of Rome, had found himself defenceless in his capital because those who owed allegiance to him had flocked to the rich and glamorous invaders. Two aims were, therefore, to determine his future policies. The first was to find a way of persuading the chief cities and provinces of Italy to join together in common defence; the second was to impose order within his own domains. For the first of these, at any rate, there was no time like the present.

Velletri, to the south of Rome in the Alban Hills, seemed to be the predestined spot to mark the new policy. There, Cardinal Cesare, riding gaily with the French army in quality of Legate and hostage, was shown a secret passage. Down it he scuttled and soon was riding post-haste back to Rome. Alexander shook his head gravely and muttered that the Cardinal had behaved very badly indeed, and Cesare carried on to Spoleto. The French then discovered that Cesare's rich baggage which he had left behind only contained rubbish. This treacherous coup released the Pope's best soldier who was to do so much to give the Papacy the temporal force it needed to give Italy effective leadership. At Velletri, too, the ambassadors of Ferdinand of Spain, suspicious of French aggression and traditionally on the side of the Papacy, tore up the Franco-Spanish treaty and threw the pieces at the feet of Charles because he refused to desist from the conquest of Naples, the right to which the Pope had denied him.

Charles, intoxicated by his easy successes, the breath of the early spring in Southern Italy, the beauty of the dark women, the spoils lying in wait and, above all, the craven attitude of Alfonso II, who had fled to Sicily, and his successor, Ferrandino, who fled to Ischia, did not bother to look back over his shoulders. Had he done so, he would have seen that Alexander was gathering together more than half Italy into his defensive Holy League, backed by Spain and the Holy Roman Empire—a treaty, announced by the Supreme Pontiff on Palm Sunday, April 12, 1495, to the delight of the Italians who believed, as they put it in a popular song, that the Borgia Pope had for once demonstrated that the laws of God could actually overcome the evils of the world. It is unlikely that Savonarola in his pro-French Florence, heard this compliment, so much in its substance after his own heart, paid to the grandest of the *gran maestri*.

By May, Charles, basking in his new kingdom, could not continue to pretend that he did not understand the signs of the times. Leaving a garrison in Naples, he ordered the retreat of his army back to France. A kind of monarchic ballet was diplomatically staged in and near Rome where King and Pontiff curvetted towards one another, as Charles sought contact and Alexander sought to avoid it. The Pope won the game, as usual, and returned in triumph to his capital and issued a Bull bidding the French King cease from warfare in Italy. Charles continued his journey north. After an indecisive battle at Fornovo, the King of France re-entered his country less than a year after his useless invasion had begun. As the Scourge of God and the renewer of His Church, prophesied by Savonarola, Charles VIII could hardly have failed more abjectly. But this failure only had the effect of encouraging the Friar to promote an early return of God's chosen forces to afflict Rome and the rest of Italy, while sparing the lilies of Florence as they flowered in company with the lilies of France.

IV. *The Conflict Begins*

HAD the proclamation of the Holy League and the departure of the French from Italy led to a general settlement of the country, it is extremely improbable that Alexander VI would ever have bothered himself greatly with the prophetical friar of Florence. Borgia had carved his own way, as Cardinal and Pope, uninterested in what other people thought of him, indifferent to criticism and measuring enemies solely in terms of the effective harm they might do to him as the supremely responsible churchman and ecclesiastical prince. He was interested in his own way and the last person to go out of that way to answer criticisms and reply to libels, an outlook which made him a great figure in the Church and the world, but has left him defenceless until recently against the criticisms and libels of posterity. Just as he chose his own private life, so he sought to carry out his public pontifical responsibilities, as the times saw them, without claiming any merit save that of the successful accomplishment of his duties. The last person to look for friends who would flatter and defend him, so he was the last person to pick unnecessary quarrels and enemies. But he was well able to assess the limitations of his momentarily spectacular success in the winter and spring of 1494–1495.

The Holy League, despite its name, was an unstable political arrangement to meet an immediate danger: some of the French were still in Naples; Charles, humiliated, would not give up the idea of trying again; neither Spain nor the Empire could be counted upon; the Italian States had not changed their characters in a season; and the Pope was still faced with the task of turning the anarchy of the great Roman military families and of the petty despots in the Papal States into an ordered and secure territory in the heart of Italy.

In these conditions the hostility of the holy city of Florence, run by a God-intoxicated Friar, determined to keep the city pro-French and outside the League—a city set at the keypoint of a French invader's route and strategically vital to the safety of Rome, was a consideration to which a Pope could not be indifferent. It is easy for Savonarola's apologists to attribute every action of Alexander to political intrigue with the Medici and other Gran Maestri (or, alternatively, to make out that the Pope, himself disinterested, allowed his hand to be forced by the politicians), but the truth is really to be found in the inevitably semi-political nature of the Pope's responsibilities at that time.

Alexander's first relations with the Friar took place in 1493 before the French invasion and the spate of prophecies about the new Cyrus. The events serve better to throw light on the Friar's character than to involve the Pope who then, not surprisingly, knew little or nothing about Savonarola.

It is the story of how Savonarola took steps to lay the foundations of his Florentine reform by first establishing more securely his own position and that of his fellow friars of San Marco as the heart of the coming reform.

The Friar's own ecclesiastical position in Florence was highly uncertain. As a member of the Dominican house of Bologna, he could be transferred by the Vicar of the Dominican Congregation of Lombardy to any of the many houses of that Congregation. He was a "religious," continuously under orders of appointed superiors. He had little patience with the laxer forms of Dominican observance and, as Prior of San Marco, was determined to make San Marco, together with other nearby Tuscan houses, conform with earlier and stricter principles of Dominican life. The realisation of this ideal would need time and his own security of tenure would be necessary. For this reason he set on foot a plan for the separation of San Marco from the Lombard Congregation, and

The Meddlesome Friar and the Wayward Pope   127

in this idea he certainly had the support of his Dominican brethren in San Marco. In any case, his moral authority over them was immense. There was precedent for this separation, since San Marco had only been united with the Lombard Congregation thirty years earlier, then separated from it, and then reunited. As he pointed out in a letter "It is quite a mistake to say that we have entered upon a new mode of life. A return to the principles and example of our saintly predecessors is not the adoption of a new mode of life. To build poor houses; to wear a rough, old and patched habit; to eat and drink within the limits of sobriety; to live in a poor cell; to cultivate silence and solitude; to separate oneself from the world; and to give oneself to contemplation—these are not innovations."

These are not innovations, but the Friar's temperament precluded him from seeing the tradition of the spiritual life in any terms but his own. He hinted that the Lombard Congregation was unsound and he saw his cause as something that would not "grow without war." Politically, he was right, for in those days even such Church affairs as monastic reformations and discipline excited the jealousies of rulers. Milan, Ferrara, Bologna, Venice and Naples opposed Savonarola's plans for the new Congregation which of course were enthusiastically backed by Florence. The Signoria wrote urgently to Cardinal Caraffa, Protector of the Dominican Order, to support this petition to make Florence independent even in so narrow an ecclesiastical matter, while strong opposition to it from other quarters was brought to bear. It was a matter for the Pope to decide.

How little Alexander at that time cared about Savonarola, one way or another, is illustrated by the story of how Caraffa obtained the Pope's favourable Brief. After a Consistory on May 22, 1493, Alexander brought the session to an end, saying that he would sign no more Briefs that day. But Caraffa was bold enough to go up to the Pope with the all-important Brief. Before Alexander could dismiss him, Caraffa, doubtless with the smile of one who knows his man and his good personal relations with him (Caraffa was one of the best of the cardinals), slipped the Pope's ring from off his finger and then and there sealed the document. When the opposition deputation came to protest, Alexander said he had no intention of undoing what had been done. The scene suggests that Alexander was very willing to be led in such matters by a worthy and holy cardinal.

As it happened, the Papal Brief just saved Savonarola from having to obey an order from the Lombard Vicar to leave Florence. The bearer of the Vicar's order had, as a contemporary put it, to go home with the blare of trumpets still in his baggage. Savonarola must on this occasion have thought the *gran maestro*'s timely action providential.

Armed with his new authority and security, Savonarola was able to put his reform into operation. This he did with such success that the numbers in San Marco rose from fifty to three hundred, and the new recruits included many from the greatest Florentine families, a proof of how effectively he had preached his reform. But in his eagerness to see it spread into Tuscany, Savonarola did not hesitate to enforce his reform even on unwilling houses. Thus in the case of Pisa (still under Florence at this time) only four subjects out of forty-four expressed willingness to be within Savonarola's reform. Nevertheless the majority were expelled to Lombardy and the Pisan house filled with friars from San Marco until, a few months later, these were expelled when Pisa revolted from its suzerain.

Two years later, in the summer of 1495, the Pope and the Friar began to take a more direct cognizance of one another.

It was just about the time when Charles VIII was retreating to France. He was in Siena, so tactlessly threatening the Florentines that even the followers of Savonarola were taking up arms in self-defence. Savonarola, writing to the King, had to warn him that his behaviour would bring adversities on him and cause the nations to rise against him. Preaching to his own people from the Duomo pulpit, he said: "Florence, this is what I say to you: God has given you his honey—in other words, he has chosen you for His own. But if you refuse to do penance and be converted to Him, He will take away your honey and give it to others. This is as true as the fact that I stand here in this pulpit." In the same sermon, he had gone out of his way for the first time to single out the Pope, though indirectly, as an example of the kind of scourge which demanded a thorough renovation of the Church. "When you see a head which is healthy, you can say that the body is healthy also; but when the head is bad, look out for the body! And so when the head of the administration happens to be ambitious, lustful and in other ways vicious, be sure that the scourge is near.... When therefore you see that God allows the head of the Church to wallow in crime and simony, then I say that the scourge of the people approaches. Mind you, I do not say that all this is true of the Church: I say *when* it happens." His disclaimer, given perhaps with a mischievous Italian smile, only made his meaning clearer.

Diplomatic and ecclesiastical relations between Florence and Rome being then very close, Alexander, of course, could not have failed to receive reports of this sermon and of others like it. Whether he was annoyed by the pointed reference to himself or whether, which is much more likely, he was irritated by the Friar's insistence that God was favouring Florence because it was pursuing under the Friar's guidance a pro-French and anti-Italian and anti-Papal policy, we do not know. Whatever his reactions, Savonarola thought it wise to write a letter (now lost) to the Pope, possibly to underline the point that he had been speaking hypothetically, and almost certainly to complain about intrigues against his mission in Florence.

In his short answer of July 21, 1495, Alexander spoke of "his great joy" at the accounts of the Friar's apostolic labours and the assurances, recently received, that the Friar was seeking to promote the service of God. But, the Pope went on, he had been informed that "in your sermons to the people you have said that your prophecies do not come from human wisdom, but from divine revelation. We desire then, as is suitable to our pastoral office, to speak to you and to hear from your own lips about these things so that, being made aware of God's will, we may the better comply with it. We therefore ask and order you, in the name of holy obedience, to come to us as soon as possible. We shall receive you with fatherly love and charity."

This letter is generally interpreted as the invitation of the spider to the fly, and Savonarola sarcastically recalled that even St. Bernardine had thus been called to Rome. It may be so, but this is not a necessary interpretation. The language sounds hypocritical in the case of Borgia, but it was in fact the normal way in which a Pope would express himself in such a letter. And we have little doubt that if Alexander had anything in mind beyond his proper wish to investigate the case of this meddlesome friar, it would not have been to clap him into a dungeon, as is so often suggested, but to try to bribe him by some honour or promotion. The plain truth is that nothing could have been more natural or normal than for the Pope or a representative of his in Rome to inquire into the political activities of Savonarola who, as a religious, did not directly come under local episcopal authority. Savonarola's claim to a special divine illumination over temporal things must also have awakened the Pope's curiosity, for Borgia was far from being a sceptic in such matters. Nor is there any reason to think that Savonarola's reaction to the letter is to be accounted for by any fear of imprisonment or poisoning. Savonarola took fright simply because he judged that the Pope might stop him preaching or remove him from Florence. If this happened after his efforts to obtain security of tenure for his work, all would be lost and, as a Dominican friar, he would have no redress at the hands of the Pope who would be acting fully within his legal competence. The only thing to do was to think up a good excuse for being unable to accept the Papal invitation.

Seeking precedents that went back as far as the twelfth century, Savonarola quoted Alexander III's command to the Archbishop of Ravenna "either reverently to fulfil our demand or give a reasonable excuse why you cannot do so." He then explained that he had been longing

The Meddlesome Friar and the Wayward Pope

to visit Rome and venerate the tomb of the Apostles, especially now that His Holiness had so graciously commanded him to make the journey, "but many obstacles stand in the way: bodily infirmity...a constant agitation of soul and body, brought on by my exertions for the welfare of this State...many wicked men who thirst for human blood and want to reduce the city to servitude." He might well be murdered by violence or poison. He goes on, "All good and wise citizens judge that my departure from this place would be to the great detriment of the people yet of little use to you in Rome." After begging the Pope to allow him a brief delay, he more clearly said: "Because of the furtherance of this work I am quite sure that these difficulties in the way of my going spring from God's will. Therefore it is not the will of God that I should leave this place at present." As for the Pope's worries about his divine revelations, he promises to send the little book (the *Compendium Revelationum*) about his prophecies which he is having printed. From this all the necessary information can be gathered. As for "the matters which must remain hidden in the ark of the Covenant (Rev. 11:19)," these he cannot reveal to any mortal man.

Allowing, as the present writer would certainly wish to do, for the widest possible interpretation of the duty of obedience from a subject to his formal and freely accepted superior—in this case from a member of a religious order to its supreme superior, the Pope, Savonarola's answer is surprising both in matter and manner. One excuse is reasonable, namely the Friar's health. But, though he constantly complains of his health and though his tense emotional disposition suggests great physical strain, it did not appear to affect his arduous work and manifold activities in Florence. The excuse that his presence is badly needed in Florence, in other words that he had much to do there, is not altogether consistent with it. The danger of being captured or murdered *en route* was also, no doubt, real. It was, however, a common risk of all travelling in those days and could be guarded against. In fact, his life had once been attempted in Florence itself where, of course, his real enemies were likely to be. Had he decided to obey his superior and been murdered on the way, would it not have been the will of God? The will of God in this instance seemed to be restricted to the divine protection of the Friar and his cause after the most careful consideration as to what suited his plans best.

In this first encounter with Alexander, Savonarola had been betrayed, as he so often was, by his fatal gift of words. Had he been content to rest his declining of the Papal summons to Rome on medical grounds for which he could, doubtless, have offered solid evidence, he would have lost nothing. Nor was it necessary for him to go to Rome in order to furnish the Pope with a reasoned defence of both the authenticity and full orthodoxy of his prophetical powers, summarised from the fuller account that was being printed. Instead of doing this, he set up his own divinely-based certainty as against the Pope's canonical authority, thus prejudging the whole case on his own behalf. It was, to say the least of it, an extraordinarily tactless letter and, whatever the Pope's true motives may have been, it was enough to justify the authorities in Rome to take further action. All, it is clear, started from this very injudicious—to say the least—first reply.

This was not delayed. The new letter (or Brief, as Papal letters are called) was sent from Rome on September 8. This was quite a different sort of document. In it the Friar is referred to as "a certain Fra Hieronymo Savonarola of Ferrara," that is, a certain named friar, among friars generally, picked out for official accusation in a grave matter. The Brief was no longer Alexander's personal work, but a formal indictment drafted by officials, whether pontifical or Dominican, who had studied the whole affair, and it was despatched in the name of the Pope.

Savonarola himself believed that Alexander had never received his previous letter, but the present Brief mentions his refusal to go to Rome and adds that the Friar was making things worse by publishing a book which anyone could read, thus adding to what he had hitherto "rashly said by word of mouth."

The Meddlesome Friar and the Wayward Pope

The Brief listed, in effect, eleven heads of accusation against the Friar. The charges made are as follows. He has indulged in erroneous doctrinal novelties. The state of affairs in Italy has unbalanced his mind. He proclaims to the people, without canonical authority and against the sacred canons, that he has been sent by God. He also claims to speak with God, as many heretics have likewise claimed, but can adduce no miracle or special backing of Scripture to support his claim. He asserts that if he lies about all this, then Jesus Christ Crucified and God also lie—a horrible and execrable blasphemy. Those who refused to believe in his rash affirmations are, he says, outside the way of salvation. It is impossible not to reprehend him for deeds, sayings and writings which could encourage the spread of false religions within the Body of Christ, thus promoting evil under the appearance of good. The Pope's hope that patience and waiting would enable him to see the fatuity of his prophetical claims has not been fulfilled. Likewise with the way in which he has rashly and evilly caused trouble in the Church. Hopes have been frustrated that his conduct would turn the Pope's sorrow into joy, a sorrow caused by his unbridled arrogance and the scandalous separation from the Fathers of the Lombard Congregation which was obtained, as the Pope later learnt, by the fraudulent cunning of some perverse friars. Finally, the Pope had to confess with sorrow that his hopes had been deceived; Savonarola had refused to come to Rome and was writing a book to be read by unformed readers setting forth the things he had rashly taught so far only by word of mouth.

In view of these charges, the Papal Brief, underlining the personal Papal preoccupation "with the great and wearing task of bringing peace back to the whole of Italy," appoints Fra Sebastian Maggi, the Vicar General of the Lombard Congregation, to examine and resolve the whole affair. As for the Friar, he is rigorously commanded in virtue of holy obedience and under pain of excommunication to accept Fra Maggi as the Pope's deputy and to obey him without delay or appeal. "Meanwhile, in this present Brief, we decree that while the matter is being examined before the Vicar, the aforesaid Girolamo be suspended from all duties of preaching to the people and lecturing in public." San Marco in Florence and San Domenico in Fiesole were to be reunited to the Lombard Congregation and all the brethren were to obey the new Vicar. Three of Savonarola's closest associates and supporters, Fra Domenico of Pescia (Savonarola's cheerful lieutenant and understudy), Fra Silvestro Maruffi (a more sinister and politically-minded aide) and Fra Tommaso Bussino were to be assigned to houses outside Florence.

Few will deny that some of the accusations in this Brief were false or grossly exaggerated in many respects, though the Brief contains some well-justified charges that Savonarola was making extravagant claims of private illuminations, while unwilling to submit them to canonical examination, and behaving in a manner that could give grave scandal. The contrast between this document and the Pope's letter of July 21 leaves little doubt that it represents the organised opposition, political, curial and Dominican, to Savonarola. This opposition, as we shall see, was never quite in step with the Pope himself who was always ready to take a more indulgent view until indulgence was no longer possible. Even so, it is to be noted that Fra Sebastian Maggi personally not only had a high opinion of Savonarola's character, but was later beatified. Savonarola's enemies could hardly have chosen a fairer judge.

Two exaggerations, at least, in this Papal Brief gave the Friar the right to defend himself against the accusations and to put forward reasons why, in his view, the Pope's orders would be calculated to do more harm than good. He did so, and he is to be commended for doing so. He had already written a long letter to "a Brother of his Order" in Rome, clearly an influential person, to persuade him to show himself a true friend by weakening the Roman conspiracy against him. To this confrère he enclosed a draft of the letter he would send to the Pope. His reply to Alexander was despatched the day after the Papal Brief had been officially received.

In his long reply he declared that all his preaching was in accordance with Scripture and the teaching of the Doctors of the Church. Hence he could not have taught false doctrine. He always submitted himself to the judgment of the Church, but he claimed that it was impossible to forbid prophecies, so long as they were not contrary to faith, morals and sound reason, for "this would be to impose a law upon God Himself." He had never claimed to have been sent by God or to hold converse with Him. Anyway who can make a law forbidding God to converse with whom He will?

For a trained theologian there is much special pleading in this part of his answer. The Pope was obviously not denying that God could inspire or speak to anyone He pleases. He was insisting that as a matter of ecclesiastical discipline and authority it was for the Church to examine and decide whether such alleged special inspirations were such as might be publicised and made the basis of general teaching and exhortation from the pulpit. The distinction is elementary and obvious, and the Friar could not have missed it but for his conviction that the Pope had ulterior reasons for his orders. It would have been better to have said so plainly.

Savonarola had no answer at all to the charge of calling God to witness for the truth of his claims by declaring that God would be false to Himself if what he said were not true. This habit of calling God to witness for his justification and even asking that God should destroy him if what he said were not true was to grow during the next three years. It was surely a sign of an increasing lack of balance in the Friar's mind. Similarly he did not defend his assertion that those who refuse to follow him are out of the way of salvation. It was not enough to explain, as the Friar did, that since grace can never conflict with truth, those who obstinately refuse to believe what they heard from his lips cannot be in a state of grace. Once again, he was prejudging the questions of whether it was a divine grace or only his own will and whether his hearers were satisfied about the question. No one, of course, would doubt that Savonarola's spiritual exhortations and calls to penance were fully within his commission as priest and preacher, and the Pope had already acknowledged this. The question in dispute was concerned with matters that went beyond this normal exercise of his ministry.

Finally Savonarola appealed against the choice of Maggi as the examiner on the grounds that as Vicar-General of the Lombard Congregation he was already an interested party in the dispute between San Marco and the Lombards. Therefore "we may without fault disobey Your Holiness" pending "a more impartial inquiry and an anticipated full acquittal from all the charges." This expectation was followed in the Friar's answer with fulsome expressions of his readiness to amend his conduct and to retract his errors.

Even this last reasonable-sounding objection was not to the point, for the Pope (or, more likely, the officials concerned) had already made the decision to reunite San Marco with the Lombard Congregation, as was entirely within ecclesiastical rights. Once this reunion had been effected, Maggi, the Vicar General, would then, as the canonical superior, be the proper person to look into a major trouble within his jurisdiction and report on it.

It is not very safe to compare the discipline of the Church in those days with the discipline of modern times. It is inconceivable in modern times that a Dominican like Savonarola would be given the freedom and allowed the moral political authority which he enjoyed save with the fullest knowledge and consent of the local and the central Church authorities. Hence the case could hardly arise. But were something of the kind to occur today, the ecclesiastical reaction would be similar in substance and the accused would have little choice between obedience and open defiance. Today, however, one hopes it could be presumed that motives would be spiritual and not political. The motives of Alexander and his advisers were without doubt largely political. To him the Friar was mainly a political nuisance, though this fact did not take away his right to act in ecclesiastical terms about a problem which fell within ecclesiastical discipline. But if one allows for all this, one is also entitled to expect that Alexander, the political Pope and *gran maestro* of such

The Meddlesome Friar and the Wayward Pope

evil propensities, would have claimed the freedom to use every means at his disposal to break the obstinate Friar, whether by hurling anathemas against him and his followers or by darker methods suited to the Borgia legend. But not at all! The really surprising and imperfectly explained thing is that on October 16, 1495, Alexander VI replied with a letter of the utmost generosity and charity.

Alexander makes it clear that he has not been hoodwinked. On the contrary his judgment of the case is plainer and severer than ever. "We are displeased at the disturbed state of affairs in Florence, the more so in that it owes its origin to your preaching. For you predict the future and publicly declare that you do so by the inspiration of the Holy Spirit when you should be reprehending vice and praising virtue. Such prophecies may easily lure the simple-minded away from the path of salvation and the obedience due to the Holy Roman Church. Prophecies like these should not be made when your charge is to forward peace and concord. Moreover, these are not the times for such teachings, calculated as they are to produce discord even in times of peace let alone in times of trouble."

Certain of his facts, the Pope went on, he had resolved to call the Friar to Rome again either to purge himself of the charges or suffer punishment for his behaviour. "Since, however, we have been most happy to learn from certain cardinals and from your letter that you are ready to submit yourself to the reproofs of the Church, as becomes a Christian and a religious, we are beginning to think that what you have done has not been done with an evil motive, but from a certain simple-mindedness and a zeal, however misguided, for the Lord's vineyard. Our duty, however, prescribes that we order you, under holy obedience, to cease from public and private preaching until you are able to come to our presence, not under armed escort as is your present habit, but safely, quietly and modestly as becomes a religious, or until we make different arrangements. If you obey, as we hope you will, we for the time being suspend the operation of our former Brief so that you may live in peace in accordance with the dictates of your conscience."

Of this reply Villari, the hero-worshipper of Savonarola and hater of the Borgias, writes: "With his usual acuteness and sagacity, Alexander VI grasped the difficulty of the case and hastened to proceed with an astuteness truly worthy of the whilom law student of Barcelona." Obviously we are not going to pretend that if Alexander Borgia wrote a letter like this such as any of his saintly predecessors or successors might have written, it was because he was a saint. But Alexander was never, in fact, unaware of what his Papal duties entailed, founded as they were on a lifetime of Vatican experience which in matters of spiritual and moral administration ran, even in those worldly days, very much as they have always run. One has but to read a few pages of Burchard's Diary to feel that behind the outward show and apart from private lives, the Vatican routine of ceremony, prayer and work was then very much what one would expect to find today. If Villari were right, why should so unscrupulous a Pontiff, at the very moment when the Medicis hoped to engineer a revolution that would be favourable to the Pope's Italian policy, allow the Friar to remain quietly in Florence? Why should he thus suspend the operation of the former Brief which would have put the Friar in an extremely awkward ecclesiastical position?

What was happening behind the scenes in Rome we do not know. Perhaps the "Brother of his Order" had taken up Savonarola's cause. Perhaps Maggi had seen through the motives that dictated the severe Brief of September 8. At any rate what is clear is that Alexander in his latest letter had distinguished between wild accusations and the real ground for legitimate complaint against the Friar, namely the illuminist nature and claims of his preaching, now indulgently, and maybe slightly maliciously, attributed to a certain simplicity of mind and misguided zeal. The reiterated order to cease from preaching was, in fact, a natural and inevitable consequence of the Friar's unsatisfactory replies to the Church's objections to unexamined prophetical claims. Equally, Savonarola in Florence remained in a position to do a great deal of mischief from the point of view of the Pope's temporal affairs, which included, for example, the defence of the West against the Turks. A religious subject, while surely entitled to distinguish between purely temporal and mixed temporal-spiritual matters, would need to have very serious reasons for setting himself up in opposition to a Pope's legitimate temporal-spiritual interests. And by now Savonarola could hardly claim that he himself was distinguishing as clearly as was the Pope himself between his own spiritual commission and the political consequences which he genuinely believed to be involved in it.

Once again, an unprejudiced approach seems to reveal a striking example of Alexander's clear understanding of the distinction between his diverse duties and the different aspects of his personality. This time, the distinction was drawn in circumstances which might well have tempted morally much better men to much less conscientious behaviour.

The arrival of the Pope's Brief was delayed, and this enabled Savonarola to justify himself (his conscience was very broad in these matters) in continuing to preach—actually a sermon of his antedated the despatch of the Brief—though the normal reaction of a priest would have been to cease until his superior had had the opportunity of replying to the self-justifying reasons put forward. It was perhaps unfortunate for him that the danger of the return of Piero de' Medici, backed by the Holy League, seemed considerable; to help prevent this the Friar's latest sermons were couched in more provocative terms than ever.

Everything now was seen in the light of a holy war, "a war which will be more bitterly fought against us than was the war of the tyrants against the martyrs or the war of the heretics against the faithful." Why, if not because of the growing intensity of the preacher's own feelings? He clearly foresaw where his fight would lead him: "We shall see excommunications, orders and things like that." "They say that I hold excommunications not to be valid. What I said was that excommunications are only to be feared when no error is to be found in them; when the error in them is patent, then they have no efficacy." And he appealed to precedents in history, to St. Catherine, to St. Peter Martyr and to St. Vincent

Ferrer, to show how saints may be unjustly condemned. Thus the story of St. Vincent which the preacher described in all detail referred to an occasion when one of his religious brethren gave money to a prostitute to make her go round saying that Master Vincent had slept with her and was a hypocrite. Later when challenged she admitted that it was another Vincent she meant, not the holy man. The comparison had little relevance to his case. And once more, despite the Pope's pointed reproof of this habit, the Friar solemnly touched the wood of his pulpit, declaring that what he said was as true as his touching the pulpit—"only if God errs, can I be said to err!"

V. *Moral Reform*

AT length the Papal Brief reached Florence, and Savonarola for the time being desisted from preaching. Villari hardly does his hero much credit when he says, "As we have seen, Piero de' Medici's expedition speedily failed, and there being no longer any pressing need for Savonarola to raise his voice in defence of the Republic, he held his peace so as to give his foes no fresh pretext for attack." In point of fact, the Florentine Government did all it could in the way of letters to the Pope and to the Dominican Cardinal Protector, Caraffa, to get leave for the resumption of the Friar's preaching during the Advent of this year, 1495. All in vain! Savonarola did not preach again until the Ash Wednesday of 1496, and then without permission.

Alexander was, however, justified in bearing in mind the distinction between the dangers of allowing the Friar the freedom of the pulpit and letting him carry on his more direct spiritual ministry in Florence. For Savonarola, temporarily accepting the ban, concentrated on the work for which he is best remembered by posterity, namely the outward purification of his holy city by an extremely effective campaign, organised in conjunction with Fra Domenico, in which the children of Florence played a leading part. This led in the last two years of his life to the famous Bonfires of the Vanities at Carnival time.

Savonarola in these pages has been criticised for many aspects of his work and the extravagances of his outlook, but his tragedy lay in the fact that these were increasingly wild deviations of a character and purpose which was on one side saintly, noble, utterly dedicated and, on the other, intellectually serious and sane. This picturesque reform which he now undertook may seem faintly ridiculous to us and in some aspects even sinister, yet at the back of it lay a sound outlook which is easily misrepresented.

Savonarola was by no means the prototype of the Puritan. He had all the vivacity, charm, humour, childlikeness, love of colour and spectacle of the Italian of the Renaissance. His gaunt worn face is as much a sad clown's as an ascetic's, and we may be sure that the twinkle in his dark eyes was as natural to him as the black look with which he could freeze his congregation. His sermons are filled with the homely colloquial touch of the people. He rarely used a delicate paraphrase where the coarse realism in word or story would be the more telling. The devotion he aroused in his followers, of every type and class, was the best tribute to a charm and attraction which perhaps today is not very easy to understand. His raw anticlericalism, impossible to imagine at the present time in a man of his position, was, as we have insisted, far less shocking to his fifteenth-century congregations, and perhaps preacher and people were all the better for a realism founded in unshakable faith. On the other hand, without in any way minimising his tremendous earnestness, one must also allow for the Italian theatricalness, the born actor sincerely believing in his lines, the Latin delight in carrying an effect to its most spectacular expression in the impassioned pleas for a revived spirituality and a religious reform. All these expansive, human characteristics good or bad, are in marked contrast with the negations and respectable repressions of the Puritan.

Savonarola's mission was not to deny the Renaissance, but to Christianise it, and he had infinitely more in common with a Dante before him and an Ignatius Loyola or Philip Neri after him than with the Protestant Reformers. He waged war on the Catholic compromisers with the paganism in the Renaissance, of whom Alexander was the outstanding example, because they were still redeemable, but his natural opponent was a Machiavelli who made a religion of an unregenerate, but immensely vital, humanity. What Savonarola wanted was to see the philosophy of Aristotle and Plato, as Christianised by Aquinas, regenerate and guide the torrent of new life which was flooding around him. Purification, adaptation of means for the achieving of their true end, a revealed supernatural order directing, but not denying, this powerfully dynamic instinctive, natural life, fed on the new wonders of human achievement and ambition—these were his aims. His insight was perhaps not great, nor was his intense vision sufficiently well served by balance and common sense, but he was no destroyer of progress and culture in themselves.

His outlook is well illustrated in his views on art itself where his behaviour has been much criticised because of the burning of the vanities.

> Creatures [he said in a sermon] are beautiful in so far as they share in and approach the beauty of the soul. Take two women of like bodily beauty, and if one is holy, while the other evil, you will notice that the holy one is more loved by everyone than the evil one so that all eyes will rest on her. The same is true of men. A holy man, however ugly in body, will be pleasing to all because however ugly he is, his holiness shows itself and makes gracious whatever he does. Think how beautiful was the Virgin who was so holy. She shone forth in all she did, and St. Thomas says that no one who saw her ever looked upon her with evil desire, so clearly did her holiness show itself in her.... But now think of the saints as they are represented in the pictures you put up in the churches. Young men go about saying, "There is the Magdalen and there St. John," and all because the paintings in the church are modelled on them. This is a bad thing that makes you greatly undervalue the things of God. You fill your churches with your own vanities. Do you imagine that the Virgin Mary went about dressed as she is depicted? I tell you she went about dressed as a poor person, simply and so veiled that her face could hardly be seen. So with St. Elizabeth. You would do well to blot out pictures so unsuitably painted. You make the Virgin Mary look like a harlot. How the worship of God is being ruined!

The picture or painting is not condemned, but the lie within it especially when that lie reflected the paganism of the times. While we may be grateful that Savonarola was not taken at his word "blot out," we must remember that living with the great frescoes of Fra Angelico and others in his home, he could not condemn art as such. His views, as we know, made a profound impression on many of the greatest artists in Florence, such as Lorenzo di Credi, Fra Bartolommeo, the Della Robbias, Michelangelo himself and, most of all, Botticelli, whose later paintings such as the National Gallery *Nativity* (the three men embracing angels in the foreground have been held to represent Savonarola, Domenico and Silvestro who were executed together) and the mystical *Crucifixion* in America, are symbolic expressions of the Friar's reform. A similar picture is the *Madonna and Child with Saints*, by Piero di Cosimo, in the St. Louis City Art Museum, U.S.A. Piero, an unlikely artist to be affected by a spiritual revival, enjoyed the patronage of Francesco Pugliese, of the rich family of Wool-Staplers, one of the most devoted and loyal of the Friar's disciples.

In poetry, the Friar expressed a more constructive piece of criticism when he wrote, "By some it is held to consist solely of form; but in this they are greatly deceived: the essence of poetry consists in philosophy and thought since without these no man can be a true poet. Should anyone think that the art of poetry only teaches dactyls and spondees, long or short syllables and verbal flourishes, he is certainly very wrong."

Another striking example of Savonarola's true outlook is to be found in the heavy financial commitments which he undertook on behalf of San Marco to ensure that the great Medici Library did not go to the French, but remained in Florence where in the San Marco library it could be freely consulted by scholars.

The same mind was behind the organisation of a new type of pageantry and social self-expression which was his answer to the traditional Carnival celebrations with the strong flavour of paganism and licentiousness which went with them. Outdoor processions, dancing, bonfires in the warm Italian evenings and nights were, and remain, a very natural expression of the Italian *joie de vivre*, and, just as with us on Guy Fawkes Day, young people were accustomed to importune passers-by for money wherewith to organise the festivities and buy the requisite materials, costumes and the like. Many earlier preachers had seen the advantage of turning these customs to religious usages, and with success; but in the ordinary way of things they were fighting a losing battle.

Savonarola was not the person to put up with half-measures. He was determined to do the thing in style, organising special reforms in the city and Christianising its semi-paganism by the brightest possible kind of religious carnival. This was obviously better than bidding good people remain indoors, wearing black and mumbling rosaries and thinking all the time how holy they were compared with the unregenerate disporting themselves to their damnation in the Piazza. Let there be jollifications, but so purposefully organised that the happy people would sing and dance the praises of God and be a judgment on the sin provoked by the immodesties of a pagan tradition. Children are always the heart of any true fun and revelry, and the child in man is awakened by dancing, fancy-dress, singing, bonfires, but the child in man soon turns into the animal when given free rein to his emotions. What more natural then that the children, still untainted by the world (though hardly in Florence on the testimony of a contemporary biographer of the Friar—"they were deeply plunged in every kind of vice so that Florence had become another Sodom") and preparing to take their places as the future generation, should be recruited, organised and given their pre-eminent importance as the leaders of the new Christian rejoicing and reform?

One may detect, too, a subtle point in the Savonarola revivalism. Often he had inveighed against religious ceremonial and the wealth and ostentation that went with it. He even stated on one occasion that if man had been created less imperfect even the sacraments would have been unnecessary. His point was that the show had replaced the interior spirit of prayer, since it was treated as mere display and ritual. By transferring the show to the unspoilt children and giving it a manifestly moral purpose, outside the already perverted liturgical functions, he was both promoting his reform and expressing his horror of the golden chalices and wooden men which had replaced the wooden chalices and golden men of the early Christian days.

And so where it had been the custom for high spirited young people to go about with long sticks holding up passers-by, wedding processions and the like to extract money for improving the evening fun, so under the Friar's directions and those of his scoutmaster-like lieutenant, Fra Domenico, the children of Florence were organised into disciplined bands going about with their sticks to beg alms for the poor and to persuade men and women in the name of Christ the King to hand over extravagant and unnecessary ornaments to improve the bonfires. Where men and women had danced and sung for the sheer fun of it, too often with lewd words and gestures, they were now to dance to the music of hymns with the friars, the older folk and the young wearing garlands on their heads cutting capers to the glory of God. In this first year of the experiment, everything was rather rough and unrehearsed, but in the two following years, as we shall see, organisation improved, the ritual became more elaborate and the spectacular burning of the vanities brought the season of festivity to an end with a mighty blaze.

It was a simple age in which people could easily take the colour of vice and virtue, changing dramatically from the one to the other so long as both were sufficiently exciting. Nor is there any doubt that the Friar at first had the majority of the people of Florence behind him in his picturesque reform. The Milanese ambassador reported that he had "all the common folk under his control." A contemporary biographer speaks of "the change, wonderful, stupendous, incredible" which came over the boys of Florence. Similarly, the girls gave up their vanities and their vices, keeping what was suitable to their mode of life and their class, but dispensing with superfluities and whatever was unbecoming, and living in the greatest charity—or so it was reported.

Unfortunately the best can easily become the enemy of the good—a point Savonarola always failed to appreciate. Seeing that he was on to a good thing, he and Fra Domenico encouraged his youthful militia pretty well to take over the moral organisation of the city.

He bade them act as spies within their own homes and in other people's houses so that they could report cases of gambling and evidence of other vices. The children (like Charles VIII) were also "the scourge wherewith the Lord purges His temple." "Children," he told them, "go round and see how matters stand.... The Board of Eight will give you permission to confiscate the cards of gamblers." Acting on such advice from the pulpit, the children's leaders called on the Signoria to report on the organisation of their reformist campaign and to obtain the Government's authority for it, sententiously assuring the magistrates that they had left aside "old evil customs and abominable vices" that they might see "holy virtues and good customs prevail in their place." Whereas Savonarola and Domenico with greater tact and understanding might have done much to give an active and practical training to children so that they could learn their responsibilities in an easy and attractive way, this kind of exaggeration has to us, who know of what children are politically capable, an unpleasant flavour of Fascist Youth. Nor can it have been good for the young people themselves thus led to believe in their own importance and virtue as expressed by their making a thorough nuisance of themselves. It should not have taken much knowledge of human nature to realise that this kind of thing could not last and would inevitably bring its own strong reaction. The possibility of this never seemed to strike the mind of the Friar who, despite his political work, had led from youth a sheltered life which all the more cut him off from an understanding of the inevitable ways of a spiritually mixed world in that he had always been so intense and even fanatical in his religious fervour, even though, paradoxically, his horizon was wide and his personality more balanced than is often the case with one-idea reformers.

VI. *Dilemma of Conscience*

THIS increasingly extravagant religious zeal led the Friar in these early months of 1496 not only to the establishment of a rigorously controlled Holy City, situated, as he pointed out in a sermon, by divine choice at the navel of all Italy, but to an absolute conviction that Pope Alexander could not really have meant what he had said when, twice over, he had forbidden the Friar to continue preaching. Or perhaps the Friar was thinking that a bad Pope, like Alexander Borgia, had no right to prevent him preaching. Charity, in the sense of love of God and of our neighbour for God's sake, makes up for all other virtues or lack of them. He had charity. The Pope had not. The Pope need not be obeyed. Such was to be, ever more emphatically, the line of his defence.

Apart from this, very heavy pressure was put on him by the Florentine government, conscious now of ever increasing unrest in the city. It did all it possibly could to persuade both the Pope and Savonarola of the imperative need for the Friar to express in the pulpit his powerful moral authority and spiritual guidance. This, too, seemed to Savonarola to be a call that set aside normal ecclesiastical authority and machinery. In fact, Savonarola did not hesitate to obey the Signoria.

It was only in March, after Savonarola had already preached three sermons, that Becchi, the Florentine Ambassador in Rome, was thanked by the Government for his "unsuccessful" efforts to have the ban on the Friar lifted and assured that this failure was not his fault, but due only to the calumnies of the Mediceans. On the other hand, there was by now talk of something said by Cardinal Caraffa which was interpreted as a hint that the Pope in fact would not make a fuss so long as Savonarola

The Meddlesome Friar and the Wayward Pope 149

in his sermons kept off political and Roman subjects. The Ambassador in a later despatch in March quotes Caraffa as saying that the Friar had promised "not to meddle with matters here as they were not his business nor appertaining to him." It is enough, he went on to explain, that His Holiness has borne with his preaching, a statement which suggests that in fact Alexander had decided once again to turn a blind eye on the Friar's disobedience rather than force an issue that must end in tragedy.

Whatever be the truth of this, one thing is certain. Savonarola, without any permission, preached again in the cathedral on Ash Wednesday, 1496, after the new type religious carnival and on the subsequent Sundays in Lent. Only his later sermons had the sanction of an unofficial Papal tolerance.

So far from not meddling in affairs, which, according to the Pope, did not concern him, these sermons, with their many references to the growing force of his enemies among the cautious *Palleschi*, or Medicean party, and the more bitter *Arrabiati* or aristocratic and moneyed party, poignantly reveal the terrible conflict that had been going on within him, together with his growing sense that he was being carried out on "a great sea." This realisation that there was now no turning back possible made his words more challenging than ever.

For this first sermon after the ban, the Duomo was specially prepared and a great amphitheatre of seats for the now privileged children was erected. One wonders about the role played by the Episcopal authority, a Medici, and the cathedral clergy, but this is a detail that is never mentioned.

As Savonarola began the sermon that must prove decisive for the future there was tense expectation in the cathedral. The preacher began with a long *apologia* for his recent absence and his presence now. Did he fear to be killed? No—else he would not be here today. Had he been excommunicated?

Who says so? And even had he been excommunicated, the excommunication would have been "worthless and of no help to those people so filled with lies." Supposing, he said in one of his rather over-simple examples, a commander had been sent by the king to fight his enemies under a general and had proved highly successful. If the general for some reason ordered the commander to stop fighting when such a command might have fatal consequences to the king's purpose, would the general be angry if the commander disobeyed his orders and carried on to victory? "Always, therefore, when it is clear that a superior's orders are contrary to God's, especially where charity is involved, no obedience is due.... When I saw clearly that my leaving the city would mean the spiritual and temporal ruin of the people, I could not obey any living man ordering me to leave it. This is so because this order would be contrary to God's orders and presumed not to have been meant; it is the intention of the laws which we are bound to obey, not the mere words."

Thinking of the Friar standing there in his pulpit below the Crucifix, arguing, gesticulating, one moment defiant and challenging, the next wooing and pleading, before his immense, hushed congregation, one wonders how far he realised the brittleness of his hold on them. Even on those who this day were intoxicated by his presence and the power of his words which was his real genius. "I cannot live unless I preach." But all present were not thus intoxicated.

Well then, you [the Palleschi and the Arrabiati] who write such lies to Rome, what will you say now?" he demanded. "I know what you will say: What, Brother?—You will say that I have said that no obedience is due to the Pope and that I refuse to obey. I never said so. If the owner of the vineyard were here and saw the harvest being gathered in, he would take no account of what you write to him." Then, turning to the mass of the people, with a knowing smile, "O citizens of Florence, if you could only know the kind of people who write to Rome and what idiocies they write, what a good joke you would think it all, and how surprised you would be to think that anyone could possibly believe them.... When I see such hostility and from so many quarters against this little man, worth not three farthings, I have said within my heart: perhaps you have really wandered from the right path and let your tongue speak falsities. Therefore I will now examine my conscience." And so the Friar did—at great length, professing his faith in the Holy Roman Church to which he had always submitted and always would submit. And in a long and moving prayer, Savonarola complained that the Lord who does all things well had deceived and betrayed him more than any man "for I have always prayed that you should give me the grace never to have the responsibility of looking after others; but you have done just the contrary, drawing me little by little to this place, without my having been aware of it. Only in ways of peace have I found pleasure, but you have snared me away from it as a little bird is snared. Had I seen the snare, maybe I should not be where I am today.... Surely we are in the centre of a deep sea and the winds break upon us from every side.... You, Lord, have proved stronger than I and have me beaten. Daily I become a mockery; every man jeers at me because I have for so long cried against evil and announced tribulations and devastations.... Yes, Lord, since you wish me to sail along so deep a sea, may your will be done!"

He ended with an appeal to the young people who had been spared the evils of the past and knew the meaning of liberty and with an invective against the incorrigible old who gossip and write to Rome. "A great war shall destroy your show and your pride. A mighty pestilence shall force your women to rid themselves of their vanities. Your tongue, you murmuring people, shall be stilled by a great famine."

It was a sermon that poignantly expressed the growing conflict of conscience within him.

In a later Lenten sermon, the preacher threatened Italy with the punishments awaiting it and seemed to revel in the heaping up of the horror to come. "O Italy, O Rome, I [God] will hand you over to those who will destroy you down to your very foundations. I will bring to Italy and Rome bestial and cruel men, starving like lions and bears. So many will die that everyone will be amazed. Italy cannot believe this, yet so often have I warned you on God's behalf. Italy, I have told you to do penance. Venice too! Milan, I have told you the same. I have warned all the wise men of the world. There is no remedy but penance.... The Lord threatens Rome and threatens the clergy." And he insisted, as so often before, that he names no names, nor were the punishments to come his own doing. He was only God's mouthpiece. "I am not here to preach to Florence only, but to all Italy." To the Florentines he gave the warning that first hinted of his own death.

"Do what you will, O Florence; play with any fantasy you like; imagine what you want to—I have this to tell you this morning. This reform, never will you be able to beat it to the earth; it will continue even after I die, for it is Christ's work.... O, my Lord, I turn to you. You know the first truth and wanted to die for this truth and, in dying, you conquered. So am I prepared to want to die for your truth.... Behold I am here, Lord. You wanted to die for me and I am content to die for you."

It was at this point that Savonarola, according to one of those present, turned to the Crucifix above him and called with such force and fervour that the people cried out, "*Misericordia!* May Christ our King live!" The commotion was so great that the preacher stopped, gave his blessing and left the pulpit.

On yet another Sunday in this Lent, he once again foretold the punishment to descend on Rome for its sins: "They have turned their churches into stalls for prostitutes; I shall turn them in to stalls for hogs and horses because these would be less offensive to God."

This series of sermons ended after Easter with a last attempt to justify himself. He now avoided all rhetoric and emotional outbursts. His position was therefore stated all the more eloquently.

His first point was to ask whether anyone could really believe that his stand was merely the result of pig-headedness.

> Do you think that if I were a liar I would lightly raise against myself all Italy, find myself in this deep sea and let myself be

accused of even being against God? Do not then believe such things for you know that I am not a fool to provoke men and God against me in this way. I know very well where I stand and not one of you would choose to be in the danger in which I now find myself. Look at it another way. If I were a false prophet, would I be teaching you the Christian way of life? ... Do you think God would let so many good people be deceived, especially as in that case it would be the deluded who lead the good lives? Do you not realise that God knows that if my work fell into ruins, the good people who follow me would say: we have been deceived and now can no longer believe in anything?

All that I have written and preached I submit to the correction of the Church Catholic and Roman. I have written as much to Rome and declared that if I have preached or written any heresy, let it be shown to me and I will gladly amend it or retract it in public. Therefore I am prepared for every form of obedience to the Roman Church, except where it commands anything against the law of charity. But you will say when I make this exception: You are not the Roman Church; you are only a man and not a shepherd. The shepherd cannot order things against God and charity.

It is worth noting here that Savonarola, as always, when he seems to be approaching the real issue of exactly when a subject may rightfully disobey his superior, slips away from it, and puts up the easy objection to answer, namely, that superiors can never err. Naturally, he went on: "That is where you are wrong! I say this because there are many who have done evil things and continue to do them. You know that an excommunication was expected. But it has not yet come. 'With what care they hatch their designs, planning treason double-dyed'(Ps. 63:7). But they have hatched them without finding any cause, for there is none to find against the truth."

"Well, we have spoken about the Roman Church," he went on. "Now let us say a word about the Pope who is head of the Church. Let us speak to the Pope who is the head of the Church. Scripture says, 'Thou shalt not speak ill of him who rules thy people' (Acts 23:5). Have I ever done this? I have never named anyone...." This argument, more than once used, is surely a patent equivocation. He went on:

> Write this to Rome: the Friar says that Rome is under a threat of a terrible scourge. The priest must be ready to give the holy oils. The traveller will not escape. Those who avoid one sword will surely run into another. And write that the Pope alone in this world can prevent such things by his good example and his call to all to repentance and conversion.
>
> Now, dear children, we shall cease for a season to preach. You know I have asked you to pray that God may withdraw the sword that is to fall on Florence and change it to the plague. But if you pray very hard, the Lord may spare you everything. If three-quarters of Florence undertook together to live good lives and to do penance, I believe that the Lord would spare you all these scourges.... Well then, though I cease from preaching I shall not leave you, for my wish is to live and die among you.

Savonarola's resolution to stop preaching in Florence had nothing to do with the Pope's orders, since he went to nearby Prato and Pistoia to continue his preaching and widen the ambit of the Florentine spiritual-civic reform. His sermons there, as well as this long Lenten series, were now causing widespread interest in Europe, even as far as in England.

The Friar, we have seen, was the first to have mentioned the word "excommunication," and the whole tone of his sermons suggests that he was expecting the worst from Rome and trying to brace himself and his followers against whatever was to come. He had already hinted that guile was at the back of the delay.

The Meddlesome Friar and the Wayward Pope

The Pope, however, was clearly most reluctant to proceed against the Friar in any canonical way. The fact is quite inexplicable if we believe Alexander Borgia to have been no more than a corrupt political Pope. He had nothing whatever to lose by applying the normal sanctions where a rebel subject was concerned. Florence was in no position at the time to make political mischief for him, and the heavy sanctions of the Church, excommunication and even interdict, would then, as they did in the end, weaken the Friar's followers, unsettle the large body of waverers and give heart to the open Miceans and the hotheads among the Arrabiati waiting to turn the tables on the Friar and his mischievous reform. Whatever political action in support of the League Alexander might see fit to take, this would be strengthened, not weakened, by the use of the spiritual weapons he had the power to wield.

The only possible reason why Alexander had so far acted so cautiously was that his conscience pricked him and that he was taking the advice of the better and wiser men in Rome. He knew perfectly well that the Friar was engaged in God's work, the work of reform which he himself would have wished to undertake had he been a better man, the work that, under the sorrow of the murder of his son, he was so soon to try to promote in a big way. In his letters to Savonarola he had plainly approved of his spiritual mission and its effects, questioning only the exceptional nature of the Friar's claims to direct illumination from God and complaining of the political and anticlerical side of his preaching. Everything suggests that the one thing he wanted to avoid was an open conflict between this undoubtedly holy, if obstreperous, man and himself whom he knew to be anything but what a Pope ought to be in example to the Church and the faithful. As against this, he had his grave political responsibilities, and the Florentine insistence of maintaining the French alliance and refusing to join the Holy League was a real political danger in view of the known intentions of France and those of the cardinals who supported the French King.

In these circumstances, Alexander did everything he could to put the onus of dealing with the Friar in his mischief making political capacity on to the Florentine Government. So it was that Becchi, the Florentine Ambassador, was reporting home the Pope's view that the city was making a fool of itself in the eyes of the world for living under the thumb of a friar and entrusting its public order to bands of children. Such things, as the Pope rightly foresaw, were bound to have bad results in the end. Alexander was entitled also to complain, as he did, about the Florentine government's tolerance of Savonarola's constant attacks on the Pope, the Papal court and the Cardinals "as though all this was his paternity's business." In another report Becchi passed on the Pope's message that the Friar should speak modestly of His Holiness and the most reverend Cardinals and prelates, and that he ought not to transgress the methods of other excellent and admirable preachers, nor open his mouth about things which do not pertain to him or his office, nor meddle in secular matters and affairs of State.

The two men were, of course, in opposition, but each of them was wrong on his main point of opposition. The Friar was certainly entitled to point to the corruption of morals, even at the Papal court and in regard to the person of the Holy Father himself, but not to deny his authority. The corruption was a sad sign of the times and the result of the lack of true spirituality and penance within the Church. Alexander was wrong to complain of the Friar's outspokenness, but right in complaining of Savonarola's political activities and the confusion in the latter's mind as to where even the worst of popes was entitled to expect obedience from his own religious subject. Indeed, the holier the Friar was—and there could in his case be no question of ignorance since he was a trained theologian—the more careful he should have been in drawing this distinction, inveighing even to the point of martyrdom where he had a right to, but scrupulous in obeying where obedience was due. But so far, it had been the bad Pope who had shown care and charity in not exercising the authority that was his, the good Friar who had taken

The Meddlesome Friar and the Wayward Pope   157

no precautions whatsoever to keep within reasonable limits of submission to the Pope's rightful authority. When the Pope had appointed the commission of Dominican theologians to inquire into the case of this strange Dominican, he had had no difficulty in concluding that the latter was "a heretic, a schismatic and a man disobedient to the Holy See and superstitious." The first two charges would hardly have stuck in an examination in modern times by a tribunal with all the facts before it, but there was certainly a *prima facie* case. Yet in spite of this, Alexander refrained from taking further action. Even now, it was sufficient for the Signoria to report to Rome that Savonarola had gone to Prato and Pistoia (there was no mention of preaching there and, no difficulty, apparently, about his personal safety) and to state that many of the accusations against him were calumnies, for the Pope to declare himself "well enough satisfied" about the business.[1]

But Savonarola, overwhelmed by his sense of the evil of the Church and of the times, mistook the Pope's forbearance for weakness, and, preaching once again in Florence in May, openly exulted in the fact that "we are still here" and it was in this sermon that he confessed that he could not live without preaching. Because of the corruption of the Church "God will unsheathe His sword and send a foreign invader" who would destroy "priests, bishops, cardinals and *gran maestri*." Now, too, for the first time, he indirectly referred to what was to become his only solution to the conflict of conscience between obedience due to the Pope and the evil of the Pope and the Church he ruled. "The anguish

---

1.   Some Italian Dominicans, intent on promoting the beatification of Savonarola, go to extreme dialectical lengths in seeking to prove that the Friar was technically justified throughout. Clearly this is not the book in which to argue these subtle matters. Nor, surely, are they really to the point. Does a saint need to be justified by highly complex legal arguments? It can hardly be doubted that Savonarola, especially in those canonically laxer days, could have achieved the spiritual and political reform of Florence, as well as shown up the corruption of the times and even of the Pope, while obeying Alexander where normal canonical obedience was normally to be expected. Why did he not do so? A little more homely charity—or even tact—would have served. Holiness is sanctified politeness, St. Francis of Sales is reported as saying.

is unbearable; nevertheless we have to remain submissive for it is not the Lord's will that the keys be changed." The keys were the keys of Peter in the hands of Alexander VI. The time was soon coming when the thought of the keys being changed so worked on his mind that he would have no hesitation in holding that it was the Lord's will that the keys be changed—by a General Council of the Church.

The renewed prophecy of the invader and of the sword falling on Italy and Rome was this time singularly badly timed. For, during the latter part of 1496, it was Florence which suffered. The wars were going badly against Pisa, and Florence was in danger of being cut off from the port of Leghorn whence its supplies came. The great popular leader, Piero Capponi, one of Savonarola's strongest supporters, was killed in battle. Funds were running out. Famine and pestilence were growing. Worst of all, Charles VIII, the hope of Savonarola and Florence, gave up all ideas of invading Italy because he was expecting a son, born in September and dead a month later. His grief was as effective as his earlier joy in putting Italy out of his mind.

But when things were going badly, no matter where the blows fell, the Friar was always in a position to say "I told you so." It was Florence now which was lacking in a fervour sufficient to stay God's wrath. Later in the year when the corn ships unexpectedly made Leghorn by the same wind that kept the Venetians off, the people went mad with joy, shouting, "The Friar's sermons have saved us again," and even Savonarola had to warn them against letting themselves be "so easily overcome by joy or by grief."

It was at this time that the Friar said in a sermon: "I want no cardinal's hats, no mitres, whether large or small; I want nothing but what you, O Lord, have given to your saints, namely death—a red hat, yes, but red with blood—that I wish for."

His words caused people to believe that the Pope had indeed tried to buy him off with a red hat or some other high preferment. The story that a Papal messenger, described in one extravagant version as being

The Meddlesome Friar and the Wayward Pope

the Pope's son, Cesare, was sent from Rome to offer him the hat rests on slight evidence, and it is hard to believe that the Pope could have been so naïve. But he might well have made a joke about it in Rome, and the story, changed in the telling, could have reached the Friar's ears. Another possible explanation is that the Friar himself, unable to explain to himself Alexander's long silence in the face of the continued challenge, imagined that the Pope might be thinking of some such base bargain and was prompted to mention the cardinal's hat as a graphic symbol of the martyr's blood, which indeed it is, in his sermon.

Alexander by the close of this decisive year, 1496, was in fact thinking along very different lines for in November, the all-important Brief *Reformationi et augmento* was published.

VII. The Last Order

NOTHING is clearer than Alexander VI's reluctance to press home anything like a personal attack on Savonarola. After the 1496 Lenten sermons, the Florentine envoy in Rome reported the Pope as saying that he was fairly satisfied with the situation as regards Fra Girolamo, "though there are many who are trying to spoil everything." We have suggested the reasons why—reasons that differ from those of most historians who are determined to see nothing but malice and guile in the Pope's behaviour. Yet Alexander's actions are equally consistent with his unwillingness to pursue a good man for his mistakes and extravagances, if this could be possibly helped. How then get round the difficulty, for politically at least the Friar's power in Florence was not to be tolerated by Rome.

The Pope's solution was made clear in this new Brief, occasioned, no doubt, by the evidence that Savonarola, so far from moderating his tone, was determined to make a martyr of himself for his cause.

The Brief did not mention Savonarola at all and indeed read from start to finish like an impersonal ecclesiastical document of a routine character. Its object was declared to be the good of the Dominican Order. It established a new Dominican Congregation "of the stricter observance," to be called the Congregation of the Roman and Tuscan Province. Among the sixteen Dominican houses assigned to this new Congregation, the name of San Marco in Florence was to be found in the middle of the list. No less a person than Cardinal Caraffa himself, Protector of the whole Order, was appointed Vicar-General of the new Congregation for two years. That in substance was all!

It will be noted that this decision indirectly upheld the Friar's original plea that San Marco, with its stricter observance, should not be joined again to the Lombard Congregation. It appointed one of the best of the cardinals of the day as the direct superior of the new Congregation. And it did not affect Savonarola's office as Prior of San Marco itself. In fact, the only indirect effect it had on him was to deprive him of his authority as acting Provincial of San Marco and the few houses joined with it.

It must have seemed impossible to the Pope and his advisers (for it is nonsense to attribute a decision like this to the Pope only), for even Savonarola to find a legitimate way round so sensible and ingenious a scheme for moderating his independence while in no way humiliating or challenging him.

But the Friar, by this time, was far beyond seeing anything objectively. His text, "we must obey God rather than men," had enabled him to justify to himself so many strange actions that he now had no difficulty or hesitation in finding an immediate answer to "this game of chess in which when one is hard pressed one moves from one square to another, and back again," as he said in the pulpit. His mind was undoubtedly expressed in the Apology of the Brethren of San Marco, the preface to which he signed.

His sophistry now seemed to have no bounds. With a great deal of scholastic jargon, he argued that the effect of the new plan would not be to extend the virtues of the strict observance of San Marco to the laxer houses of the new Congregation, but to infect San Marco with the tepidity of the others. "We know what we have done at San Marco. We know what goes on in other houses. Humanly speaking the reform of those houses is impossible. We are to consider not what God can actually do, if He should choose to work a miracle, but rather what He is wont to do." And, carrying all the members of San Marco with him in this rather uncharitable judgment, he declared with them in a joint statement: "This union, therefore, is impossible, unreasonable, mischievous, and the brethren of San Marco cannot be bound to accept it, for superiors cannot command what is contrary to the constitution of the Order and contrary to charity and the good of souls."

It is hard, however much one may wish to defend a person of such virtue and zeal for true Christianity, not to throw up one's hands at this reaction, especially when one remembers that the Pope had acted in concert with Cardinal Caraffa and the Dominican General, Fr. Torriano, a man of the highest reputation, and appointed Caraffa as the Friar's immediate superior. As for the argument that the bad must drive out the good, this view obviously ran counter to the whole theme of Savonarola's apostolic life. If it was not to be expected that a house like San Marco could exert a spiritual influence by its example on weaker houses of the same Congregation, how could the Friar have supposed that his followers in Florence could drive out the bad in the city?[1]

Here, surely, was the real test-case in the Friar's life—the point which separates actions, however surprising, but about which one may retrospectively argue, given the sharp contrast between the Friar's spiritual zeal and the personal unworthiness of the Pope, from a perfectly

---

1. Father Lupi, O.P., writing in *Blackfriars* (December 1952)—his argument has been expressed by other contemporary Dominicans, defending Savonarola—says that the Brief would have virtually compelled the Friars of San Marco to give up their stricter observance "since it was obvious that they would not be able to maintain it against the greater number of relaxed religious with whom they were now to be joined and among whom they would be scattered. So they would not accept the Brief; and Savonarola supported their resistance with a clear conscience. To him and them alike it seemed that the Pope could not really mean such a thing." In fact, the Pope did not mean it. He was to make it clear that there was no question of moving friars from the stricter houses to the laxer. Apart from this, the fact that Cardinal Caraffa and the Dominican Superior-General were associated with Alexander might surely have suggested to Savonarola that they knew what they were talking about, where the Order as a whole was concerned—knew better, in fact, than he. It is true that no superior, even the Pope, can command anything against charity and the good of souls, in the sense of something sinful, but, apart from the general and obvious truth of this, the matter here refers to the special case of a religious Order which, as in the case of all religious Orders, depends on the Pope for authority and approbation. Fr. Lucas, S.J., suggests that Savonarola's argument could, a fortiori, have been used to justify Jesuit disobedience to Clement XIV when he suppressed the Society of Jesus under political pressure. In the end, of course, the Congregation of San Marco, famed for members such as St. Antoninus of Florence and Blessed Fra Angelico, was destroyed and only reinstituted as late as 1934.

The Meddlesome Friar and the Wayward Pope

plain issue of ecclesiastical discipline and obedience at its highest level and in itself absolutely distinct from the wider conflict between a bad "right" and a wrong "good."

Yet he seems to have hesitated even less over this act of defiance than over the previous objections. He was indeed being tragically carried by a great tide towards his own doom and towards the inevitable destruction of his own spiritual work. Many have even held that he was being rapidly carried towards the great break, which was to be God's permitted scourge for the laxity of so much in the Church: the Reformation itself. Doctrinally and spiritually, Savonarola was fully orthodox, but so was a great deal of the positive teaching of the Reformers. Horrified as he would have been by the idea, it is not easy to deny that his complete defiance of the rightful authority of the Pope, even when a bad Pope, must make him in some sense a precursor of the Reformation which likewise rebelled against Papal authority. Thus Savonarola was, paradoxically, a victim of the divine scourge which he prophesied for others.

Savonarola's intention to disobey the instructions of the Brief, expressed so clearly in the "Apology," technically at least involved him in excommunication, for the Pope's order had been given "under pain of excommunication." He realised this and formally said that the fact would not deter him. He would "rather face death than submit to what would be poison and perdition for our souls."

Cardinal Caraffa proceeded with the work of creating the new Dominican Congregation, and the Pope himself made it clear that it had never been the intention to move friars from stricter houses to laxer ones. But even now nothing was attempted to force Savonarola to take action. Indeed, his refusal to obey brought the situation to very much where it had been before. Either the Friar's disobedience must be tacitly condoned for the moment or the full canonical attack on him personally must be launched. Alexander once again could not bring himself to do this.

Meanwhile Savonarola carried on into 1497 as though nothing had happened. In this year, the religious Carnival was carried to even further lengths and it ended with the first of the two Bonfires of the Vanities.

An immense fir tree, whose lower branches had a circumference of two hundred and fifty feet, had been placed in the Piazza, with large boards lying on the many tiers of the flat green branches. At the heart of the great pyramid, wood and a keg of gunpowder had been placed. The people of Florence had been exhorted by the children, better organised than ever, to place their "vanities" on these mounting shelves. "Vanities" meant anything which in the heated religious emotionalism seemed to their owners—or to the children—to be temptations against the life of perfect purity and of perfection. Women's finery, make-up, powders, false hair (much of this was, not surprisingly, secured by the youthful militia holding up people with their sticks of office) vied with the cards, dice and other means of gambling taken from the men. Volumes of Boccaccio and Petrarch and other immodest writers jostled against pagan and worldly pictures. Tapestries, musical instruments and the fancy-dresses used in the old-type carnivals, all these were contributed with an uncritical fervour which, one hopes, exceeded in the general excitement the prescriptions of the Friar himself, though probably not those of his artistically coarser-grained lieutenant, Fra Domenico. And near the summit of the giant bonfire there was placed, with a more typically Italian sense of fun, the effigy of a merchant who, so it was said, had offered a high price for all the "vanities" to be sacrificed in the cause of the new order. All through Shrove Tuesday, the boys in white, wreathed with olive branches, the friars in their albs, likewise garlanded, and soberer citizens, whose holiday clothes added to the gay scene, were busied around the tree, helping or watching.

After nightfall, as the eager excited crowds, mostly composed of the Friar's followers, but well spiced with his mocking enemies, watched, the great Bonfire of the Vanities was fired and the trumpets sounded a fanfare.

The Meddlesome Friar and the Wayward Pope

Whatever we may think of the methods and character of the Friar's revivalism, we can at least be sure that he scored the triumph of his life as the men, women and children of Florence feasted on the wonder of the crackles, the smoke and the flames that mounted up to the dark skies, warming the cool winter night, a spectacle to out-carnival any carnival of the bad old days. Did the Friar, perhaps already at his prayers while the vanities curled, twisted, melted, crumbled and burnt in the all-devouring flames of God's judgment, have any presentiment that not many months ahead another bonfire would be lit in that same Piazza where flames would claim the mortal remains of the most hated man in Florence?

After the Carnival came the new course of Lenten sermons, plainer, more vehement, more accusatory than ever: "You have become a shameless harlot in your lusts," he said of the Church. "Once you were ashamed of your sins; now you are shameless.... O prostitute Church, you have displayed your foulness to the whole world, and you stink to high heaven. You have multiplied your fornications in Italy, in France, in Spain and many other places." Admitting the worst about the Renaissance Church, which, after all, produced far more canonised saints than at any time since and millions of whose members, priests and layfolk, lived their humdrum Christian lives very much as today, the persistence, the language and the continued heightening of Savonarola's invective, even in the presence of the children of Florence, suggests that he must have been ever more the victim of his oratorical intoxication, as he was certainly becoming the victim of his *idée fixe* about his mission.

As to the excommunication, he defied them, as we saw in the Prologue, to carry it "aloft on a spearhead.... Let the gates be opened to receive it. I have my answer..."

Savonarola's tone was now beginning to correspond to the increasingly strained nerves in Florence itself. The Frateschi were losing political ground and the Palleschi and Arrabiali growing bolder in their hostility. Bernardo del Nero—the same Bernardo who, as we have seen, was to be condemned to death without benefit of the appeal which the Friar had done so much to establish—was elected Gonfaloniere or Head of the State. The Ferrarese Ambassador was reporting home that the Friar had now little hope that Charles VIII would ever return to Italy and support the city against the Pope's Holy League.

These conditions again suggested to Alexander that the time was propitious for persuading the Florentines themselves to rid themselves—and him—of the troublesome priest who kept Florence out of the Italian alliance. He asked that a special envoy be sent to him in Rome and the Signoria despatched Alessandro Bracci (a more important person that Becchi) who earned the name of a stout ambassador with a thin commission. When he promised the Pope that he would do his best to get Pisa returned to Florence if it joined the Holy League—"a final expedient of truly diabolical ingenuity," according to Villari—Alexander cheerfully answered: "My Lord Secretary, you are as fat as I, but pardon me if I tell you that the commission you have brought with you is a pretty thin one." Bracci, in fact, had to refuse the bribe, and Alexander, referring to Savonarola as "that chatterbox," said if only he himself could personally go to Florence he would be able to make its people see through that Friar "whom your lords and citizens tolerate even when we are slandered and scorned, threatened and trampled upon by him, we who after all occupy, however unworthily, this Holy See." It must have seemed a fair enough comment.

But though the popular government of Florence, still possessing a precarious majority, was able to resist the Pope and stand by the Friar, the Mediceans and the Arrabiati were growing bolder. At the end of April 1497, anyone less foolish than Piero could have made an attempt to regain power with good hope of success. Piero indeed tried, but he mismanaged things so badly that he never got beyond the gates of the city. Within them, however, a gang of Compagnacci, tough young bloods who liked to make trouble, decided to have done with the holy Friar's preaching.

They made their preparations on the eve of the feast of the Ascension when the Friar was due to preach in the cathedral. In the darkness the gang smashed the door of the Campanile, entered into the Duomo and climbed into the pulpit which they covered with filth. It was a gesture worthy of their type.

Next morning, after the pulpit had been cleaned, Savonarola courageously mounted and stood before the nervous and excited congregation which was expecting further trouble. The Signoria, in fact, had forbidden any more preaching in the city, giving as an excuse the recurrence of the pestilence but really because of the danger to law and order. This was to be the last sermon.

"You thought I would not enter the pulpit this morning," the Friar said. "But you see I am here. Is it because I have been well guarded? No, it is because I come and will always come when the Lord inspires me to. No man in the world, whoever he be, will be able to stop me." He went on in an unusually moderate tone, explaining his actions as inspired by the will of God. "But you say: Brother, you are the cause of our war; but my answer is that your evil lives are the cause of the war. Christ did not come to make peace between the good and the evil. He came to make peace among the good."

After he had been preaching a little time, loud noises were heard. Intruders had entered and were banging on benches and beating a drum. "I hear a noise," the preacher said. "It is the evil people who are determined to have their say." The congregation began to panic and to try to push their way out of the building. Savonarola held up his hand. "Wait a little! Be patient! If you knew what I know you would be sorry for me. Have no fear! God is on our side." Meanwhile, Savonarola's supporters rushed to get their arms and quickly surrounded the pulpit where the preacher was holding high the Crucifix. "Believe in this!" he cried. "Fear nothing!" He dropped to his knees. Then, supported by his followers, he left the cathedral and walked to San Marco surrounded by his defenders, crying, *Viva Christo!* in a procession with spears, swords and crosses waved on high.

Within a week of this extraordinary Ascension Day, Alexander VI at last acted. He affixed his seal to the Bull of Excommunication.

VIII. *The Last Defiance*

EVEN now it had required two things to persuade Alexander to take the final decision. The enemies of the Friar in Florence had been bringing stronger pressure to bear on Rome and they had been eagerly supported by Fra Mariano who had recently left Florence determined to get his revenge on the man who had humiliated him by depriving him of the congregations which he had once held as the fashionable preacher of the day. But just as important was the fact that Cardinal Caraffa saw no other solution to the continued defiance by his own Dominican subject in the face of the ecclesiastical orders contained in the Pope's last Brief establishing the new Tusco-Roman Congregation. Genuine religious motives were mingled with political ones and the Pope had to act.

The decision was fully expected in Florence itself for the Friar anticipated the half-sought blow by sending a letter to Alexander denying that he had attacked the Pope and accusing Mariano of having done so. If the Pope, as reported, was once more moved by this letter, one can only be surprised at his readiness to believe the holy man in the face of the plain facts of the case, almost as though he had a superstitious horror of excommunicating a man so obviously belonging to a different spiritual world from that of the easy-going degradation of the court of the Vicar of Christ.

But at this stage even the Pope could hardly stop the processes of the ecclesiastical law—Savonarola's letter of May 20, 1497, was dated twelve days after the Brief of Excommunication, though the latter only reached Florence in June—and, despite the nervousness of the Papal messenger who carried the Brief to Florence, causing these delays in publication which were used as excuses to suggest invalidity, the Brief of Excommunication was duly published in Florence and affixed to the chief churches of the city.

In it the culprit was described as "a certain Fra Girolamo Savonarola of Ferrara, Vicar, so it is said, of San Marco," a mode of reference quoted as showing the special malignancy of the Pope, though there was nothing unusual about it in a document of this kind, the Friar himself by his disobedience having weakened his title to be still the Vicar of San Marco. The Brief recounted the previous disobediences and the fact that the last one had automatically involved censure. Now the truth was to be publicly established that "the said Fra Girolamo was to be held excommunicate by all men for his failure to obey our apostolic admonitions and commands. Under pain of the same penalty, all are forbidden to assist him, hold intercourse with him, or approve him by word and deed as a person excommunicated and suspected of heresy. Given in Rome, May 13, 1497."

The text of the excommunication, which was considered by some to be canonically badly worded, made it clear that disobedience to the Pope's repeated orders and, specifically, disobedience in refusing to accept the union of San Marco with the new Congregation was the cause of the solemn publication of an excommunication, already incurred, yet without accusation of heresy. Much has been made by apologists of the Friar of the introductory accusation of spreading "a certain false pernicious teaching with scandal." What pernicious teaching, they ask? Another point they make is that Savonarola was not the only person not to take any steps to establish the Tuscan-Roman Congregation. But Savonarola's reaction alone was positively disobedient. Time would obviously be needed for the implementing of the Papal order by the others whether they approved or disapproved, and the latter could afford to wait on events, as Savonarola much more wisely might himself have done. As for the alleged "false doctrine," it is true that the Brief was clumsily worded, but it formally declared that heresy was only

The Meddlesome Friar and the Wayward Pope

"suspected," and the possibility derived, no doubt, from the Friar's persistent refusal to submit his illuminations to the examination of the Church authorities.

Politically, an excommunication in those days could be a much more serious matter than it would be today, and this despite the fact that the abuse for temporal purposes of the spiritual weapon had weakened its impact. Directly or indirectly, governments could be shaken by a condemnation which commanded the consciences of the people. General disobedience might involve the imposition of a Papal interdict whose effect could be to isolate a State or city with disastrous effects on its trade. It required a delicate balancing of probable effects to decide whether the Pope's censure was to be defied or obeyed. In Florence just now the Friar's supporters were again in the ascendant—the rapid changes in political ups and downs were due to the very short terms of office—now that the Medicean plotters had been executed. The political atmosphere therefore encouraged those who wanted to defy the Pope, though the diplomatic correspondence shows the great nervousness of the Government about the possible longer-term consequences of this defiance.

Much more surprising and much more difficult to defend was Savonarola's own reaction to his formal condemnation. Regarding it as unjust, he continued to celebrate Mass and to fulfil the other sacred functions of his priestly office. However unjustly condemned he might believe himself to be, the act of excommunication affected him as a priest and as a Catholic in that it derived, not from the stated grounds of the act, but from the Pope's positive authority and jurisdiction over all the clergy and faithful. It did not affect his priesthood or his Catholicity, but it affected his right to exercise the offices of his priesthood which are always under the Church's jurisdiction. More unexpected perhaps, though entirely defensible, was the fact that Savonarola after having been excommunicated should undertake the writing of one of his best and most orthodox works, the *De Triumpho Crucis*, a book which anticipated the modern science of apologetics and has since been constantly used in the training of priests and religious. This is one of the many paradoxes of Savonarola's life.

Despite all this, it is not hard to understand why the Friar, believing that matters had now gone beyond the limits of law, felt himself to be justified in carrying on his normal priestly work within the privacy of his convent and in continuing his urgent public ministry to the dying and the suffering from the plague which prevented people congregating in the churches and therefore prevented him from preaching again. Indeed, in so far as there was urgency about the need by the sick of his ministrations, he was entirely justified in his action.

At this time, whatever deep conflicts of conscience were at work within Savonarola's spirit, the Pope too had his own. For it was now that the murder of his son, the Duke of Gandia, took place, and we have already described Alexander's grief and his short-lived emotional reaction by putting into operation a major reform of the Church. (See Prologue.) Did the Pope connect the loss he had suffered with the warnings of the Florentine Friar and with the final decision to call so holy a man an excommunicate? It is hardly possible to think that he did not, particularly so when he received from Savonarola a letter which demonstrates once again the two sides of this terrible, yet gentle and understanding Christian figure.

This letter, the text of which we previously gave (p. 10), seems to sweep us away from the bitter public conflict between Pope and Reformer and disclose behind the public scenes two different men, a sinner and a saint, united at the deepest level in the consciousness of their humanity that could be raised by Christ to the highest ideals just as the hand of Christ could reach deep down to support in his distress the weakest of his followers who happened at that moment to be His Vicar. Respecting the Pope's grief, the Friar avoided all allusion to the wrongness of the Pope having a son at all.

But to the world at large Savonarola also issued what Fr. Lucas calls "a private encyclical." In this manifesto he uses his old all-embracing argument that since he is right, whatever may happen is further evidence of that rightness. The excommunication is all a necessary part of the work of the Church's renovation. In it his enemies, just as much as his supporters, are active, despite themselves, just as Herod and the Jews were instrumental even against their wills in the fulfilling of the prophecies of Christ. The excommunication is but another predestined step along the road to the "great victory." "Do not believe that these excommunications have any validity, for they depend on the false suggestions of men. It may be true that some say that when a man refuses to obey in those things that are expressly contrary to God's will, this is disobedience, but it is fatuous to suppose that we are bound to obey in all things. For we ought to obey our superior in so far as he holds the place of God; but he does not hold the place of God, and is therefore not our superior, when he commands what is contrary to God."

It was the old story—the refusal to admit the right of third parties to judge between the contestants, the inability to distinguish between rightful authority even in a bad superior and illegitimate authority in a good one, the refusal to consider when in practice a command was "contrary to God." At this time, the Commission of Cardinals for the Reform of the Church, which the Pope had set up after the loss of his son, declared to the Florentine Ambassador, Bracci, that it could hold out no hope of an absolution so long as the Friar refused to obey in the matter of the new Romano-Tuscan Congregation. Yet Bracci himself reported that even now the Pope himself was disposed to lift the excommunication. One cannot but deduce that, whatever the political intrigues, the excommunication, so far from being an act of Papal bad temper, sprang from ecclesiastical necessity, as the considered view of the best churchmen of the time.

These facts, it seems, prompted the Friar to write a letter to Alexander in October, the changed tone of which is illustrated in its abject expressions: "a child grieving at having incurred the displeasure of its father...fly eagerly to your feet, begging you at length to give ear to my cries...to whom should I go if not to the shepherd." Even so, the Friar was careful to express nothing but general and vague submissions with no reference to the specific differences in question, and in a sermon, just before the 1498 Carnival, he denied ever having sought absolution, despite pleas that he should do so.

It has been suggested that Savonarola never in fact wrote this uncharacteristic letter. It has also been suggested that if he did, it never reached Rome. The evidence of the Pope's readiness to forgive, if he was given the slightest chance, is clear. However this be, the Friar can gain little moral credit from expressions of repentance so curiously sandwiched between defiance immediately before and immediately after. If the letter was really written, it prepares us for the hesitations and weaknesses which the Friar was to show when he was finally tried. There is a suggestion here that Savonarola was never by any means as certain of his own rectitude as he appeared outwardly to be. A highly emotional character like his is often by no means as strong as it looks when carried on waves of holy excitement. The likelihood that this may be true surely adds a further note of tragedy in his life.

Two months later, on Christmas Day 1497, Savonarola, as we have related in the Prologue, took the decisive step of publicly celebrating the three Masses of the Feast in the church of San Marco and himself giving Holy Communion to the people. This was followed by a solemn procession round the Piazza, led by the Friar and his community.

The gauntlet was now indeed truly thrown at the feet of Alexander. The visible Church was openly defied. This was of all his actions the hardest to defend, for even the preaching which he was about to resume, now that the pestilence was over, was a much less sacerdotal and sacramental act than the public celebration of the Mass and Communion from which he had been solemnly excommunicated. The scandal caused was inevitably great and disapproval was shown even among his followers. Nevertheless, the Signoria, at present still supporting him, did not hesitate on the feast of the Epiphany to go to San Marco, to bring the

The Meddlesome Friar and the Wayward Pope

traditional gifts and to kiss the Prior's hand. Even while doing this, however, the government was busy trying to get an absolution from Rome, despite the news that the Pope and the Cardinals took a very grave view of these latest events. Alexander, nevertheless, still hoped to avoid further action and made another attempt to persuade the Florentines to renounce their Friar's policies and join the Holy League.

On Septuagesima Sunday,[1] Savonarola, in the face of the opposition of the Vicar of the Archbishop of Florence, Leonardo de' Medici, but with the consent of the Signoria, returned to the cathedral to preach to the by now thoroughly excited people, following with mixed feelings this dramatic struggle between Savonarola and Alexander.

The Friar's state of mind at this moment is described in a despatch by the Ferrarese Ambassador to the Duke d'Este. "I went to see him," writes the Envoy. "He told me quite plainly that he had made up his mind to preach during this Lent. I asked him whether he was awaiting orders from the Pope or from the Signoria. He replied that he would not be persuaded to undertake this work by command of the Signoria, nor even by command of the Pope, considering that the evil life of the latter was continuing. He was well aware that the Pope made no secret of his determination not to take back the excommunication. The upshot of it was that he awaited the commands of One who was superior to the Pope and to all creatures. He added that he made no account of the excommunication, the injustice of which would soon, he hoped, be made clear, as well as the whole truth about it."

At last, after nearly three years of conflict during which he had again and again held back his hand, Alexander VI was now making it clear that he could stand no more. Lumping together Florence's persistence in standing by the French King—all the ambassadors could promise the Pope was that they would behave as "good Italians"—and the outrageous conduct of their Friar, Alexander during an audience with the

---

1. See above, pp. 25–28.

envoys rose in fury and broke off the conversation. As he left, he turned and said: "Let Fra Girolamo preach forsooth! I should never have believed that you could treat me so!" Alexander, like Savonarola, was an emotional man.

After this scene, the crestfallen ambassadors requested fresh instructions. They realised, as the Signoria as yet had not, that times had changed and that there was now no chance whatever of further relenting from the Pope and Rome. On the contrary, as the Pope clearly warned them in a further audience, the next step could only be the declaration of an interdict on Florence. "Neither Turk nor infidel would tolerate such behaviour," Alexander bitterly exclaimed. The next day Alexander himself wrote a letter to the Signoria in which he referred to the Friar as a "son of iniquity." In it he recounted at some length all that he had suffered at the Friar's hands and went on: "We therefore strictly command you to send Fra Gerolamo to us, promising that if he comes and shows himself penitent, we shall receive him and treat him kindly, both for your sake and because we do not seek the death of the sinner. At least we command you to confine him, as a rotten member, in some private place where he can be cut off from communication with others. But if these orders are not obeyed and you go on giving your support to this man, pernicious, publicly excommunicate and suspect of heresy, we shall lay your city under an Interdict or even proceed to severer measures." Even now the Pope's tone, given customarily ecclesiastical terminology in these matters, remained moderate and, in particular, he still avoided any direct charge of heresy.

The list of charges were: spreading various errors; seducing the people with the pretence of not having been excommunicated; publicly organising and taking part in processions; celebrating Mass and giving Holy Communion; the conduct of the citizens in aiding and abetting him.

This Papal ultimatum was dated on the morrow of Quinquagesima Sunday, that is, during the Carnival of 1498, February 25 to 27. On that Carnival Sunday, the last of his life, Girolamo Savonarola seemed to sum up in his sermon the very heart of the attitude he had taken up from the beginning: "by their fruits you shall know them."

> Laws [he preached] are made to do good; they must therefore be in accordance with reason and love. If the purpose of the law is good, the fact will show itself in the fruits derived from it. Where you see good fruits, you see good laws; where the works are evil, there will be no good laws—"But, Father, if everyone turned away from you, what would you do?"—I would stand firm, because my teaching is a teaching of the good life, and therefore comes from God. This excommunication stands out in contrast with the good life and therefore proceeds from the devil.—"But, Father, the canons state that when an excommunication is unjust and its error unseen, it must be respected lest scandal be born."—This is true when you are excommunicated for a sin you have not committed, but of which people believe you to be guilty. You are then obliged to submit in order to avoid giving scandal. But when your innocence is manifest to the whole world, as in our case, why should any scandal be feared? I will go farther and say that if you are excommunicated in circumstances which force you to act against charity, then you are not obliged to abide by it. If you are prohibited through excommunication from helping someone in extreme necessity, it is your duty to disregard it.... If unjust sentences were to be accepted as valid, a bad Pope could ruin the whole Church and we should be obliged to accept the fact.

The argument was, again, correct in principle, but was stated in generalisations which took no account of the real nature and cause of the present case which, we must remember, now proceeded not only from the Pope personally, but with the general approval of many good prelates and authorities in Rome. On Savonarola's argument, any man of good intention could flout any authority which he believed to be harmful to his own good works. Of the rightness or wrongness of his behaviour there could be no judge but himself. Anarchy would be the result, whether in Church or State.

Stranger and more ominous were the concluding parts of this sermon, for Savonarola, despairing of earthly judgment, was prepared to demand that heaven itself should aid him.

"That God may be all the more ready to hasten matters," he said, "I propose that on the Carnival day we should all join earnestly in prayer. I will say Mass and take the Sacrament in my hands, and let everyone pray that if this thing proceeds from me and I am deceiving myself, Christ shall send fire from heaven upon me to swallow me up in hell.... Write this everywhere and bid mounted messengers ride to Rome praying that if this thing is not from heaven, destruction shall fall upon me."

Ominous words indeed, as we shall see, and in their demanding a miracle for self-justification strange words to come from a trained theological mind. Yet Savonarola repeated them in even more dramatic circumstances on the morning of Shrove Tuesday when the last day of Carnival opened with High Mass at San Marco. After the Mass and a procession, the Friar mounted a pulpit erected outside the church. From it he blessed the crowd with the Blessed Sacrament, saying, "Lord, if I am not doing this work of yours with a full sincerity of heart, if what I say is not inspired by you, may I be blasted at this very moment!" His face was lit up and his eyes blazed as he spoke, unaware in his excitement, we must suppose, that he was laying down his own conditions to God under whose inspiration he had throughout been claiming to be acting.

With greater solemnity than ever, the festivities of the Carnival were carried out that day. The Bonfire of the Vanities was crowned by a tableau of Lucifer in the midst of the seven capital sins. After the vanities had been burnt away to the delight of the great crowd, the Crucifix was carried in procession to San Marco. In the Piazza outside, priests and people danced in circles, hand in hand and carrying olive branches, singing psalms and hymns.

IX. *A General Council*

By the beginning of this last Lent of his life, Savonarola seemed to have completed the process of his emotional and spiritual development. He was now the real Savonarola, prophet of the Lord and called from on high to the mission of cleansing the Church at all costs to the established authority, jurisdiction and discipline of the Church. He had finally burst through the reflexes of his normal Catholic training as a friar and a priest. His ever fiercer and more simplified zeal for the victory of good over evil, of sanctity over sin, was leading him to a position that corresponded up to a point with that of Wycliffe in England. Though he avoided working out a theology of his position, his attitude amounted in practice to holding that no authority and power can be legitimate, either in Church or State, in the case of anyone who is not in a state of grace, who has not charity, who is not among the saints. It was in the logic of things that he should come to persuade himself before he died that Alexander's badness and simoniacal election should find their ultimate explanation in the fact that the Pope was not a Christian at all and had never been baptised. True, in this as in so many other matters he was far from consistent, applying quite a different measure to Alexander and to Charles VIII. Among the many Scriptural texts he used, he never quoted: "All things whatsoever they shall say to you, observe and do; but according to their works do ye not." Nor did he, towards the end, stop to consider that his ever fiercer attacks on the Pope and his advisers involved both a refusal to listen to the judgment of any third party and a virtual denial that there was anything to choose between Alexander Borgia and advisers like Cardinal Caraffa or the

Dominican Master-General, Fr. Torriano, so far as criticism of his views was concerned.

One cannot withhold a certain admiration for his fierce refusal to compromise in a fallen world where compromise is necessary for the survival of man and society. One can easily understand how his blinding vision of the good and his life-long horror of the evil which corrupted the Church, especially where her pastors were concerned, led him into his tragedy and martyrdom. And indeed Savonarola remains in history a great witness to the highest ideals which man has conceived. But equally he left no choice in the end to those whose duty it was to judge him on earth, however unworthy they might be as individuals to compare with him. Many a better Pope than Alexander might have dealt with Savonarola's case in essentially the same way. Would the Friar's conduct have been different? And, if not, what becomes of the attempts to defend him?

On this Ash Wednesday, he told the people in the Duomo: "Let the Pope be as much of a *gran maestro* as you please, I will have no peace with him if he does not live well." And, calling to Alexander, he cried: "If you wish to fight against me, you will fight as a pagan; for we live in a Christian manner, but your life is in opposition to Christ. If I am a martyr, you will be a tyrant persecutor. I must necessarily behave towards you as St. Ambrose did when he rebuked Theodosius for his sin." The omission of Alexander's actual name did little to offset the direct aim of the attack, especially as he recalled how Jacopone da Todi, preaching before "that wicked Pope, Boniface VIII, said 'I marvel that the earth does not swallow you up!'"

This was the last sermon he ever preached in the Cathedral because the Government, after a long debate, felt sufficiently disturbed by the Pope's ultimatum of February 26 to insist that he must continue his Lenten sermons in the relative privacy of the Church of San Marco. There he preached to the men. To the women he preached on Saturdays in another smaller church.

The Meddlesome Friar and the Wayward Pope

The situation now was such as to cause increasing disquiet within the Florentine government. The Signoria which had been just elected contained a majority against him. In his sermons, he himself had to answer the current criticisms that his followers were falling away from him. All through his career it is not easy to assess, in the complexity of Florentine political parties and constant elections, as well as in the generalised reports of ambassadors and early biographers, the movements of public opinion about the prophet.

It is impossible to doubt that many of the ordinary people had enthusiastically welcomed a spiritual revival of which they themselves were the heroes. His had been a movement of genuinely popular appeal, both spiritually and socially. The Florentines revelled in the Friar's prophetical claims, in the colourful oratory which flattered and lashed them, in the personality so evidently capable of inspiring both personal and mass devotion. They were living the drama which they adored—a drama constantly presenting them with the hope of an apocalyptic denouement all in favour of the poor and the oppressed. But we must also suppose that many gradually grew sick of the cult of virtuous living, of the prohibition of easy ways, of the forbidding of gambling and drinking, of the snooping of the self-important children. Preachers rarely change human nature in the mass.

At the governmental level, support for the Friar was much more definitely political. The popular government was committed to the French alliance and could hope for little from the Pope, the Medici Cardinals and the Holy League. Yet as time passed, the wind began to blow steadily against this policy, and the Mediceans and the *Arrabiati* came out more and more into the open, working on the people and forcing the Government into an ever more difficult position. Those who hoped for a return to the old oligarchic ways pressed it on one side and those who felt discouraged by the Friar's loss of ground undermined its own confidence. But it had no choice but to hold by the Friar as long as it possibly could. Even now, while the Signoria was unfavourable to the Friar, other governmental elements, such as "the Ten" in charge of foreign affairs, still had majorities in his favour.

Despite this partial change of orientation, the Government as a whole continued to defend him and this, it seems, for an odd reason. While those who supported him were obviously honest in their intentions, his opponents, who took a more realistic view of the situation and better appreciated what was involved in the Pope's anger, were ready to force matters to a head—in other words, to give Savonarola enough rope wherewith to hang himself and his *Frateschi*.

Alexander himself was satisfied that his Brief of February 26 would bring the Florentine Government to its senses, thus at length putting the tiresome Savonarola affair into the perspective he had always believed it really had. He was furious, therefore, when the envoy brought him a letter from the Signoria in which the Friar was still defended, though in rather more guarded terms. After the letter had been read to him by the Bishop of Parma, he called it "a sorry missive" and poured out his grievances. It was too bad of the Signoria to say that he had been misinformed. Misinformed? The Friar's sermons were in print for anyone to read, and he quoted passages. What was the use of this withdrawal to San Marco, if the Friar still preached there? What guarantee was there that he would not preach again in the Cathedral? As for the arguments about the invalidity of the excommunication, they were simply laughable. Anyone could see that the Friar himself had dictated the Signoria's answer.

Despite his anger, Alexander VI was still prepared to give Florence its last chance of avoiding the Interdict, assuring the Ambassadors that he was still prepared to forgive, if the Friar would seek absolution. But Savonarola this time really must stop preaching. So he sent a further Brief to the Signoria, dated March 9. The Pope again emphasised, and more emphatically than ever, that his quarrel was not with Savonarola's spiritual mission. "As for what you say about his virtuous life and the fruits of his preaching, these things we have never disapproved and we do not disapprove of them now. On the contrary, we greatly commend such good works which are most pleasing to us; what we condemn is the obstinacy, the pride, the mischievous boldness he shows in contemning ecclesiastical censures and in leading others to contemn them so that he has infected the whole city with the poison of his evil example." And the Pope demanded that the Signoria should either deliver the Friar into his own hands or detain him themselves until he asks for absolution. He promised to receive the repentant Friar with a kindly welcome, to absolve him and restore him to the Church so that "freed and delivered from his bonds by apostolic favour, we may send him back to you so that he may further spiritually enrich souls by preaching the word of God."

Was this a further invitation by the spider to the fly? We simply do not know. It depends on what view one takes of Alexander Borgia. But if one bears in mind the consistency of his policy from the start and the fact that in ecclesiastical matters, at least, the Pope's behaviour was normal and carried through with normal curial advice, there seems to be little reason to suppose that the Pope did not mean what he said.

The Florentine Envoys underlined in their dispatches home that there was no hope at all in Rome. "The printed sermons of the Friar have so exasperated the minds of men here that there is absolutely no remedy but submission." Bonsi, a supporter of Savonarola, had in fact been completely converted from his original belief that Florence and the Friar were in the right. Now he knew that it was not only a matter of an irritated Pontiff of poor moral reputation, but of Rome as a whole.

The Pope's latest Brief led in Florence to lengthy debates in the so-called Collegio or Consultative Assembly where the leading citizens sat. The debates, detailed reports of which have survived, reveal the highly perplexed minds of the chief spokesmen who seemed to agree on one point only, namely that the discussions were the most important ever held in Florence.

They had to weigh in the balance the very real sense most of them had of the Friar's good work, spiritual and temporal, in the city; the natural pride of the Republic in the face of a political, as well as a spiritual, challenge by the Pope of Rome; the danger of an Interdict, never far away from the mind of any merchant ("I have trade all over Italy and if the sentence is passed I shall be bankrupt," one speaker said); the possibility of the Friar being after all in the wrong ("Even a good man may err, and mistake his own imaginings for the spirit of prophecy," said another. And another: "He may create a new sect of *fraticelli*[1] of which we have had previous experience."); the legitimate spiritual authority of the Pope; the foolishness of trying to recover Pisa while continuing to defy Alexander; the thought that "a sermon unheard will not be the cause of anyone missing heaven." In fact, the discussion seemed to bring up every possible consideration without however throwing any light on the question at issue: what should be done in practice? The decision had in the end to be left to a small committee which, in the circumstances, could do nothing but reach the most obvious compromise solution that the best thing to do would be to persuade the Friar to be his own willing executioner.

In a different sense from that of the Commission which had hoped that Savonarola would get Florence out of its difficulty by a gracious gesture to the Pope, the Friar did become his own executioner. He knew that the tide in his holy city was turning at last—and turning fast, as popular tides usually do. He knew that forces in Florence were preparing to bring him to his knees and, if possible, kill him. He knew that once they were strong enough, the thousands who had supported him as a saint would jeer at him as a lunatic. He himself had despaired of the Church as it was then constituted. He was caught between a spiritual power which he had rejected as a prostitute power and a temporal power, now insufficiently confident of itself and no longer determined to stand by him in his extremity. Nothing was left to him but one last desperate throw, the one on which he would be judged in the end and fairly found guilty.

---

1. Extreme and anarchic off-shoots of the Franciscans, condemned by the Church.

Already, in his Ash Wednesday sermon, he had given a further hint of the plan which had been slowly maturing in his mind. "The time draws near," he told the people, "to open the casket. And if we do but turn the key there will come forth such a stench from the Roman sink that it will spread through all Christendom and stink in the nostrils of everyone." In other words, the government of the Church will be undermined and broken, laying bare the filth which lies behind its façade. There was only one way in which this could, in theory, at any rate, be effected: by the calling of a General Council of the Church to declare Alexander VI no true Pope. Savonarola, aware undoubtedly of the pressure put upon Charles VIII by Cardinal della Rovere to do just that, must have had the idea at the back of his mind for a long time, though he had held, as we have seen, that God had not willed the key to be turned. Coming from a simple Dominican friar, the coup would indeed have been audacious and dangerous. But now it was all or nothing.

"I tell you," the Friar said in this last of his Cathedral sermons, "that when the ecclesiastical power ruins the Church, it is no longer the ecclesiastical power: it is a power from hell, a diabolical power. I tell you that when this power supports harlots, love-boys, robbers, persecuting the good and trying to destroy Christian living, it is a Satanic and infernal power.... I tell you that every time the law is contrary to God's purpose, it is no law. You have understood that when normal rulings are useless and harmfully affect the Church, it is time to turn to Christ and say: You are my prelate, you are my parish priest, you are my bishop, you are my Pope. O Lord Jesus Christ, look after your church, look after your world, rid us of this wicked influence. Make a vendetta, O Lord, for we can no longer bear it."

In his further sermons in San Marco, the theme was the same, and the Friar's preaching made an unfavourable impression on Machiavelli, who went to hear him. Admiring his courage at least, Machiavelli, writing to a friend, said: "Starting with very terrifying words and with arguments such as seemed most convincing to those who did not discuss them, he declared all his followers to be excellent and his adversaries most vile.... Of the Pope, he says all that could be said of the vilest wretch you please; thus, in my opinion, he goes on favouring the times and giving colour to his falsehoods."

Now the Friar passed beyond any mere hints of a General Council and said: "Tell me, O Florence, what does this Council mean? Men have even forgotten what a Council is. How can it be that your children know nothing of it? What is the significance of the fact that they no longer happen nowadays? ... I tell you a Council means the gathering together of the Church. But be sure that there would be no question of the Church, if the grace of the Holy Spirit were not present. Where shall we find the Holy Spirit in these days? Perhaps in some humble little man. So long as this is so you cannot say that a Council could not exist. In a Council the wicked priests can be chastised and a simoniacal or schismatic bishop deposed.... Pray to the Lord that in the end a Council may be gathered together to help those who wish to do good and fight the wicked."

Thus, the long litany of sermons drew to their close, and at the end, Savonarola had these last defiant, sad and moving words to say:

> Boldly I will say this morning: If I have deceived myself, O Lord, it is you who have deceived me. Holy Trinity, if I have deceived myself, it is you who have deceived me. Ye Angels, if I have deceived myself, it is you who have deceived me. Every word of this is true—and yet impossible, for everything that God, His angels and His saints have said is most true. They cannot lie—nor I, saying what they say, can lie. I knew what I was doing when I entered this sea. But I was told not to doubt. We shall cross this sea, I was told. Had I foreseen everything then, from the beginning, maybe I should have run away. Everyone has mocked me. I have become the world's joke. I am called an idiot, a madman, because I do no more than call everyone to penance and prophesy tribulations. For so long have I cried to all Italy

and to Rome that they will be devastated and meet the barbarians. Because it seems that nothing of all this has happened, my enemies believe nothing any more. Instead the whole world has a good laugh at me and I am dishonoured by all. I have sometimes thought, as I came down from the pulpit, that it would be better if I talked no more and preached no more about these things—better to give up and leave it all to God. But whenever I went up into the pulpit again, I was unable to contain myself. I could do no other. To speak the Lord's words has been for me a burning fire within my bones and my heart. It was unbearable. I could not but speak. I was on fire. I was alight with the spirit of the Lord....

They are saying around me: let us see if we can catch him and send him to Rome.... Florence, Florentines—I mean the evil men among you in Florence—arm yourselves as you will and prepare what you need for the assault. You will be vanquished again, for you cannot kick against the goad. The Lord, indeed, is with me, a strong companion in arms. Therefore I tell you that those who pursue me will fall, some by the sword, some by pestilence, and all will be overthrown and scattered across the face of the earth. Their strength will be weakened and wasted, like ants. They will be utterly confounded and their confusion will be very great.

In his last sermon on earth, suitably preached in San Marco itself, Savonarola took final leave of his people.

Yesterday evening, at the third hour after sunset, a spokesman of the ruling party came over and told me that, for various reasons, they wanted me to preach no more. I asked if he came from his masters. And when he said, "Yes," I said, "I, too, must consult my Master. Tomorrow I will give you my reply." Now I give my reply from here. My Master has granted your demands and yet not granted them. They are granted in so far as my abstaining from preaching is concerned, but not granted in so far as your salvation is concerned. Bad news is predicted for Florence and misfortunes will fall upon the city. You fear the Interdict but the Master will lay one on you which will deprive the wicked of life and living. Our prayers will make up for the loss of our preaching. We beg the good people to join with us in these prayers. O Lord, I beg and pray you on their behalf that you will no longer delay your promises.

This request from the Signoria was the result of the great debate following the Pope's Brief, and if the Friar obeyed, it was not because of either the Pope or of the Government, but because he knew that all hope had gone, save for the chance of his last blow in the cause of God and His justice. At his trial, he said that he feared to be killed, if he continued to appear in public.

Now he wrote his final letter to Alexander VI. "I had always supposed that it was the office of a good Christian to defend the faith and to work for the reform of morals. But in carrying out this work I have met with nothing but trials and tribulations. I have found no one to help me. I had hoped in your Holiness, but you have instead turned against me and have put it within the power of savage wolves to wreak their cruelty on me.... I cannot hope any longer in your Holiness, but must have recourse to Him alone who chooses the weak things of the world to confound the strong.... As for myself I do not seek the glory of this world; I only expect and desire death. Your Holiness will do well not to procrastinate any longer, but to make provision for your own salvation." "I had hoped in your Holiness"—an avowal hardly consistent with his present claim that Alexander was illegally elected and therefore no Pope and his later denial that he was even a Christian.

Savonarola had by now set in motion his last plan, the summoning of a General Council of the Church to dethrone his enemy.

The Meddlesome Friar and the Wayward Pope

As we have already mentioned, in connection with the efforts to do the same by della Rovere and the rebel Cardinals in 1494, one cannot view such an idea in the fifteenth century in quite the same light as it would be viewed today. General Councils, convoked without Papal authority, had been held in the life-time of men of seventy. The great theologian, Jean Gerson, was freely quoted as holding that a General Council was superior to the Pope. Indeed, the upsurge of the Universities, together with the rapid growth of nationalism, had inevitably created a challenge to the weakened Papacy whose authority in practice largely rested on tradition, precedents of Canon Law, Papal Bulls, decisions of Synods, in which the Pope's spiritual and canonical authority, still more, infallibility, were not clearly distinguished from the mixed authority developed in history. The Papal authority was a living thing, subject to adaptation, rather than a finally coded and settled formula. But already by Savonarola's time, the picture had become clearer, and this in part because of that same growth of nationalism. Its establishment was rapidly destroying the sense of the Papacy's wider temporal authority as well as the sense of a universal spiritual-temporal authority in Christendom that might challenge the Papacy's sovereign authority. In other words, frontiers were becoming clearer, and the Pope's authority, if diminished, was at least more clearly defined. Already by the time of the Renaissance Popes, the reaction had set in sufficiently to enable Pius II to go back on his own earlier views before he was Pope, and issue the Bull *Execrabilis* in which he formally condemned, on the basis of tradition and the sacred canons, any appeal from the Pope, Vicar of Christ, to a Council.

Despite this, however, the matter was not so clear as to prevent Cardinal della Rovere, the future Julius II, from taking steps similar to those the Friar was contemplating, nor to prevent the Sorbonne from supporting Charles VIII's timid hopes from a Council. Della Rovere's excuse was that Alexander was not a lawful Pope at all, having been invalidly elected. But even Julius II, when he issued the Bull defining for the future that simoniacally elected Popes were no true Popes at all, restricted objections, on the ground of alleged simony, to the cardinals present at the election.

We cannot doubt that Savonarola, as a strictly trained Dominican theologian, could not, in a cool hour, have found any solid justification for his present action, as an ordinary priest. It was not for him to assume the simoniacal election of the Pope whom he had long regarded as a true Pope, still less to defy on his own account the Bull of Pius II, whose Vice-Chancellor, it will be recalled, Rodrigo Borgia had been. But, however, these canonical complexities might stand, the Friar could not have been unaware that the climate of the times, with the growing disunion and secularisation of Europe, made any practical possibility of his convening a General Council against an established Pope, through the European monarchs, a mere dream. His dream of a holy city of Florence was practical politics by comparison, besides being in itself orthodox and wholly worthy of his vocation. The present dream necessarily involved him, according to Fr. Lucas, in constructive heresy and while not absolving his judges as regards the manner of his trial and condemnation, it gave them a charge against which there could be no defence.

It is clear that by now Savonarola had gone well beyond calculating his steps. He was the tortured victim of a lifelong frustration in his pursuit of a tremendous ideal, directly inspired by God, as he certainly believed. His uncontrolled imagination and will hurled him forward, ready to grasp any means that miraculously could keep him on his way. He confessed at his trial that he had had no great hopes of succeeding in this last throw.

Having made his decision, which, as we have seen, must have been at the back of his mind for some time, he naturally enough thought of the King of France as the obvious agent for the plan which had for so long formed part of the latter's general strategy against Italy. But it was presumably his own idea to add the sovereign of France, with whom he had a real hope, the sovereigns of England (Henry VII), Spain and Hungary, and the Emperor, none of whom could be supposed to be favourable to the anarchic plan. About Henry VII he said that he had heard he was a good man.

For each of them he drafted a letter, substantially the same in each case, but with a special appeal for each of the princes as a bait.

> The time for vengeance has come [he wrote] and the Lord wishes me to unveil new secrets which will make clear to the world the danger which besets the bark of Peter, thanks to your long indifference. The Church is chock-full of abominations from the head to the soles of the feet, but you do nothing to cure the evil, being content to worship the cause of the evil which defiles it. The Lord is therefore angry and for some time past has left the Church without a Shepherd. I solemnly declare to you in the word of the Lord that this man, Alexander, is no Pope and cannot be held as such. Therefore, leaving to one side his most wicked crime of simony with which he bought the Papal See and daily sells to the highest bidders the benefices of the Church, I affirm that he is not even a Christian and that he does believe God to exist, and this scales the height of all faithlessness.

The Princes were then invited to summon a Council in a suitable and free place. He would prove them to be right even by miraculous signs. Then he added his special message to each, but unfortunately the letter to Henry Tudor has not survived.

To prepare the way for the delivery of these letters to the exalted addressees, the Friar got in touch with a number of influential Florentine citizens with good contacts in the countries to which the letters were to be sent. These men were thus to prepare the way for the official despatch of Savonarola's letter to the Potentates. This his friends did by writing about Savonarola and his plans to a highly-placed Florentine representative abroad, enclosing the rough draft and a copy of the Friar's last letter to Alexander.

This was an added risk when letters were liable to be intercepted by spies or stolen by robbers, though obviously necessary if the sovereigns were to understand what it was all about.

Tragically for the Friar, the letter sent to the Florentine Ambassador in France fell into the hands of Milanese spies who immediately sent it to Ludovico Sforza. From the Milanese tyrant to Alexander VI the way was direct—through Cardinal Ascanio Sforza.

The evidence was damning; but before the consequences could be foreseen, Savonarola was involved in the lamentable episode of the ordeal by fire which brings us back from the relatively enlightened values of the Renaissance to an affair of the truly dark ages.

X. *Ordeal by Fire*

BY April 1498, the Florence of Michelangelo, of Marsilio Ficino, of Machiavelli, suddenly found itself the stage for a trial by fire in which not two crazy men only, but a hundred and more of enthusiastic spiritual volunteers, were ready and prepared to risk being burnt alive in front of the people to prove that they were in the right and their opponents in the wrong over the heavenly credentials of Girolamo Savonarola in his prophetical claims and in his defiance of the Pope's excommunication.

How the strange business started is not very clear. But a year earlier, the preaching rivalry between the Franciscans and the Dominicans worked itself up to such a pitch in Prato that Fra Francesco di Puglia challenged Savonarola's aide, Fra Domenico, to enter into the fire with him and see which of them survived. For some reason, however, Francesco backed out. It could hardly have been fear because now that Savonarola himself had been silenced Francesco repeated his challenge to "the adversary" who may have been Fra Domenico or Savonarola himself.

Savonarola at first would, quite rightly, have nothing to do with the business, and we do not know how far the Franciscan was really in earnest. But the irrepressible Domenico took up the challenge with enthusiasm, drawing up a list of points for the truth of which he was prepared to enter the fire. These included, with the general lines of Savonarola's claims, the bald statement that "those who do not obey the excommunication do not sin."

The challenge had become so much of a public matter that the Signoria felt obliged to look into it, and, surprisingly enough, accepted the situation, taking steps only to see that both parties played fair. At this point, Francesco, for the second time, stepped back, and the initiative, from now onwards, was with the Dominicans. Fra Domenico, declaring himself ready for any ordeal, even one worse than being burnt alive, protested at the idea of Savonarola himself being chosen since he was destined for greater things. The latter, who doubted whether anything would come of it all, also insisted that he must reserve himself for a greater work. The reason for both these reserves seem to have been the attempt to convene a General Council.

It must be said that though the Franciscans took the initiative in the sorry business their motive was different from that of the Dominicans. They did not expect a miracle to prove them right; they expected that the lack of any miracle—in other words, that both parties would perish—would prove the Dominicans to be wrong. Theirs was the more self-sacrificing attitude and considerably the more realistic.

Fra Domenico's enthusiasm for entering the fire and being miraculously preserved was catching, for all the friars of San Marco wrote to the Pope to say that each was ready to go into the fire, and they were joined by large numbers of men, women and children. A chronicler described their enthusiasm as being comparable to going to a wedding. This letter from San Marco, as well as the despatches to the Florentine Envoy, brought the news of the affair to Alexander and the Cardinals. They expressed the strongest disapproval of the ordeal, but Alexander did not take steps to stop it, presumably because this would have suggested that he feared a miraculous outcome. In fact, he seems to have thought, as many in Florence thought, that the whole business would come to nothing.

However, the champions were finally chosen: Fra Domenico for Savonarola and San Marco and the Franciscan, Fra Giuliano Rondinelli, for the convent of Santa Croce.

The Signoria proved itself a good deal less sensible than the Pope, for it formally approved of the grim proceedings. The debate on the matter, however, furnishes us with some shrewd views of the minority. Nothing, for example, could have been more sensible than the view of one

The Meddlesome Friar and the Wayward Pope

magistrate that if the friars insisted on making a test of this kind, why not do so without risk of life, as for example to see which of them could cross the Arno without getting wet. Another rightly pointed out that their ancestors would have blushed to think it possible that they would make themselves the laughing-stock of the world by discussing this issue. A third could not help noting that anyone who was prepared to risk being burnt alive should not be nervous of going to Rome. Such views did not however prevail, for the Signoria drew up a long document in Latin laying down the detailed conditions of the heavenly experiment. The most important decision concerned the fate of the unsuccessful contestants. The death in flames of the Dominican would involve the perpetual banishment of Domenico (who anyway was to be the subject of the experiment) and of Savonarola. The same penalty would fall on the Franciscans if their champion was burnt. But if both perished, as indeed seemed inevitable, only the Dominicans would be punished. This decision logically expressed the attitude of the respective contestants, since the Franciscans did not expect a miracle, merely asserting that there would be no miracle to save Domenico.

We may charitably hope that the Signoria never really expected the ordeal to take place or that, if it did, both parties would draw back from the appalling test itself. It did, in fact, order its postponement from Friday, April 6, to Saturday, April 7. In Rome, too, it was not expected that the trial would be proceeded with, though Burchard gives a long account of it all, hostile, naturally, to Savonarola, but without comment.

Now that all was decided, Savonarola, though he had never really approved of the experiment, made sure that there should be no cheating. He insisted that on the platform to be erected on the Piazza della Signoria on which the faggots were to be heaped, leaving a central passage for the contestants, the fire should be lighted first at the farther end and then, as soon as the Friars had begun to walk forward, the fire behind them should be lit. Thus neither champion could escape. Savonarola, however, stated at his trial that his object had been to frighten off the

Franciscan champion. This appears to be a far more sensible reason, but it is, oddly enough, discounted by biographers because of its supposed unworthiness and is therefore considered to have been extracted from Savonarola under duress.

When the day of the ordeal dawned—not a fine day, it seems, the orders of the Signoria were carried out. Foreigners had been excluded and the gates of the city were closed. The Piazza itself was also closed, save for one guarded entrance. Fear of trouble clearly exercised the magistrates, for careful military preparations were made outside the city, inside it and on the Piazza itself. Unfortunately, both interested parties found themselves championed by military formations, the Compagnacci, under their leader, Doffo Spini, representing the anti-Dominican cause and a friend of Savonarola commanding a guard near the Palazzo.

The Dominicans, under their Superior whose life and work were thus to be tested, made rigorous spiritual preparations, with fasting, High Mass and an address from Savonarola himself. In procession and singing the sixty-seventh psalm, "Let God bestir himself, needs must his foes be scattered, their malice take flight before his coming," the friars, led by the cross-bearer, with Fra Domenico in a cloth of gold cope, and Savonarola himself carrying the Blessed Sacrament at the rear, moved on to the Loggia where an altar for them had been prepared. One Franciscan chronicler makes a charming comment about the story that the Dominicans, while singing the Litanies, forgot their own saints, but included the Franciscans. The explanation, he says, was that they realised that the Dominican saints would know about their excommunication, whereas perhaps, they thought, St. Francis and his fellow saints had not as yet been apprised of the facts.

The Franciscans had preceded them, but they had come without any ceremony and had proceeded to the chapel of the Signoria for private prayer. Apparently, their simplicity met with the disapproval of the crowd who did not want to be cheated of as much pageantry and prayer as possible, thus heightening the excitement of the final consummation.

What was the general annoyance then when the hours passed without anything further happening. Behind the scenes, the Dominicans and the Franciscans were wrangling about the detailed conditions of the trial. The Franciscans insisted that Domenico should change his clothes before entering the fire in case they were enchanted. The Dominicans, it seems, were agreeable so long as the Franciscan champion, Rondinelli, did the same. Then objection was entered against Domenico carrying the crucifix. But the real bone of contention was Domenico's insistence on carrying the Blessed Sacrament itself. Domenico firmly believed that he had been inspired to do this, and at his trial insisted that when he got to heaven he would make it quite clear "to all these people" that he was moved by divine inspiration and not self-will. The Signoria and other officials "for many and evident reasons" sided with the Franciscans.

This dispute continued while the day passed and the weather worsened. The irritated crowd, deprived of their thrill, had been soaked by a heavy shower. The wood must have now been wet and could hardly have been easily fired. It became evident that the experiment would have to be postponed.

However the rights and wrongs of the whole affair, as well of the dispute during the day, be interpreted, the people could not be blamed for viewing it all as primarily a Dominican trial. It was Savonarola's teaching and heavenly *bona fides* which were behind the whole dispute. Inevitably, the disappointment, the pathos, and sense of having been let down were vented on Savonarola and his community. They could only leave the Piazza under an armed escort and they made their way back to San Marco in the face of the jeers and insults of the crowds which were now entirely hostile to them.

One might leave the scene, thankful that the only clear divine intervention, namely the rain, had prevented a totally useless tragedy, but alas this cruel and grim day, lit only perhaps by Domenico's naïve faith, had worked up feelings to such a pitch that greater tragedy had become unavoidable.

X. The Last Defence

NEXT day was Palm Sunday but after the excitements and the frustrated feelings which had marked the collapse of the ordeal on the previous evening it was not to be expected that even this Sunday would pass without trouble.

Savonarola himself now knew well enough where he stood, for in a short sermon in the church of San Marco he told his faithful followers sadly and in moving terms that he foresaw his coming tribulations and was ready to offer the sacrifice of his life for the good of his flock.

None the less, it seems that it was the Dominicans, not apparently realising the fullness of their danger, who made themselves the occasion of the first trouble. For Fra Mariano Ughi, one of the friars who had signed a statement volunteering to enter the fire on behalf of his Superior, was to preach in the cathedral after Vespers. It was an open invitation to the troublemakers to restage the Ascension Day riot of the previous year. Nor did the cathedral authorities measure the seriousness of the danger for, instead of prohibiting the sermon, they thought it would be sufficient to postpone the time of Vespers.

By then, of course, the Duomo was full of people, uncertain whether the sermon was to be preached or not. Many of them had come to give the preacher moral support, but more had come to take advantage of the opportunity of making mischief. Soon the great church was in confusion with those hostile to Savonarola banging loudly and insulting those who had come to hear and support the Dominican preacher. As on Ascension day, one of the Compagnacci mounted the pulpit, hammered on its wooden sides and told the women to go home as there would be no

The Meddlesome Friar and the Wayward Pope

sermon. The threatening demeanour of the Compagnacci provoked retaliation from those who had remained faithful to the Friar and one of these drew his sword. The ensuing scene is best suggested by the remark of one who was present: "Blessed was he who could find the door."

But as the people poured out of the cathedral the trouble grew, for the Friar's reformed children, or so we must suppose many of them had been, returned with a vengeance to the time-honoured Florentine game of stone-throwing, selecting now for their target the friars and their followers hurrying for refuge down to the little streets towards San Marco. The mêlée grew, the house of a well-known partisan of the Friar being attacked. Here the mob received as good as they gave. Once fighting had started in earnest, the Compagnacci found the excuse they had been looking for to turn an unpleasant brawl into a dangerous and bloody riot. Soon, two inoffensive followers of the Friar, one of them walking quietly and saying his prayers, were murdered. By this time, the mob, doubtless cleverly led by the Compagnacci who knew their business and had long been awaiting just this opportunity, had reached the walls of San Marco.

There Vespers were being sung, but the noise and temper of the crowd drove the worshippers out of the church and the whole convent was locked and barred against the intruders.

Even now all might have been well if Savonarola's own instructions had been scrupulously obeyed by all of his three hundred strong community and the lay people who had remained within. But some days earlier a few of his friends had introduced within the cloisters some helmets, body-armour, muskets, bullets and, mysteriously, two small pieces of artillery. Though the weight of the evidence suggests that the mob outside, with many boys and young people armed with their stones among it, was at this time more noisy than dangerous and that, short of the doors being set on fire, the walls were thick enough to ensure the inmates' safety, some of the community, together with the lay people, made the great mistake of arming themselves, and we are left with Villari's description of these men "with breastplates over their Dominican robes and helmets on their heads, brandishing enormous halberds and speeding through the cloister, with shouts of 'Viva Christo,' to call their companions to arms." So accoutred, they made a sortie from the convent into the Piazza and engaged in a hand-to-hand fight.

In this unfortunate business, how glad one is to be able to record that Savonarola stood out as the great and holy man he was—how glad to record that the boisterous Fra Domenico would have nothing to do with such folly on the part of the hotheads. At about this time a messenger from the Signoria came to San Marco with an order that all were to lay down their arms and that Savonarola was to be banished from Florence. The Friar could now hardly be prevented from going out alone, armed only with the crucifix. "It is on my account," he said, "that this trouble has arisen. Let me go out and face it." But his community, fearing to lose him and certain that he would be killed, barred his way, so he led them in procession and prayer into the church.

One of the leaders of this counter-attack from the convent was Francesco Valori, a leading figure in the political struggle against the Medici and one of Savonarola's closest and most influential supporters. He had recently been a prime mover in ensuring the execution of Bernardo del Nero and the other Medicean conspirators. During the lull which may have been the result of the arrival of the heralds from the Signoria, Valori left San Marco, possibly to obtain new defenders, but, more likely at the Friar's suggestion, to protect his family and his house, for there was a vendetta against him because of the execution of del Nero.

By now the civic authorities and their soldiers were taking charge, but, alas, not to restore peace. It seems that they allowed themselves to be led by the Compagnacci into an armed attack on Valori's house. There Valori's wife was killed at a window by a shot from a crossbow and Valori himself, called to the Signoria, was murdered on his way. Other houses of influential and humbler supporters of the Friar were also sacked. Its blood still further heated by these deeds, the armed mob, more or less officially led, returned to San Marco, as the light was failing, to be met once again by its small band of determined defenders. To make matters worse, the great bell of San Marco was tolled to summon help. Fra Domenico, at least, was running about vainly endeavouring to prevent all this useless and provocative fighting and to stop the ringing of the alarm bell.

Soon to the moving lights of the lanterns and flares of the assailants in the Piazza were added the mounting flames from the bonfires of wood and other inflammable materials which had been erected against the doors of the convent, for it was clear that only by such incendiarism could the place be entered.

Savonarola, realising that it could only be a matter of time before the mob would break through, gathered his community—and some of his friends, among them Francesco Pugliese, Piero di Cosimo's patron—together and led them in procession, singing the Litanies, as for the last time they proceeded round Michelozzi's cloisters and entered the church, solemnly carrying the Blessed Sacrament. There, the community remained in prayer for many hours, each member feeling certain that these were his last moments on earth. One was heard to say as he strengthened the resolution of the younger brethren, "We shall sup with God." It is a moment of truth and courage like this which has made posterity feel that despite all his mistakes and extravagances, Savonarola stood for values, absolute and imperishable, a witness and martyr for truth and goodness.

By these standards not all of the community could live and die, for when at about midnight the doors had been burnt down and the invaders burst into the church, a German friar, called Enrico, and another picked up a musket each and fired at the assailants. Retreating slowly to take cover ultimately behind the altar, they maintained their armed resistance—to the deep sorrow of the Prior himself who led the community away from the church into the library and forbade others to imitate this understandable example. There had already been casualties and from among them; one young layman, lying mortally wounded, received, as he lay on the altar-steps, the Viaticum from Fra Domenico and another, less badly wounded, was received into the Order.

If only the tragedy could have ended with that prayerful and sublime resistance, but the final scene was now inevitable. A message from the Signoria arrived ordering Savonarola, together with Domenico and Silvestro Marulli, his two closest aides, to leave the convent and come to the Palazzo. While this order was being authenticated, Savonarola addressed his community for the last time. In the presence of God and before the Blessed Sacrament he affirmed again the teaching he had given them. "What I have said I have received from God and God in heaven is my witness that I speak the truth." He said that he had not expected the city to rise against him as it had done. "I do not know whether they will take my life, but I am certain that, being dead, I can help you in heaven more than I was able to do in my lifetime on earth." Savonarola then made his confession and received Communion at Fra Domenico's hands, for by now it was well past midnight.

There was some discussion as to whether he should try to escape, but the resolution to surrender was soon made. Savonarola and Domenico stepped forward to give themselves up, but Silvestro was not to be found. He was discovered next morning in hiding. The two friars, each carefully bound, were led out in the night, but so menacing was the attitude of the crowd that they had to be protected by the soldiers who made a fence around them of crossed spears and shields. In a manner that could not but remind onlookers of another procession in Jerusalem, those who had so recently praised Fra Girolamo now hurled insults at him, crying: "Now give the key a turn!" "Prophesy who it is who has struck you!" And as he passed into the Palazzo, one man kicked him from behind and shouted, "That is the seat of his prophecies."

The prisoners, after questioning, were separately lodged in cells in the bell-tower, where next morning Silvestro joined them. So ended that Palm Sunday and so began the Monday of Holy Week in that year, 1498.

XII. *Trials*

GIROLAMO Savonarola has lived in history as an outstanding religious figure. We need to recall this as we reach the story of his trial and death, for if so controversial a figure has left such a deep impression on posterity we cannot be surprised at the degree in which he affected the emotions of his contemporaries, whether in love or in hate or, as so often, in the quick change from love to hate. His life was publicly lived at a period when men very directly and very vividly lived that which they were and felt. During the years of his public ministry he, a simple Dominican friar, had played a decisive part in the political life of his country and his city, both in connection with the great French invasion and with the political revolution in Florence against the Medici and for popular government. Though he had not been unique as a prophet, he had made uniquely detailed prophetical claims, directly referring to political events, and he had made these at a time when the trend of thinking was becoming increasingly rational and naturalistic. Above all, he had openly challenged Church, Pope and the *Gran Maestri* in unprecedentedly clear and unguarded terms, so much so that Luther had no hesitation in claiming him as a proto-martyr of the Reformation. And all this highly controversial work had been effected by a personality possessing remarkable powers of influencing people to love and to fear—of causing them to follow him and then to turn against him and to hate him for having stood on so high a pedestal and then, apparently, for having fallen so low.

Undoubtedly, ever since the ordeal by fire had been conceived, large numbers of the people of Florence had been mainly thinking in terms of a miracle—a miracle which would at last justify his life; a failure to effect a miracle which would damn him. Failure to produce the sign or miracle even at the supreme testing moment when the end was near and his ungodly captors were leading him through the mocking crowd must have broken the faith of many who most enthusiastically believed in him.

Such was the emotional atmosphere in Florence when it came to trying Savonarola himself, his two closest friends, the friars of San Marco and other personalities closely associated with him.

In Rome the picture was different, but even less favourable to the prisoner. For Rome had not experienced the personal sincerity and charm of the man, nor had had direct evidence of his self-dedication and holiness. All this had been reported and, as we have seen, Alexander himself had been ready to believe in the quality and fruits of Savonarola's missionary zeal. Cardinal Caraffa, Protector of the Dominicans, and Fr. Torriano, the Vicar-General, both men of high spiritual and moral reputation, had for a long time defended him. But seen from two hundred miles away and from the seat of ecclesiastical authority, Savonarola's anti-Roman and, as it seemed, anti-Italian political activities, his persistent disobedience of orders, universally regarded as within the Church's jurisdiction, his personal defiance and criticism of the Pope and the Roman Court, spread abroad without thought for misunderstanding and scandal, his denial of the validity of the excommunication, and, above all, his attempt to procure a General Council with its inevitable result of a new schism in the Church, all these cannot but have created a certainty that his purpose was to overturn and destroy the Church, for the sake of those private illuminations of his which he consistently refused to submit to the Church's judgment.

It is evident that, whether from the point of view of the civic authorities in Florence or from the point of view of the ecclesiastical ones in Rome, there was never any question about the guilt of Savonarola himself and of Domenico and Silvestro. It was simply a matter, according to the juridical practice of the time, of extracting from them, as "kindly" as might be, the necessary confessions, and for the secular arm to carry out the inevitable punishment of death. The "kindly" means involved the use of as much torture as might be necessary to get a sufficient confession. Horrible as the whole business seems to us, Savonarola himself, as Fr. Lucas insists, in principle approved, since he had approved of the use of similar torture in the criminal code of Florence. This is not to say, as we shall see, that the Florentine government, deeply nervous about the state of public order after all the excitement and frightened, as every Florentine government was, of rapid changes of opinion due to the shortness of the terms of office in the various governmental committees, did not use arbitrary measures to effect their purpose. But their motive in doing so appears in the light of the story of the trial, or rather three trials, to have been at least as much a desire to finish with the business as revenge, hatred or still more cruelty for its own sake.

Savonarola, as already described, was taken in the early morning of the Monday in Holy Week, and one would have thought that he would have been left in peace throughout that sacred week until after the week of Easter. But it seems that the general nervousness was such that his followers dared not show themselves for fear of being killed. In this general state of tension and unrest there was universal agreement to deal with the unhappy business as though it was a normed season of the year. In fact, the government decided to anticipate the Pope's permission to begin the questioning and they took measures to give authority to those in power to carry the inquiry through to its end. Though the questioning and the use of torture began on the morning of Palm Sunday itself, the commission of seventeen examiners was only appointed on the Tuesday. It was, needless to say, largely composed of enemies of the Friar, but it is interesting to note that one member refused to serve on the grounds that he would have "no share in this homicide," while Doffo Spini, the leader of the Compagnacci, who was also on the board, insisted that all should be done "with mercy and reason" and later declared that if he had known the Friar better he would have been one of his followers. If Spini could act thus, we may take it that we are not dealing with a gang of monsters but with men who might be prejudiced but who remained human and susceptible to Savonarola's spiritual appeal.

The mode of torture used was to hoist the prisoner by his arms with a rope over a pulley. The prisoner was then allowed to drop rapidly when the rope was suddenly jerked back. This caused a more or less sudden dislocating pull on the hands according to the speed of the fall and the quickness of the jerk. Even Villari, who views the whole trial as a cruel and illegal farce which proved nothing against the prisoners, admits that it was by no means one of the cruellest tortures, and in fact we have no means of knowing with what degree of severity it was used on this occasion. That Savonarola, apart from the delicacy of his health and the weakness due to his austerities, was a highly sensitive and nervy person is hardly in doubt, and it may have required little of the torture to weaken him into making the needed confessions. His left hand, not needed for him to sign his confessions, was rendered almost useless.

The more important subjects investigated during these interrogations were the Friar's claim to supernatural powers, his relations with European rulers, his political record, the ordeal by fire and the riot and last resistance in San Marco.

Unfortunately, the efforts of the Florentine Government to secure a confession adequate for their purposes under these different heads led them into a piece of trickery which has made it extremely difficult for posterity to obtain a satisfactory idea about the Friar's defence and his admissions. Apart from the suspicion that necessarily falls on anything extracted under torture—then, of course, a universal practice, even confessions described as having been made "without torture" only meaning that they had been "freely" confirmed *after* torture had ceased—the Government employed a notary, called Francesco di Ser Barone and known as Ser Cecchone, to edit the printed record of the depositions. Such factors would incline anyone to dismiss the whole evidence as fraudulent and valueless. But in fact the curious mixture of ensuring an adequate confession and yet trying to play as fair as possible within the conditions led to the production of a document which cannot by any means be wholly disregarded.

Much of it is very much to Savonarola's credit and Ser Cecchone did his editing so badly that his interpolations are fairly easy to guess. The general result, in fact, was so unsatisfactory that orders were given to destroy all copies, though some survived, and to hold a new trial. Moreover, in addition to the doctored deposition of Savonarola himself, we have the depositions of Domenico and Silvestro, as well of those of other prisoners, which have a bearing on the conduct of the Friar.

For example, in his deposition Savonarola described as we know it the beginnings of his work and recounted how he began to feel himself "impelled to affirm these things more positively than I had yet done, although, in fact, they were my own inventions"—the latter a clear addition by Ser Cecchone. "And seeing that the affair prospered, and that my reputation with the people was on the increase, I began to say that I had these things by revelation. And very often I repeated things which Fra Silvestro told me, deeming them to be true; nevertheless, I did not converse with God nor God with me in any special manner, as is His wont to speak to His holy Apostles or the Prophets." But Vivoli, Savonarola's disciple and the reporter of so many of his sermons who is said to have had access to Cecchone's notes, says that the Friar's actual words were: "This is not a matter which concerns the State; whether I am a true prophet or not God will show. Other prophets have been brought to a worse plight than that in which I am." Vivoli's report is far more like Savonarola and what it says is common sense, for the claim to be a religious prophet had nothing to do with civic authorities except indirectly, for example, by disturbing the public peace. Another piece of editing by Cecchone, according to Vivoli, involved the suppression of the Friar's words about his moral reform: "Let it be; if it is of God, He will give a manifest sign; but if it be of man it will fail"—another typical attitude of the Friar.

On the other hand it is admitted by the defenders of the Friar as it was vigorously asserted by those who tried him that his evidence was inconsistent and that under torture he admitted dishonest and self-regarding motives which he otherwise denied. His invincibly dialectical mind also, it seems likely, enabled him to have recourse to phrases like "for glory" which could be interpreted either as "for the glory of God" or "for his own fame and reputation." Fr. Lucas calls these "downright lies" and "prevarications," and adds: "It is hardly the line of conduct which we usually associate with the idea of a martyr." This is surely a harsh judgment. Though it is true that the tough and faithful Fra Domenico, whose behaviour under trial and torture was throughout magnificent, admitted nothing and supported the Friar's highest claims throughout, we must surely reckon with Savonarola's different physical temperament and strongly emotional disposition. Savonarola, as we shall see in the third ecclesiastical trial, did not bear up well under torture, but we cannot see that this physical weakness in so highly sensitive and emotional a person is necessarily to his moral discredit. The weakness is his make-up was part of his nature from the beginning.

As regards the accusation of interfering in the political life of Florence and pulling strings from behind the scenes, the examiners, even with the help of Ser Cecchone, really established nothing to his discredit. On the contrary, the picture that emerges is one of a religious who felt himself called, as any priest has a right to be, to elaborate moral political principles, to give moral advice and, in a general way, to give political advice. But he clearly did this while taking the greatest trouble to have as little to do personally as possible with the individual politicians, even those who felt closest to him. Certainly nothing was shown to suggest that either Savonarola or Domenico used their priestly authority to influence the actions and decisions of the politicians who accepted his principles and general advice. Here it was Silvestro who was at fault for he seems to have thoroughly enjoyed political gossip and intrigue with the distinguished visitors who came to San Marco. The care that Savonarola took to avoid this precise charge ever being made against him was amply demonstrated in the attestation of various witnesses whose custom it had been to visit San Marco. They made it clear that they went to the convent for spiritual reasons and their testimony in this regard is entirely edifying in the picture it conveys of the convent life.

One should not, however, pass over the evidence of a leading friar, Ruberto Ubaldini, which surely rings true. He said: "I could not but see that it was a cause of scandal that there should be three *gran maestri* [unkindest cut of all] in the house who usurped all authority, and claimed for themselves every kind of liberty and exemption and practised none of that subjection which their profession required. It was evident that everything was settled among these three and that the business of the rest of the community was to assent to whatever was done or determined by these three." This was perhaps not very charitably expressed, but the moral force of Savonarola and his special association with Domenico and Silvestro, the first his enthusiastic lieutenant, the second a much shrewder and more complex man of affairs, acting as a natural channel with both the community and the outside world, must have made their quasi-dictatorial authority inevitable, and it throws light on the real initiative behind the Apology of San Marco.

On the question of his relations with foreign princes and his attempt to have a General Council called (which surely was an ecclesiastical rather than a State matter) Savonarola's evidence added little to the facts made known in other ways.

He said he had "great things to do in Italy and beyond Italy, with the help of the princes with whom I have made friends." When asked whether he wanted to make himself a Cardinal or the Pope, he answered that if he could carry through the work he envisaged, he would in any case be the first man in the world. A man "devoid of virtue" could be Pope, but what he was undertaking required "the highest spiritual force."

It seems unlikely that the above strange sentiment represented Savonarola's mind, nor, in view of his behaviour on Palm Sunday in San Marco, can one easily accept the confession in the second trial that he arranged for arms to be brought into the convent for its defence, though on general principles he would have had no objection to such a course since he habitually went about with an armed escort.

This first deposition was signed: "I, Fra Hieronymo di Nicolo Savonarola di Ferrara, of the Order of Preachers, of my own accord confess to be true all that is written above in this document and I faithfully declare that I sign with my own hand on this 19th of April, 1498." But, according to his friends, the wording was altered because of the interpolations to which the Friar had objected. Another account says that Savonarola reconciled himself to signing with the mental reservation that he was only signing what he himself had really written. Turning to the witnesses, who included many of his own brethren, he said: "My teaching you know and all men know it. In my present tribulation I only ask you two things: to look after my novices and to preserve them in the Christian teaching in which we have kept them faithful. Pray to God for me whose spirit of prophecy is now taken away from me."

While this first examination was taking place throughout Holy Week and on until the middle of Easter Week, the Signoria was busy negotiating with the Pope on two oddly related matters. The first was the disposal of Savonarola himself and the second was the protection of their own souls in view of the coming Easter feast since ecclesiastical law had been broken over the excommunication, the fighting in the church of San Marco and the start of the examination with torture, without waiting for Papal leave. Their anxiety about this spiritual self-protection seemed greater than about the fate of Savonarola.

As soon as he heard the news of the Friar's arrest, Alexander wrote to express his delight at the measures Florence had taken "to repress the mad folly of that son of iniquity" who had deluded the people with his "vain and pretentious promises" and had resisted "with the force of arms,

The Meddlesome Friar and the Wayward Pope

together with his accomplices." So, of course, it must have looked from the Roman end. Leave was then granted to examine the Friar "*etiam per torturam*" and absolution was given for irregularities in connection with the excommunication and the attack on San Marco. A plenary indulgence was granted for Low Sunday. Finally, the Pope demanded that once the examination was over, Savonarola and his associates should be delivered to him in Rome.

The Papal absolution and indulgence were far from satisfying the Signoria, deeply worried as it was by having started proceedings without Papal permission. Insistently it urged by return of messenger that its members should be specifically absolved for that part of the interrogation and torture which had taken place before the Pope's leave; but Rome had foreseen this scruple and a letter came, giving permission for the appointment of a suitable confessor to deal with any matter of this kind.

All this may be read as arrant hypocrisy, as Fr. Lucas says, but it also seems not unreasonable to view it as a genuine scruple on the part of politicians who then, as so often since, viewed the urgency of matters of State as overriding the normal channels of morality and justice. That they had a conscience at all is not wholly to their discredit.

Far more reprehensible was the bargain which was avidly discussed in debate immediately after the receipt of the Pope's first letter. The Government had no intention of handing over Savonarola, Domenico and Silvestro to Rome. The real motive for this is not very clear. It was stated that the prisoners should be punished where their offences had been committed and that to yield them to the Pope would go against the dignity of Florence. There was the general fear, too, that in view of the rapid changes of power which the Florentine constitution allowed there could be no real guarantee, if he were allowed to live, against the return, doubtless in triumph, of the man who had meant so much to the people. But there was also another preoccupation in the minds of the magistrates. They had long been pressing Rome to allow Florence to exact a tithe on ecclesiastical goods and property. The Pope's pleasure at the capture of "that son of iniquity" seemed an excellent opportunity to get Alexander to allow this tithe. The Signoria's rather ugly problem was therefore to get Savonarola executed in Florence against the Pope's desire while also persuading him to allow them, as a mark of his gratitude, the coveted ecclesiastical tithe. One cannot but think that the Signoria would have been better advised in the circumstances not to refuse the Pope's request that the Friar should be sent to Rome. Can it be that they feared lest the Pope's justice prove less severe than their own? It had only been in February that Alexander had pledged himself not to will the death of the sinner but to receive and treat him kindly. Since then Savonarola had delivered himself into Alexander's hand through the scheme of the Council, but Borgia was not a vengeful man especially where ecclesiastical affairs were concerned. We really have no reason for supposing that he would have killed him.

The results of the first trial or examination having proved so unsatisfactory, despite the help of Ser Cecchone, the Signoria ordered the second one to begin on April 21. Meanwhile the other prisoners, apart from Domenico and Silvestro, nineteen of them, some clerical and some lay, were examined and in their case, too, torture was used. This was in fact normal procedure even if serious guilt was not suspected. They were confronted with Savonarola's doctored confessions. Whatever the Signoria might think of the shortcomings of the document, it had a devastating effect on the Friar's disciples. But there was one touching and noble exception. Nothing could shake Domenico's faith in his master, neither torture nor his master's present weakness. But Fra Ruberto Ubaldini, once the Friar's secretary, and now speaking for his brethren, confessed that though he himself had always thought so highly of him that he would have suffered any kind of death to bear witness to him, yet "since he has so subtly been dissimulating and deceiving us, I thank God and Your Lordships that you have cleared things up for us. I pray you to look after these good sons of yours and not to allow them to be dispersed, but rather to help and keep them so that they may persevere to the end in the way in which they have begun."

These same brethren in a joint letter to the Pope expressed the gratitude which they owed, after God, to the Pope for the fatherly care with which he had saved them from "the depth of the darkness of error" into which "the deceit and cunning of their Prior had led them." Landucci, the diarist and close friend of Savonarola, insisting that he had expected Florence to prove a new Jerusalem whence good laws were to come forth for the renovation of the Church under the splendid example of a virtuous life, confessed, after reading Savonarola's deposition: "My soul was deeply grieved to see so great an edifice cast down by reason of having been built on the bad foundation of a single lie."

It is right to remember that the members of the community of San Marco and the closest of the Friar's lay followers were the sincerest and deepest type of Catholic. They had been carried by Savonarola's powerful personality, his patent virtue and the very boldness of his supernatural claims to believe in this almost new dispensation in the dark days of the Church. Once the bubble had been pricked they could not but fall back into their normal orthodoxy in whose light such things as false prophecy and the Church's excommunication became only too sinister. Those who had followed him for more emotional and often for mainly political reasons had every excuse for abandoning him when he had become an abject failure and the government, following the rule of far better governments that "the safety of the people is the supreme law," had no hesitation in expediting the inevitable with the help of illegalities and fraud. It is a sorry tale, but neither unprecedented nor necessarily the mark of criminals.

Savonarola's second examination took place between April 21 and April 25. Once again, and to no useful purpose, the poor victim had to go through similar questioning and endure similar torture. This time Savonarola signed his deposition with the addition "even though Ser Francesco di Ser Barone has added glosses in some places." Rather than add further confusion to a doubtfully successful business, the Signoria determined to forget about the new version and revert to the first.

At last, under the persistent requests of the Signoria, the Pope granted permission for the Friar to suffer in Florence and he sent two clerical commissaries or examiners to satisfy himself that all was in order. It is, no doubt, too much to expect that Alexander at this stage should have acted with any idea that he could still save the Friar's life or felt any keen sense of duty to do so. After all, Rome held the most damning evidence of all—the intercepted letter to the French Ambassador in France about the General Council. Romolino, the senior of the designated commissaries, made no bones about the certainty of the issue when he reached Florence. "We shall have a fine bonfire," he said unfeelingly, "for I have the sentence of condemnation with me." This presumably referred to the damning evidence. It looks as though Alexander, having made his effort to ensure that everything should be done properly in regard to this manifestly guilty, if not mad, "son of iniquity" against whom, despite much provocation, he had never shown himself personally hostile, decided that no further efforts were demanded of him. Let the Church do its duty by the formal examination of a cleric; let it degrade him and then hand him over to the secular arm. In the same mood of finishing with the business, he granted Florence, now presumably inoculated against its recent political errors, the tithe it had petitioned for, a gesture which caused the Friar's faithful friends to say that Savonarola had been sold, like his Saviour, for thirty pieces of silver, for three tithes made thirty.

The second of the examiners chosen by the Pope was the Master-General of the Dominicans, Torriano. The choice could not have been more fair, both in view of Torriano's excellent reputation and of his official position. We cannot believe that a Dominican like Torriano would have concurred in all that took place unless he believed that it was right. Romolino, chosen as virtual prosecutor, was a Spaniard and a Papal official who was afterwards created a cardinal. But he was a cleric of poor moral reputation and in addition to his remark about the "fine

The Meddlesome Friar and the Wayward Pope

bonfire," he is supposed to have said "one little friar more or less does not much matter" when, having tried to save the brave Domenico's life, he found Florentine opposition against him too strong. If so, it was something in his favour that at least he tried to save one man who made no pretence of doing more than follow his master, come what might.

XIII. *Martyrdom*

WE are aware that we have only briefly and superficially dealt with Savonarola's two examinations at the hands of his secular judges and with the examinations of Domenico and Silvestro and all the other friars involved. These last, we may say in passing, were only given relatively light sentences. To have described the first two trials in detail would have involved, in view of the complexities and uncertainties of the evidence, a long and tedious description and discussion. Nor was this necessary, for we agree with Fr. Lucas that the real capital guilt of Savonarola in the criminal law of the day was to be found in his initiative, both political and ecclesiastical, to disturb both the peace of Europe and the peace of the Church through the calling of a General Council of the Church. The attempt could never have succeeded, but had it done so and in so far as it might have done so, the results would have involved a fresh Great Schism and all the political disorders that in those times must have gone with it. The Church and Europe were to suffer heavily enough through the coming Reformation, but a Schism at this moment must have involved even more serious consequences. Savonarola, with his prophetical gifts, did not apparently foresee this, nor did his judges anticipate it in so many words, but it is not unfair when a man undertakes something formally against the rules, to see in his punishment a safeguard against possible dangers which only posterity can guess at in retrospect. Nor, as we have said, would Savonarola himself as a political adviser in Florence have quarrelled with the view.

It was this head of accusation which chiefly concerned the ecclesiastical examiners. For this reason and because the deposition in this third trial is so graphic and so calculated to make us see the torment which Savonarola underwent in these terrible days, that we feel it to be necessary to summarise the evidence in greater detail.

The examination took place between May 20 and May 22 in the presence of the commissaries and of some half-dozen representatives of the Florentine Government.

"All that you have confessed to their Lordships and which you have signed," Romolino began, "is true? You have signed the deposition and you have admitted it all freely and not simply because of the torture?"

"It is true," answered the Friar.

Asked, in connection with the project of the Council, whether he had had dealings with other ecclesiastics as regards the things he had admitted, he answered: "Now that I have broken with my sins and repented of them, I say before God—may He save me and be my witness!—that I have never communicated any of these things to any person, save only those three Friars, Domenico, Silvestro and Niccolo, I had a great desire to do so and though I did not have any great hopes of bringing about the Council, I tried to interest others; but, even so, I never confided with anyone and when I caused those friars to write the letter I made them do it as though in confession."

Savonarola then explained why he rested his hopes in the different princes to whom he intended to write, relying principally on the King of France, the Emperor and the King of Spain. The Italian princes he looked upon as his enemies, and he reaffirmed that he approached no prelates.

Asked which cardinals were his friends, he answered that he looked upon Cardinal Caraffa of Naples as a friend until Piero de' Medici and his brother, the Cardinal, turned Caraffa against him. Lately, he had no dealings with cardinals.

When asked whether Fra Domenico and Fra Silvestro revealed to him what they had heard in confession, he answered that they did not and that Domenico did not hear confessions.

Had he observed the excommunication? He answered: "I confess having done evil and that I am a sinner; but I ask for mercy."

Had he said that the Pope was no Christian, not even baptised and no true Pope? "I never said so; but there was a letter in my cell which said so. I wrote it; but never published it, and I have since burnt it."

Insisting that he tell the truth and nothing else, Romolino then ordered him to be stripped and put to the rope. In the greatest terror, he fell to his knees and said: "Listen to me! O God, you have me caught. I confess that I have denied Christ and that I have lied. O Lords of Florence, be my witnesses that my denial is due to my fear of the torments. If I have to suffer, let me suffer for the truth. What I have said I have said because I had it from God. O God, you punish me for my denial. I deserve it." Then he was stripped, as he prayed. He fell to his knees again and showing his maimed and weakened arm, he went on to say: "I have denied God for fear of the torments." And as he was drawn up on the rope, he said, "Jesus, help me. Now you have me caught!"

The unemotional language of the deposition conveys better than any fine writing the horror of such moments of torture on the terrified and weakened mind and body.

When asked, as he was hanging by the rope, why he said such things, he answered: "So as to seem good. Do not tear my body. I will tell you the truth, the certain, certain truth."

Why then did he just deny it? "Because I am a fool.... When I see the torture, I forget myself, but when I am in a room with a few kindly people, I do better."

Asked whether the deposition made by him was wholly and entirely true, he answered that it was true and that was why he always admitted it. Why then had he just denied it? "I have told you. I thought you would have feared to lay your hands on me. That was why I said what I did."

Did Fra Silvestro tell him what he heard in confession? He answered that he never revealed anything specific. But in general and by accident, he may have said certain things but without saying that he had heard them in confession. And he added that he had no need of the confessional material of Fra Silvestro to know what was happening in Florence. Nothing happened in Florence which he could not get to know in other ways.

How? "From the citizens and from Fra Silvestro who often talked to them, quite apart from hearing confessions. Besides, I would not have had much faith in Fra Silvestro nor in Fra Domenico in such matters for they were inclined to talk, Fra Silvestro especially; he was an easy-going man whom I considered unreliable and not so very good. Fra Domenico was, I thought, good and sincere. I was the worst of them, and because of my subtle pride I wanted to be thought a prophet and a saintly person. I could not confess this sin because I did not want to be found out. None the less, I knew I was doing wrong."

Romolino then proceeded to sum up the points made under eight heads, and Savonarola answered them along the same lines. When asked whether he had preached a new form of Christianity and divided the seamless robe of the Church, he denied the charge, admitting only that he had not feared censures and excommunications. To the question whether he did not fear to give scandal through trying to bring about a General Council, he answered: "It was my pride, my folly, my blindness which drove me to it I was so stupid that I did not even see the danger to myself and others. I had planned to write to the Pope to ask for his forgiveness and to turn to him like the Prodigal in the Scriptures."

Further questioning, that day, concerned Florentine politics, the execution of the Medicean conspirators—though what business this was of the ecclesiastical commissaries is not clear—and the ordeal by fire. About the defence of San Marco he said: "You can see for yourselves how idiotic I was, for I had twelve hours in which to escape, but I never went."

The interrogations of the second day, May 21, began with a question about his previous confessions. Savonarola explained to Romolino that he had spoken like a man beside himself through fear of getting entangled in the business, for the anticipation of those bodily tortures was worse than ten pulls on the rope. If he had not confessed everything, it was because he was trying to hide his pride. Seeing, however, how kindly he had been treated, he wanted to tell the truth. "If you think I have not said very much, do not be surprised because the things I undertook were few, but very important. When I denied and retracted yesterday, it was through fear. It was wrong of me and I apologise to Your Lordships."

The interrogation continued.

Asked if he had concealed smaller matters, he answered: "I have given you a million ducats. I should be a fool to hide one away now."

Then came far-fetched questions such as whether he denied the divinity of Christ and what he had said about Muhammad—questions, put to him perhaps to enable him to deny having done things no one ever imagined he had done, just to make the process more plausible and convincing. Naturally, his denials to such questions were strong.

"What have your dealings been with women and have they helped you with your revelations?" He answered: "At first, when I began to maintain these things, I did have dealings with them and I learned from them things which I preached as revelations through my own mind. But lately I have not done so because I did not want women to take advantage of having spoken to me."

He admitted to having disregarded the excommunication in his charge of the spiritual life of his community, even though he really knew that it had been valid.

With the threat of further tortures, Romolino turned again to the great matter of the General Council. Savonarola called it a fantasy the business of which had occupied him for three months. It was due to his great pride. But further long descriptions of his movements added little to what had already been confessed. He said that Cardinal della Rovere knew about his plans, because through a third party he had heard from him that a number of cardinals were coming to Florence to form a

The Meddlesome Friar and the Wayward Pope 221

Council. But he took no notice because he thought della Rovere "shifty and a liar."

Here apparently Romolino did his best to involve Cardinal Caraffa in the Council affair perhaps because he had been told to do so in Rome, perhaps because he had a grudge against him. Using the torture again, he extracted from Savonarola rather half-hearted admissions that he believed that Caraffa disliked Alexander and wanted to gather together a number of cardinals to dethrone him. He first denied having written to him and then admitted having done so, but only in hints and in general terms. Indirectly, he admitted, Caraffa had encouraged him "to stoke and kindle the fire."

Returning to the point of the confessional secret, the Friar admitted having cleverly and subtly dragged out of Silvestro, not what he had heard about sins of the flesh and the like, but political matters so that he might know who were his friends and use the knowledge he obtained to strengthen the appearance of his being a prophet.

On the third day, the report of which is very short, Savonarola took back all he had said the day before about Cardinal Caraffa with whom, he now said, he had had no dealings. What he had said he had said through fear of the torture.

At last, he was told by the Pope's messenger to be ready to appear next day to finish and to hear his sentence. He answered "I am in prison; if I can I will appear."

We do not know how far this graphic deposition of the ecclesiastical trial was edited by Ser Cecchone, and the reader will have little doubt of how effectively the torture, and still more the anticipation of the torture, had drawn from the Friar admissions which in no way fit with his character and all we know about him. Yet it is impossible to dismiss it all as fraudulent and valueless. Over three weeks separated the second trial from this last one, three weeks during which Savonarola remained in prison—hardly indeed in comfort, but at least in peace and, so far as we know, not unkindly treated. During those weeks, this indefatigable preacher and author wrote two of his most beautiful meditations—the meditations of a man who has lost every earthly hope and looks only to God.

In the first on the fiftieth Psalm "Have mercy on me, O God, as thou art ever rich in mercy," he wrote. "Unhappy am I, deprived of the help of every man, I who have sinned against heaven and earth. Where shall I go? To whom shall I turn? Who will have mercy on me? I dare not raise my eyes to heaven, for I have heavily sinned against heaven. I can find no refuge on earth, for in it I have been made a scandal. What can I do? Shall I despair? Indeed I will not. God is merciful; my Saviour is full of pity. God alone, then, is my refuge. He will not turn away from the creature he has made nor hide His face." And, later in a very moving passage, "Lord, do not call it over-boldness on my part that I want to teach evil people your ways for it is true that as I am, evil myself, my reputation lost and bound in chains, I do not wish to do so; but if only you will give back to me the bliss of the love of Jesus and sustain me with a sense of strength, if you will but let me go free once more, then, indeed, I shall teach your ways to the wicked again."

The second meditation—both read very like his sermons, for he was always a preacher and teacher at heart—on the thirtieth psalm, "In thee, O Lord, I look for refuge," was a long wrestling within his spirit in search for confirmation of the truth that no sin is too great to cut off God's mercy from the truly repentant sinner, and the last words which Savonarola ever wrote affirm a faith undying to the end: "My heart is comforted and in joy I begin to sing, 'The Lord is my light,' yes, Lord, my light and my deliverance. Whom have I to fear? The Lord watches over my life; whom shall I hold in dread? And throwing myself at the feet of the Lord, I said with tears: Lord, even though a whole host were arrayed against me, my heart would be undaunted for you are my strength and my defence, and for your own honour you will guide and nourish me."

Magnificent in their expression of faith as these last meditations of his are, they are certainly the work of a man conscious of failure, if

The Meddlesome Friar and the Wayward Pope

not guilt—of degradation and sin in the face of which his great faith in God refused to despair, refused too to deny the truth and value of his vocation.

They are consistent also with the view that the depositions at his trial reflect what a reader would naturally see in them: documents too lively, too spontaneous, too illogical, too repetitive, too direct in their expression to be wholly artificial and essentially fraudulent. Everything has been done by Savonarola's apologists to argue their worthlessness, but for our part we find no cause for "dis-edification" in accepting them as, in their main flow, the true evidence of a man in anguish of spirit, in natural terror, weakened as he was, by the barbarous methods of questioning then taken for granted, and of a genuine admission of having made grave mistakes that seemed to him in those conditions to be the result of his own sins and especially of his own folly. The saint is not the man who is rarely tempted and never falls: he is the man conscious of the spirit of God and the greatness of his vocation, the man who in the face of his shortcomings, mistakes and errors in carrying out that vocation yet is unmoved in his living faith in God and unshaken in his resolution to accept and serve His will until the end. To say this, however, is certainly not to deny the distressing nature of the methods used to degrade him, to exaggerate and distort the admissions—still less to deny the viciousness of the letter which Torriano and Romolino sent to Alexander VI on the last day of the trial, May 23.

In this letter, Savonarola's confessions were accepted to the letter and interpreted in the most outrageous and even ludicrous way, as when the Pope is informed that the Friar had not made a sincere confession in fourteen years! This conclusion was apparently based on the Friar's agreement that he had not confessed things which he had not regarded as sinful and, on being pressed further, had answered that when a man has lost the faith, "he does worry much how far his soul wanders," admissions clearly indicating the confusion at the time in his tortured being. And whereas he specifically denied having tried to get Silvestro to reveal confessional matter to him, admitting only having indirectly tried to pump him on political matters—another clear attempt to avoid or to diminish the torture—he was found guilty of ordering Silvestro and others to break the seal of confession.

The puzzle is how the Master-General of the Dominicans, who must have known better than we can the moral possibilities of conduct of a man like Savonarola, came to set his hand to the document with Romolino, with whom doubtless almost anything was possible. But in view of Torriano's reputation one must in fairness say that the puzzle is two-edged. While it cannot but suggest an astonishing cowardice in Torriano, it must also suggest that Savonarola had in a good man's view at least given cause for unsatisfactory findings.

The letter to the Pope reads:

> We examined the three Friars, one after the other, and learnt that they had all fallen into errors greater than can easily be expressed. First of all, Fra Girolamo admitted that for fourteen years he had never made a sincere confession of his sins and, making matters worse, had continued to say Mass. Moreover, he declared that he had taken measures to ensure that Fra Silvestro and many others should hear confessions and report to him what they had heard. And afterwards he inveighed against these reported sins both publicly in the pulpit and privately. He pretended that he had learned by revelation what he had in this way come to know. Further he has committed such heinous and detestable crimes that it would not be suitable to make them known now. He also confessed to have caused sedition among the people, scarcity of provisions and thus deaths among the poor as well as the killing of many citizens of rank [presumably the Medicean conspirators]. He also admitted that he had abused the Church's sacraments [possibly the reference is the carrying of the Blessed Sacrament at the ordeal by fire].

The Meddlesome Friar and the Wayward Pope

After dealing with the consequences of his refusal to accept the excommunication, the letter goes on:

> He has also admitted that he tried with letters and messages to incite the Christian princes to cause a schism against your Holiness. So wickedly did this Friar, or rather this most evil of monsters, behave that his appearance of virtue was only a pretence and cloak for his ambition and his desire to obtain worldly glory. It was his habit to turn to the crucifix and say to Our Lord, "If I lie, you lie too."

This, if it was a crime was certainly for once a true charge.

The sentence of the ecclesiastical court, pronounced on the last day of the trial, May 23, was that Fra Girolamo, Fra Domenico and Fra Silvestro "having been found to be heretics and schismatics and having predicted rash innovations are condemned to be degraded and consigned, or rather left, to the hand of secular justice. So be it!"

The secular sentence given on the same day reads:

> Given that the trials, confessions and crimes perpetrated and committed by Fra Girolamo Savonarola of Ferrara, Fra Silvestro of Florence and Fra Domenico of Pescia, of the Order of Preachers and of the convent of San Marco in Florence, have been heard and that all their wicked crimes, described therein, have been examined and understood; and given that their degradation has been pronounced before the people by the Bishop in the presence of the General of the whole Order of St. Dominic and the most worthy commissary of our Holy Father the Pope; and given that the most worthy commissaries, under the authority of the Supreme Pontiff, as has been made known by the latter's brief, have given them over into secular hands that justice may be administered lest they remain immune and

unpunished; wherefore the Lords of the Council of the Eight, here present, have condemned Girolamo Savonarola, Silvestro of Florence and Domenico of Pescia, to be, each and all, hanged by a rope and their bodies burnt, that the soul may be separated from the body, in public in and on the Piazza of their high lordships.

The sentence of death was, as we have seen, a foregone conclusion, for the Signoria, probably with good reason from its own point of view, dared not take the risk of allowing Savonarola to live and make a "comeback" one day. He was still a relatively young man at forty-six and we have no reason to suppose that his health was not basically sound. A change of political climate in variable Florence or a new Pope (Alexander was succeeded in 1503 by Cardinal della Rovere, as Julius II, after twenty-seven days of Pius III's pontificate) might easily result in the findings being quashed. Yet a Romolino was prepared to plead for Domenico's life and the sentence itself was merciful in that Savonarola was not condemned, as so many still believe, to be burnt alive. Moreover during the last hours of the life of the famous Friar and his two companions, humanity and kindness were shown.

A *Battuto*—a member of a self-flagellating (hence the name) confraternity to assist the dying—was allowed to go to his cell and he persuaded the Signoria to let the three condemned men to meet together for an hour. Eager to the last, Domenico prayed that he might be burnt alive, but Savonarola told him that it was not for them to choose how they should die. "How can we know that we shall be strong enough to bear the death we have to face? That depends, not on ourselves, but on God's grace." He ordered Silvestro not to protest his innocence at the time of his death since Our Lord did not do so on the Cross. Both these commands, as also his last prayer, suggest that he realised the mistakes he had made, even though they had always been made with a complete sincerity of intention.

Savonarola had been to confession to a Benedictine before this meeting and during his last night he slept peacefully, his head resting on the knees of the *Battuto*.

On the morning of the execution, May 24, 1498, the three were allowed to be together again for the last spiritual rites. Savonarola gave himself Holy Communion and gave Communion to his two brethren with the prayer: "O God, I acknowledge you to be the perfect indivisible Trinity, Three in One, Father, Son and Holy Ghost; I acknowledge you to be the Eternal Word who descended into Mary's womb and mounted the Cross to shed your blood for our sins. I pray that by that Blood I may be pardoned for my sins and I beg you to forgive them. I pray also that you will pardon every offence and hurt brought on this city and every error that I myself have unwittingly committed."

The three Friars were then taken to the Piazza della Signoria where platforms had been erected outside the Palazzo and from the corner a long platform had been built leading to the scaffold not far from the centre of the Piazza itself. On the platforms stood the members of the Council of Eight, the Papal Commissaries and the Bishop of Vasona, a Dominican who had for some years been the auxiliary bishop to the Archbishop of Florence who resided in Rome.

The Piazza was said to be crowded and with a hostile crowd described as composed of the dregs of newly-released prisoners. That it was crowded we can hardly doubt, though oddly enough the well-known picture of the scene, painted by an unknown artist a few years later, shows the Piazza almost empty. We know too that supporters of the Friar were also present, so we may presume the crowd to have been the normal throng of sightseers, good and bad, who cannot be kept back from witnessing such an occasion.

The Friars were led to the steps of the Palazzo where their religious habits were taken from them, leaving them in woollen under-tunics, with hands bound. They were then taken to the platform where the Bishop stood. His responsibility was to carry out the ceremony of degradation. They therefore had to be clothed again with the white Dominican robe and the black gown. The Bishop, who had been a friend of Savonarola, stumbled over the words in his emotion. "I separate you from the Church Militant and Triumphant," he said. He had spoken two words too many. Immediately Savonarola answered him in a loud voice: "From the Church Militant, not from the Church Triumphant. That is not within your competence," a retort which has fitly been immortalised for it epitomises Savonarola's position and most decisively gives him the last word.

The Friars, once more despoiled of their religious habits, were then taken to the platform where stood the Papal Commissaries and formally heard the Church's judgment. When Romolino asked them whether they wished for absolution, they bowed their heads in assent. At the third platform, the members of the Council of Eight, in whom Florentine justice was vested, awaited them. There the civil sentence was read.

The last moments had come. Savonarola, Domenico and Silvestro were taken along the platform on to the Piazza, leading to a circular stage from the centre of which rose the high gibbet ending in a cross-bar, pictorially badly-chosen from the point of view of those whose business it was to avoid suggesting an infinitely greater Sacrifice. Against it a tall ladder was leaning and under it the great fire of wood which would consume the dead bodies.

Silvestro, the first to suffer, had recovered his courage before the example of his master and he died bravely. Domenico, going to his death "as though to a dance" and being prevented with difficulty from intoning the *Te Deum* at the top of his voice, was next to die exultant.

Savonarola, when his turn came to climb the ladder, is described as seeming already to have passed from this earth, wrapt as he was in silent prayer. But when he reached the high summit, he took one last look at the people of Florence over whom he had exercised such moral sway and who now in a deathly silence were watching him die, degraded and disgraced. With the rope around his neck and as he was thrust into the void and to death, someone shouted the last mockery: "Prophet, now is the time for a miracle!" But after the fire had been lit and the three bodies consumed, some of Savonarola's followers succeeded in cheating the authorities who had ordered the ashes to be thrown into the Arno. They gathered together relics of a prophet and a hero whom many then and ever since have deemed to be a saint.

Despite an attempt to make out that Pope Benedict XIV included Savonarola in a list of blessed servants of God and other venerable persons illustrious by their sanctity, the Church has never sought or attempted the rehabilitation of Girolamo Savonarola. His name appears in the above catalogue not as one of the list of saints, but as an objection to the canonisation of Catherine de Ricci on the grounds that she had prayed to him. This objection was waived, and that is the nearest Savonarola has ever come to posthumous spiritual honours, even though many, including St. Philip Neri, in every age have regarded him as an uncanonised saint. At the five hundredth centenary of his birth in 1952, Florence solemnly made reparation for his execution.

The task of rehabilitating Savonarola and working for his beatification continues in Italy, but the present writer finds it quite impossible to accept the general line of subtle and complex argument adduced by a few contemporary Dominican defenders of the great Friar. It may be that Savonarola, had he lived and worked under a saintly Pope, freed from the political responsibilities which weighed on Alexander and of which he certainly made the best for himself and his family, might well have become a formal saint, for his personal holiness and heroism are not in doubt. But in fact his character received its special test under Alexander Borgia, a Pope who represented for him the widespread corruption of the clergy and laity at the time, but who, in fact, in the specific conflict between them, treated him indulgently until the end and as fairly and correctly as any Pope could have done, once the affair had started. This fact suggests doubts about whether he would have obeyed any superior thwarting his mission. Under that test Savonarola's temperament rather than his intelligence failed him and he was unable to follow the right road between his reformist vocation and the obedience which he owed as a friar to the proper authority of the Church. Accidentally, however, one regrets that the cause of his beatification has not been introduced since it would serve better than anything to clear up, from a rigorous historical point of view, the fantastically differing readings of the lives and characters of the two protagonists in this story.

So far as we know, Alexander's concern with the Friar entirely ended with the latter's death, but both as an example of human credulity, as well as to afford a scale by which to measure the Pope's own dealing with the Florentine Friar, it seems worthwhile giving Burchard's character sketch of Savonarola in his diary for May 1498. Presumably he was reporting the gossip of Rome and the lower reaches of the Roman court.

> Brother Hieronymus was imprisoned and seven times put to the question with torture. He begged for mercy and volunteered to confess in word and writing all his crimes. The torture was then stopped and he was returned to prison. Given paper and ink, he wrote the story of his evil-doings and his misdeeds, taking eighty folios to do so, they say. Among other things, he said that he had never had any divine revelations. Instead he obtained his knowledge from several of the friars inside Florence and outside it. What he knew was obtained through these friars who heard many thousands of the confessions of the faithful. Such information he sometimes made public, asserting that it had been revealed to him by Christ. For twenty years and more he had not confessed any mortal sin even though he had committed many, chiefly of the flesh in which he had sinned often and in diverse ways—even though, too, he had said Mass almost daily and yet for all those years had never pronounced the words of consecration, often giving Communion to the people with unconsecrated hosts. He had told his brethren that it had been revealed to him

to warn them against being killed by poison. That is why he once ordered the cook, the cellarer and the servers of the convent not to touch the fish that had been given one June day. He arranged with an outside friend that a beautifully prepared, but poisoned, lamprey should be sent. At dinnertime, with all the community present, he put forward the divine revelation made to him and to prove his point he had all the fish, raw and cooked, brought to him. He and the brethren prayed on their knees to God that the community be protected according to the usual divine mercy. To point the moral, he had a cat brought in. He gave it the poisoned lamprey. As soon as it had eaten a mouthful, it collapsed and died. When the brethren saw this, they praised the Friar and thought him greater than ever.

Burchard may well have told his master this gossip, and we can imagine Alexander laughing, not least at the gullibility of the kind of people who spread equally absurd tales about himself.

Alexander's interest in the Savonarola affair is generally held to have been mainly political. The charge is made that he was working all the time hand in glove with the Florentine Mediceans, the Sforzas and others who combined a hatred of popular government in Florence with support for the Holy League, however temporarily. No doubt, this is true. But the truth throws an interesting light on Alexander's character. His temptation must have been to use all his immense powers to destroy this tiresome, if stubborn, zealot. But he did nothing of the kind. On the contrary, again and again he forgave the Friar, hoping that the machinery of the Church and State, mobilised for action, need not be actually set in motion—and that machinery itself was not wholly in the hands of vicious men. Once Charles had gone, the Florentine government was never in a position to defy the forces at the Pope's disposal. Moreover, better than Savonarola himself, he continued to distinguish between the Friar's fruitful missionary zeal and those exceptional powers and illuminations which the latter refused to submit to the proper examination of the Church. Yet this was elementary routine if hundreds of self-appointed reformers were not to rise up, as indeed shortly they would. The Pope's dealings with Savonarola, in other words, seem to harmonise with the picture we have tried to draw in these pages and to be quite inconsistent with the view that he was as bad ecclesiastically and religiously as he was morally.

As for Alexander's political aims, they remained for the rest of his reign steadily set on two ends: to try and keep Italy out of the hands of France and Spain and to strengthen and organise the Papal States as a strong bastion at the heart of Italy. "We have already told you," he once said to the Venetian Ambassador whom he was trying unsuccessfully to persuade to promote an alliance as between the only two really independent powers in Italy, "that though we are by nationality Spanish and may seem in a certain manner favourable to France, we are in reality Italian. Our root is in Italy; it is here that we must live; here that Cesare must live. Our affairs are insecure without Venice. It mistrusts us, and this mistrust means that since we cannot base our actions upon Venice, we are compelled to do things which otherwise we should not do." And on a later occasion: "Ambassador, we must look to our interests. Let us unite our poor Italy; it would be united if your Most Illustrious Signoria would deign to reply to what we have so often asked without its ever doing so."

Had Alexander's chief purpose been to destroy Savonarola for the sake of the Medici, one might have expected that the Medici would have returned, or attempted to return, to Florence after his fall and that of his supporters. But it was not until fourteen years later that the Medici regained their ascendancy in Florence, a chief influence in Florence in the meanwhile being Machiavelli, the leading adviser of Piero Soderini who was made Gonfalonier of Justice under the existing constitution with the sole amendment that this highest office was now to be held for life. This change was one which Savonarola had recommended.

The Meddlesome Friar and the Wayward Pope   233

Savonarola's constitution, in fact, endured until the city in 1512 came under the virtual rule of Cardinal Giovanni de' Medici. Afterwards Florence was ruled by other members of the Medici family, aggrandised by titles and marriage alliances, while the status and creative power of Florence declined.

It is strange that Machiavelli, the one Florentine political figure of his day comparable in historical stature to Savonarola should have succeeded to his work and in doing so bridged the gap between one age and another. It is strange, too, that Alexander whose political views for the security and unity of Italy corresponded so closely with those of Machiavelli should have survived in Italian history as a villain, while Savonarola, whose pro-French policy was a step on the way to the long Italian decline, should have survived as a hero. A high spiritual ideal, combined with a genuine love of the people and of their liberty, has defeated in the eyes of posterity the realism of Pope and political philosopher. But the historical record itself, alas, has gone to show that realism rather than idealism in politics has the better survival value.

Savonarola's death as a martyr, albeit a controversial one, has given to history one of its unforgettable pictures. The character of the victim and the issues at stake in his quarrel with the Pope are likely always to be discussed, but no one will be found to deny the essential goodness and purity of his vision in those dark days for the Church, nor the quality of the spiritual inspiration and zeal which enabled him to dedicate his adopted city to Christ the King—the divine title which Pius XI has made so popular in our own day of post-Christian denial of any sovereignty on earth save that of the so-called will of the people, however manipulated and travestied.

Alexander Borgia died in Rome five years later and for a long time people believed that the bad Pope expressed in his manner of death the vices of his life and the damnation to come. He was poisoned in seeking to poison others, some said; he was poisoned by accident, others thought. He was poisoned by his own son Cesare, a third version had it. However poisoned, it was at least certain that Rodrigo Borgia manifested in the hideous corruption of his gross, blackened body, with his swollen tongue hanging out of his mouth, as he lay in state, the evil of his damned soul.

Alas for the moralisers, religious and political! Alexander, hale and hearty to the last, though saddened by the death of two nephews in the then always dangerous heat of a high Roman summer, himself fell sick of the fever on August 9, 1503. He gradually grew worse and, after receiving the Last Sacraments, he died a Christian death on the evening of August 18. It is true that his body turned black and swelled up soon after his death, but that was not an abnormal thing to happen after the fever and in the heat of the summer. He was buried with all the normal pageantry when a Pope of Rome dies.

Through the murdered Juan, Duke of Gandia, Alexander Borgia was great-grandfather to Francis Borgia, Saint and third General of the Jesuit Order. The patterns of Providence can seem to us strange. May we hope and believe not merely that Saint Francis Borgia redeemed by his austere and mystic life the sins of his Papal ancestor, but drew something from that same ancestor's better side as shown in a surprising (in the circumstances) ecclesiastical fidelity and in his fairness to the spiritually dedicated friar, Girolamo Savonarola? May we hope, too, that Savonarola in a heaven where earthly conflicts are better understood, helped to form the sanctity of that saintly figure of the Church's true Reformation, the great-grandson of his Papal foe?

Designed by Fiona Cecile Clarke, the CLUNY MEDIA *logo
depicts a monk at work in the scriptorium,
with a cat sitting at his feet.*

*The monk represents our mission to emulate
the invaluable contributions of the monks
of Cluny in preserving the libraries of the West,
our strivings to know and love the truth.*

*The cat at the monk's feet is Pangur Bán, from the
eponymous Irish poem of the 9th century.
The anonymous poet compares his scholarly
pursuit of truth with the cat's happy hunting of mice.
The depiction of Pangur Bán is an homage to the work
of the monks of Irish monasteries and a sign
of the joy we at Cluny take in our trade.*

"Messe ocus Pangur Bán,
cechtar nathar fria saindan:
bíth a menmasam fri seilgg,
mu memna céin im saincheirdd."

www.ingramcontent.com/pod-product-compliance
Lightning Source LLC
Chambersburg PA
CBHW060556080526
44585CB00013B/585